Reflection to Transformation

Reflection to Transformation

A Self-Help Book for Teachers

edited by
Nick Zepke, Dean Nugent and Linda Leach

Dunmore Press

©2003 Nick Zepke, Dean Nugent and Linda Leach
©2003 Dunmore Press Ltd

First Published in 2003
by
Dunmore Press Ltd
P.O. Box 5115
Palmerston North
New Zealand
http://www.dunmore.co.nz

Australian Supplier:
Federation Press
P.O. Box 45
Annandale 2038 NSW
Australia
Ph: (02) 9552-2200
Fax: (02) 9552-1681

ISBN 0-86469-435-0

Text:	Times New Roman 11/13
Printer:	The Dunmore Printing Company Ltd
	Palmerston North
Cover design:	Creative Rage, Palmerston North

Copyright. No part of this book may be reproduced without written permission except in the case of brief quotations embodied in critical articles and reviews.

Contents

Introduction		7
PART I: The Reflective Practitioner		15
Overview		15
1.	Reflecting–Learning–Teaching *Nick Zepke*	17
2.	Collaborative Learning Using Reflective Storytelling *Maxine Alterio and Janice McDrury*	34
3.	Action Research Transforming Practice *Pip Bruce-Ferguson (with Anne O'Brien Kennington)*	52
PART II: Working with Learners		69
Overview		69
4.	Teaching for Learning *Dean Nugent*	71
5.	Inclusive Teaching: Making Space for Difference *Nick Zepke*	89
6.	Beyond Independence *Linda Leach*	105
PART III: Supporting Learning and Teaching		121
Overview		121
7.	Preparing for Teaching *Robin Graham*	123

| 8. | Collaboration for Learning and Teaching
Linda Leach and Michele Knight | 139 |
| 9. | Course Design and Assessment for Transformation
Linda Leach, Guyon Neutze, Nick Zepke | 155 |

PART IV: Contexts for Learning and Teaching 179

Overview 179

10.	Making Sense of Our Contexts Brian Findsen	181
11.	Teaching and Learning in the Global Village Nick Zepke	196
12.	Transformative Learning : A Spiritual Perspective Dean Nugent	213

Index 229

Contributors 231

Introduction

Nick Zepke, Dean Nugent and Linda Leach

Purposes of the book

If you help adults learn, this book is for you. You may be a teacher, lecturer or tutor working in formal settings such as private training establishments, polytechnics or universities; an educator, facilitator or mentor working in non-formal settings such as community organisations; a trainer in local or national government agencies or businesses. In this book, terms such as 'teacher', 'learner' and 'student' apply to you and the people you work with, regardless of your context.

From Reflection to Transformation continues the work done in two previous books edited by Nick Zepke and Dean Nugent – *The Teacher Self-Help Book* (1987) and *The New Self-Help Book for Teachers* (1996) (with Christine Roberts). Both focus on a learner-centred approach to adult education and on a systematic and self-reflective approach to the development of adult educators' knowledge, skills and attitudes.

This latest work, however, while retaining its foundation in practical teacher skills, takes you to a deeper consideration of reflection and transformation. Hence the title *From Reflection to Transformation*. Our concept for this book is inspired by the work of Jürgen Habermas (1987). We have adapted his idea of three domains of human interest as a framework for this book:

1. *Technical or work interests*
    These interests enable us to control or manipulate our environment. They are also known as instrumental interests. Good teachers have a toolkit of technical knowledge and skills to inform these interests and their work. All of the chapters provide you with specific teaching skills and strategies to practise and develop.

2. *Practical or communicative interests*
   These interests take us away from the technical into the domain of interpretive and communicative actions. Humans share and negotiate behaviours and meanings with one another. Teaching and learning are communicative processes always involving others. Good teachers are able communicators and skilled at helping learners to construct meanings. This book emphasises communication and interaction – between teachers and learners; between learners; and between the 'classroom' and the wider community.

3. *Emancipatory interests*
   Habermas's third domain is the emancipatory interest. Through self-knowledge or self-reflection we realise the limitations that impact on our capacity to learn and act in the world. While the book is rather loosely based on Habermas in this respect – with different chapters tending to have their own understanding of *emancipation* – all emphasise the importance of self and contextual awareness whereby, through action, we can change or transform ourselves and the contexts within which we live and work.

All three interest domains are about relationships. In the book we explore and critique complexities in teaching–learning relationships. Using reflection in various ways, we can achieve deeper understandings as we construct our own meanings. Indeed we can change or transform our relationships with each other, with our learners, with our environment and within ourselves. While the book is a 'self-help' book, it is also a call for greater collaboration, for connectedness, for going beyond our individual points of view, for going beyond our usual 'selves'.

Themes in the book

This book features a number of themes about adult learning and teaching. We think about them using a model of teaching and learning developed by Hall and Kidman (1996). Their model (see Figure 0.1 on page 9) illustrates learning and teaching as a three-way process concerning the learner, the teacher and the content. Learners and teachers establish rapport; teachers have content expertise; and students develop understanding of content as a result of the teaching–learning process, a process that occurs within institutional, local, national and international contexts.

Each aspect of this three-way process, as well as a wide range of contextual issues, is discussed. Each chapter discusses several issues. While rapport between teacher and learner gets the spotlight in many cases, teacher expertise and student understanding also feature. Underlying these discussions is a view that teaching is a complex process. It is not simply a matter of developing a discrete set of skills and using them. It is the multi-faceted interaction of people, information and contexts that is a daily challenge and excitement for educators.

Although the authors have different views on some issues, a number of themes emerge across the chapters.

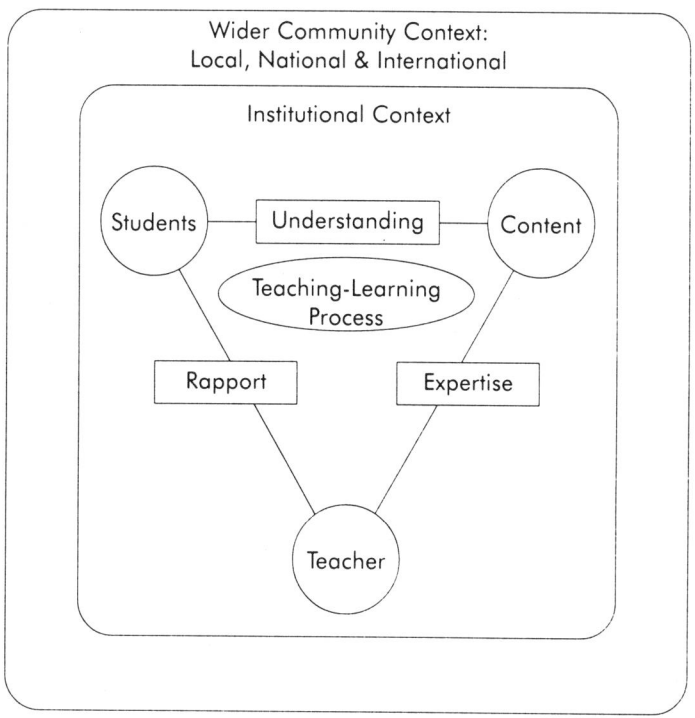

(Hall & Kidman, 1996).

Figure 0.1. A relational model of teaching and learning

Reflection, critical reflection and transformation

Reflection, a key concept in adult education, concerns our ability to think things over: to make sense of, and meaning from, experiences for ourselves. This can be both an individual and a collaborative process. Critical reflection goes beyond reflection, adding a questioning dimension. Critical reflection is not necessarily negative and destructive but does put ideas under a microscope, checking them to ensure that they make sense in particular contexts. Both forms of reflection are essentially thinking processes, widely advocated within Western education. Transformation originated in work done by Mezirow (2000). It concerns our willingness to question and change attitudes, values and assumptions we hold about the world and how it works. We free ourselves from unconsciously held beliefs that constrain our ability to live, learn and work well in society.

Political contexts

Context is the multi-layered environment in which we work – classroom, institutional, local, national and international. Underpinning the authors' discussions is the assumption that context is a major factor influencing our work as adult educators. While some chafe at constraints within their organisations, too often they are unaware of the impact of their wider contexts, for example, how government policies, international events, funding agencies and industry or professional organisations influence their teaching. Contextual issues are closely associated with questions of power – who makes decisions for whom; whose knowledge is valued; whose ways of working are privileged.

Teaching skills

Although we maintain that teaching is a complex process, the authors accept that skills are vital. There is a wide range of skills and strategies you can use to help students learn. These include skills in planning, design, organisation, preparation, presentation and assessment. Interpersonal skills and personal qualities are also important. Within individual chapters authors identify specific skills and suggest ways to develop them. These are often provided as activities for you to try.

Holistic learning

Learning is not limited to the intellectual dimension. It includes the whole person – physical, emotional, social and spiritual. Teaching–learning relationships and exploration of topics are designed to honour all aspects of each person in their learning, not just their ability to understand content. However, spirituality, in a broad sense that is not restricted to religions, gets special emphasis in this book. At least two factors influenced this emphasis. Growing concerns about the world, people and the environment, alongside increasing interest in what First Nations people such as Maori, Australian Aborigines and American Indians have to offer the West, have resulted in a new emphasis on our spiritual dimension. How this may be played out in adult education situations is a recurrent theme in this book.

Difference and diversity

Difference and diversity deal with the whole range of characteristics of learners in a group. These may be gender, race, class, culture, age, (dis)abilities, prior experience, knowledge … the list is endless. Here the authors assume that difference and diversity are to be valued and welcomed, not treated as a problem. For decades in adult education writers made generalisations about adults as learners and about how they prefer to learn. This resulted in a one-size-fits-all approach that required adult learners to conform to the 'norm'. Those who didn't conform were a problem. The more we learn to appreciate different perspectives, branches of knowledge and ways-of-being, the more our teaching can cater appropriately for difference and diversity.

Independence, interdependence and collaboration

Within the book there are some tensions around independence, interdependence and collaboration. Some authors advocate the development of independence in adult learners. Others, while valuing independence, argue that we need to move beyond it to interdependence in learning; drawing people together to foster their learning. Others support the use of collaborative learning as one way of responding to holistic learning, difference and diversity. These authors argue that learning together, in a positive and supportive relationship with both the teacher and other learners, results in enhanced achievement. This assumption contests the view that competition and individualism are the primary spurs to achievement.

Constructivism

One theory of learning – constructivism – is central to most chapters. Put simply, constructivists maintain that we each make sense of our experiences and information for ourselves. Each person, influenced by, for example, their past experiences, their characteristics, personality and existing knowledge, creates their own understanding of new ideas. Constructivism has different branches: one sees the knowledge construction process as an individual, cognitive one; another views it as a social process in which interaction with others plays a critical role in the construction of understanding.

Technology

Technology has an ever-expanding influence on teaching. Communications technology makes it possible for us to contact one another across the planet almost instantaneously. At the same time adults are under constant pressure to increase their qualifications and to continue learning. As a result, adult educators are often compelled to use communications technology in their teaching and to find alternative ways of working with learners. A range of on-line options is supplementing face-to-face teaching. Several authors offer some guidelines for practice.

The structure of the book

The book is divided into four parts, each representing overlapping aspects of the teaching process.

The reflective practitioner

Reflection is introduced as a central feature in self-development, teaching and learning. It is portrayed as learning from experience alone, in groups and by way of a transformative process – action research.

In Chapter 1, *Reflecting–Learning–Teaching*, Nick Zepke introduces some theoretical underpinnings for reflection but concentrates on describing practical techniques that can help you become a well-rounded reflective practitioner. Where Chapter 1 focuses on the individual, Maxine Alterio and Janice McDrury in Chapter 2, *Collaborative Learning Using Reflective Storytelling*, suggest that stories enable group processing of ideas and feelings. In Chapter 3, *Action Research Transforming Practice*, Pip Bruce-Ferguson uses a case study to show how action research can be used to transform your practice.

Working with learners

This concerns teaching practice – what you actually do with learners. The focus is on practical skills development but also on the political elements in teaching.

In Chapter 4, *Teaching for Learning*, Dean Nugent draws on his extensive personal experience to introduce practical ways of making teaching an interactive, power-sharing process. Nick Zepke in Chapter 5, *Inclusive Teaching: Making Space for Difference,* also discusses techniques for coping with individual differences; he also looks at some of the political reasons for difference and suggests ways of addressing them. Linda Leach uses Chapter 6, *Beyond Independence*, to suggest a transformation in teaching – a shift from focusing on autonomy in learning to interdependence.

Supporting learning and teaching

Here the focus is on the activities you carry out for your students outside the classroom.

Chapter 7 is another practical chapter. In *Preparing for Teaching*, Robin Graham describes some basic techniques for preparing for the classroom. In particular she suggests ways in which you and your students can become information-literate in this technological age. Linda Leach and Michele Knight collaborate in Chapter 8, *Collaboration for Learning and Teaching,* to advocate for students and teachers learning together. They explore the benefits of collaboration as a support for learning, discuss issues with the technique by reflecting on their own collaboration, and offer ideas on how to introduce collaboration to the classroom. In Chapter 9 Linda Leach, Guyon Neutze and Nick Zepke, in *Course Design and Assessment for Transformation*, present a practical approach to curriculum design and assessment. This chapter also offers a critique of the rather technical way these processes are often seen.

Contexts for teaching

The final part looks at the contexts within which we teach. It assumes that our work and our lives are profoundly affected, shaped even, by the contexts within which we live. The chapters in this section explore the ways in which we can make sense of the immediate context we work in, how we can be effective practitioners in what has become a global village and what we need to do to prepare for the future.

In Chapter 10, *Making Sense of Our Contexts*, Brian Findsen discusses global, national and local contextual issues and explores how they affect institutions, teachers and work in classrooms. Nick Zepke, in Chapter 11, *Teaching and Learning in the Global Village,* examines social, economic and political processes, globally and locally, through the lens of knowledge, which is the foundation of teaching and learning. In Chapter 12, *Transformative Learning: A Spiritual Perspective,* Dean Nugent introduces us to a spiritual view of learning and teaching which he links to global, political and environmental issues.

Introduction

Weaving the themes

The following table shows the chapters in which the various themes appear.

Theme	The Reflective Practitioner Ch1	Ch2	Ch3	Working with Learners Ch4	Ch5	Ch6	Supporting Learning & Teaching Ch7	Ch8	Ch9	Contexts for Learning & Teaching Ch10	Ch11	Ch12
Reflection	❖	❖	❖	❖	❖							❖
Critical Reflection	❖	❖	❖			❖				❖		
Transformation			❖	❖			❖		❖	❖		❖
Political Contexts			❖		❖	❖			❖	❖	❖	
Teaching Skills	❖	❖	❖	❖	❖	❖	❖	❖	❖	❖	❖	❖
Holistic Learning	❖	❖			❖			❖			❖	❖
Difference and Diversity	❖				❖	❖	❖	❖	❖		❖	❖
Independence		❖			❖	❖	❖	❖				
Collaboration		❖	❖	❖	❖	❖		❖	❖	❖	❖	❖
Constructivism	❖	❖	❖		❖	❖	❖	❖			❖	
Technology				❖			❖				❖	

Figure 0.2.   **Chapter themes**

Towards an inclusive style

We accept that in form and structure this book leans towards the European academic tradition in the way it portrays learning and teaching. No chapter offers a specifically Maori perspective, or considers skills that specifically address Maori learning needs. We have some regrets about this, for we want to honour the Treaty of Waitangi in our practice.

We are also conscious of gender issues. While women's voices are well represented among the authors and we have tried to use non-sexist language, we have not specifically considered feminist perspectives. Indeed, we regret that so many voices found in our classrooms are not heard in the book.

The most compelling reason for the unheard voices was our wish to develop a book that leads to valuing *all* difference. This book emphasises the importance of building quality relationships, open communication, co-operative effort and reflection: qualities that we believe will lead more easily to an understanding of the learning needs of Maori, women and others than a token chapter on any individual perspective could provide.

We want our book to reflect our belief that good teachers find out how others want to be treated and then treat them that way. If learners want their culture, their gender or their differences empowered, then as good teachers we note this and act accordingly.

We hope this book is interesting and helpful to you on your self-help, professional development pathway. Enjoy the journey.

References

Habermas, J. (1987). *Knowledge and Human Interests*. Translated by J. Shapiro. Cambridge: Polity Press.

Hall, C., & Kidman, J. (1996). Student-Centred Learning as Viewed through a Relational Model of Teaching and Learning. Paper presented as part of a Symposium on Student-Centred Learning at the New Zealand Association of Research in Education Conference, Nelson, December.

Mezirow, J., & Associates (2000). *Learning as Transformation: Critical perspectives on a theory in progress*. San Francisco: Jossey Bass.

Zepke, N., & Nugent, D. (ed.) (1987). *The Teachers Self-Help Book*. Wellington: Tutor Publications.

Zepke, N., Nugent, D., & Roberts, C. (ed.) (1996). *The New Self-Help Book for Teachers*. Wellington: WP Press.

— PART I —

The Reflective Practitioner

Overview

It is said that in these days of dramatic change, learning the job *is* the job. Teaching is no exception. It is a complex craft and requires a great commitment to ongoing learning. This first section focuses on the concept of the reflective teacher as a means for teachers to manage their learning and to develop their professional accountability.

Reflective teachers, most fundamentally, are ones who are consistently bringing a renewed awareness and understanding to their practice of teaching. There are a series of identified steps in the process. Teachers make observations about their practice in action, they identify aspects for improvement and change, plan these changes, enact them, and again make observations in order to reflect upon further changes.

In Chapter 1, *Reflecting–Learning–Teaching,* Nick Zepke considers reflective practice for self-development. He outlines the key ideas behind reflection and offers practical ways for becoming a reflective practitioner. He guides the reader in a systematic approach to practice. The chapter also indicates the limitations of simple reflection and argues for a critical reflection whereby the teacher learns to rigorously examine all ideas and so-called truths. However, there are more dimensions to reflection than the conceptual-thinking mind, and the final part of the chapter points the reader to emotional and spiritual aspects.

Chapter 2, *Collaborative Learning Using Reflective Storytelling* by Maxine Alterio and Janice McDrury, develops from the final part of Chapter 1. The authors explore the relationship between reflective learning and the creative act of storytelling and how this can be used by teachers to develop awareness of, and insight into, their various intentions, feelings and motivations. A 'levels of engagement' model analyses the various roles and perspectives listeners and tellers may take. The chapter concludes with practical suggestions for using storytelling with learners.

In Chapter 3, *Action Research Transforming Practice*, Pip Bruce-Ferguson introduces action research as a means for systematic reflection and teacher development. She outlines a history of action research in the USA, the UK and Australasia; examines three different ways of carrying out action research and the role of Habermas's critical theory perspectives; and considers and contrasts solitary and collaborative action research. She illustrates key points with reference to a case study with Anne O'Brien Kennington.

In an age that recognises the importance of diversity and plurality, a means of accountability that validates many different possibilities is essential. The reflective teacher notion provides such a means. It enables teachers to develop the capacity for critical evaluation of their practice and the re-evaluation of their values in collaboration with others. Competent practitioners do not only have a tool bag of teaching strategies and methods. They also have an understanding of the consequences of their practices and are able to provide a rationale for *why* they do what they do. These three chapters offer a variety of means for reflective teachers to recognise the many aspects of their practice and to plunge, should they so choose, into deeper waters of transformation.

— Chapter 1 —

Reflecting–Learning–Teaching

Nick Zepke

Introduction

Reflection is to self-development what a recipe is to cooking. Reflection is a process to help us learn from our own or others' experiences and to turn that learning into action. Just like cooking by recipe, reflective learning is an orderly, logical and rational process. In adult education, indeed, reflection is not just any recipe: it has become *the* recipe for self-improvement. Unless we are reflective practitioners, we somehow lack something. In this chapter, I present reflection as a valuable self-development tool, although I do not suggest that it is the only tool.

Simple reflection can, of course, be criticised. Two critiques are examined at some length. One is that reflection by itself may not make much difference to our development. Reflection can be a comfortable process, where we do not challenge ourselves or the world in which we live. Without critique we may learn nothing new at all. So in this chapter I also examine critical reflection, a way of learning that challenges us to change not only ourselves but the world around us. Another criticism of reflection, and of critical reflection, is that it is so rational and orderly. It is straight-line learning. When we use it we are educating ourselves from the neck up. But we are more than head. We have emotions, values, soul. This chapter also looks at the important role that emotion, spirituality and meditation can play in reflection. So, this chapter has the following ingredients:

- After looking at some underpinning ideas about reflection, it will offer some practical ideas for becoming a reflective practitioner.
- It will then examine four key purposes of critical reflection and build on these with some practical suggestions on how to be critically reflective.

- Finally, it will survey a couple of ways to reflect with more than our heads: to engage spiritually and emotionally with our experiences.

Reflective practice for self-development

Thinking about reflection

Reflection is a "process whereby knowledge is created through the transformation of experience" (Kolb, 1984, p. 38). We constantly reflect on, learn from and rethink our experiences so that we can understand what is happening to us and the world. And we learn from all our experiences – thinking, physical, social, emotional and spiritual. Experiential learning is vital to reflection because, first, our life experiences and background provide necessary building blocks for learning. We can reflect on past experiences to make and re-make meanings. Second, even where the actual experience is the same, different individuals construct different meanings. This suggests that knowledge is constructed by us and not just received from others. *We* do the cooking, not the cookbook. Next, the learning process usually involves learners' active engagement. They cook what they eat, they don't just sit in the restaurant being waited on. Finally, adults' life situations form unique contexts for their learning. The kitchen they cook in is different from other kitchens.

This leads me to constructivism. This is a "view of learning that involves the learner in active, individual processes of knowledge construction based on their previous experience" (Arlidge, 2000, p. 33). Knowledge is not transmitted from 'on high' and is never set in concrete. It is fallible – a recipe, for example, will never turn out quite the same with different cooks or on different occasions. Constructivism values learners' experiences as the foundation on which to build new knowledge. Learners are seen as reflective thinkers because reflection enables them to learn from their experience and prior knowledge. In this process, the teacher is no longer 'the body of knowledge'. She becomes one of many resources for the learner to tap into. Teachers guide, encourage and support the process of learning by creating environments where learners can reflect on their experiences in order to construct and explore new meanings.

The process of cooking has been my greatest teacher about reflection. When I first started cooking I kept closely to the recipe book. I learnt that when I followed instructions to the letter, the dish would turn out right. Then came the day when I could not find a recipe to suit the occasion. I decided to combine the ideas from two recipes. The result was a disaster and I finished up feeding my guests on fish and chips. I reflected on this experience. I looked closely at all the ingredients I had used, decided to change the measure of some and eliminate others. I eventually wrote down a new recipe. In doing this, I constructed new knowledge. It took me a while to cook my new recipe, and I have played around with it ever since. When I cook now, I use my experience to change recipes with some success ... and some failure.

Reflective learning as self-development

Much is expected of us as teachers. We are expected to be content experts when our study years often lie well behind us. We must plan and deliver programmes in tight time frames, often without much formal training or many resources. Our assessment must survive the scrutiny of our profession, the public at large and the demands of students who expect to pass because they have paid good money. Our employers expect us to meet a raft of quality-assurance requirements. Our students perceive a confusing number of conflicting weaknesses in our teaching when giving us feedback. We are faced with having to upgrade our performance in a number of different areas, but we can't get the time or money to help us do so. Enter reflection. It is an ideal self-development tool and does not need money or much extra time to help us lift our performance.

Why is it such a good self-development tool? The short answer is that reflection is a rational and deliberate process leading to planned improvements in clearly specified and focused areas of performance. Let's see how this process might be carried out.

A systematic view of learning

Reflection is based on a systematic view of how learning occurs. I have already mentioned experiential learning and constructivism: the idea that when we learn we construct knowledge actively from our experience. Kolb (1984) constructed a four-stage systematic learning cycle from this notion.

- The first stage is having the experience. Here you read, view a video, have a conversation, hear criticism or praise, teach something new or something you have done before, have an adventure. This is the stage of having 'concrete experiences'.
- In the second stage you review the experience. You cast your mind's eye over it recalling what happened, what you did and felt, noting ideas down in a diary, discussing them with colleagues, a near relative or students, asking questions about them. Kolb calls this stage 'reflective observation'.
- Next you draw conclusions from your experience. You compare the experience with others you have had, pinpoint how this experience confirms or changes your store of existing knowledge and, as a result, revise existing knowledge, behaviours or beliefs. This is the stage of 'abstract conceptualisation'.
- In the final stage you plan to use or apply your conclusions. Here you set objectives, plan new experiences, plan for change and set the stage for a new experience and the cycle to be run again. This is the stage of 'active experimentation'.

Although they don't have to be in any particular order, together the four stages describe the process of reflection.

Exploring the known, revealing the unknown

Self-development is not just about fixing problems. It is equally about recognising strengths. It is also about uncovering unknown corners of our being. Reflecting on our experiences reveals our many strengths and weaknesses as well as revealing things we didn't know about ourselves. By reflecting on strengths, weaknesses and the unknown, we can plan a self-development process. Many years ago, Luft and Ingham (1955) developed a useful tool, the Johari Window (see Figure 1.1).

	Things I know about myself	Things I don't know about myself
Things other people know about me	Open	Blind
Things other people don't know about me	Private	Unknown

Figure 1.1. The Johari Window

The window has four panes; each reveals something about us.

- The open pane is clear and public. It reveals those things both I and other people know about me. In reflecting on my experience to construct new knowledge I can draw on my own and others' knowledge of me.
- The blind pane hides things from me. I don't know things about myself that others do. In reflecting on my experience, I get only a part picture of me. I have to ask others for extra information.
- The third pane is private. It hides part of me from others. When reflecting, only I can get this information. I may never share it with others.
- The unknown pane is hidden to all. It signifies ignorance. Although no one knows what knowledge is hidden behind it, this is a most useful pane. It helps us recognise our own ignorance and open our minds and hearts to new ideas (Chapter 11 has more on the importance of ignorance in learning and teaching).

The panes in the Johari Window are not necessarily the same size. Some of us are very self-aware and open to the scrutiny of others. In such cases the unknown pane is relatively small. People who don't reflect much may have very large unknown areas. Whether large or small, a key purpose of reflection for self-development is to reveal more and more of the unknown self. The Johari Window also shows that in pursuing self-development we must rely on our own devices at times, but must also draw on the knowledge of others.

Reflecting–Learning–Teaching

Prompts for reflective practice

We have many great strengths as well as some weaknesses in how we teach. The *unknown* pane in the Johari window suggests that some important information is hidden from us. We can't develop all our strengths, fix all our weaknesses and push back the curtain of the unknown all at the same time. So, just as a chef plans her menu, we would benefit from planning our self-help programme. By carefully selecting what we want to develop, we can make best use of the reflective process.

I use questions adapted from a set of prompts first published by the Higher Education Research and Development Society of Australasia (HERDSA) to start me off. HERDSA (1992) described the job of teaching as a number of processes:

- designing for learning
- relating to students
- teaching for learning
- assessing and giving feedback
- developing professionally
- influencing our place of work.

The developers then prompted readers to reflect on their practice by asking some pointed questions about each of these processes. I have reduced the number of questions in my version of these prompts. Figure 1.2 summarises my prompts for good practice.

Designing for learning
1. To what extent do you find out your students' expectations about the subject and try to meet those expectations in your planning?
2. What opportunities do you give students to be involved in making decisions about how the course is taught and assessed?
3. How do you explain requirements and standards that cannot be negotiated?
4. How do you build on students' life experiences in your teaching?
5. How do you cater for difference in your students: their gender, culture, value orientations, learning styles, abilities?

Relating to students
6. How do you show students that you respect their values, beliefs and customs without necessarily accepting them?
7. How do you help students to reflect on their known and unrecognised values?
8. How do you help students recognise and value ethical behaviour?
9. How do you help students build confidence in their own abilities to learn and to reflect?
10. In what ways do you provide personal help to your students?

---

cont'd ...

Teaching for learning
11. How do you show students that you are passionate about your subject and about teaching them?
12. What do you do to create passion for learning in your students?
13. How do you develop new approaches to help your students learn?
14. What do you do to discover and to address learning difficulties and/or the needs of particularly able learners?
15. How do you enable students to learn and participate in different ways?
16. How do you help students develop a critical eye for the subject matter you teach?
17. How do you introduce your students to the values and customs of your subject?

Assessing and giving feedback
18. How far do your assessments accurately assess the learning outcomes you intended?
19. What do you do to give timely, constructive and precise feedback to your students so that they can readily improve their performance?
20. How do you help students to routinely assess their own work?
21. What do you do to ensure that your assessments are fair and consistent?

Evaluating teaching
22. What forms of information do you collect about your teaching on a regular basis?
23. How do you use this information?
24. How do you use student feedback to improve your teaching?

Developing professionally
25. How do you keep your expertise in your subject up to date?
26. How do you stay up to date with developments in teaching and learning?
27. What strategies do you use to reflect on your teaching and identify areas for development?

Influencing our place of work
28. In what ways do you keep up to date with national and/or local policy directions affecting learning and teaching and attempt to influence those policy directions?
29. How familiar are you with the decision-making processes used in your place of work and how active are you in attempting to influence decisions?
30. How do you use membership of your professional association to enhance teaching practices in your place of work?

Figure 1.2. Some prompts for reflective practice

Using the prompts for reflection

Just as you can't use all the ingredients listed in a cookbook in one meal, it seems impossible to reflect on all prompts at the same time. Serious self-development using reflection takes effort and you will want to be certain that your precious time leads to real learning. So focus on one prompt question at a time and employ a systematic process to choose it. For example:

Carefully examine each prompt on the list. Now rate your responses to each prompt. Give each prompt a rating indicating how you feel about it:

1. very knowledgeable
2. reasonably knowledgeable
3. partially knowledgeable
4. not very knowledgeable
5. not at all knowledgeable.

Prompts marked with a three (partially knowledgeable) are probably the ones to tackle first. You already have some knowledge on which to build. After succeeding with the threes, try prompts rated four and five. The latter will really help you push back the pane of ignorance.

If you finish up with a whole raft of prompts graded three, employ a secondary selection process. Try grading them according to their importance to you as a teacher. For each prompt, decide whether, for you, feeling more competent about it is:

1. very important
2. important
3. reasonably important
4. not very important
5. not important at all.

Prompts receiving a one (very important) are the ones to explore further.

Having chosen the prompt to respond to, record your current state of knowledge, skill levels and attitudes towards it. Take prompt four as an example: *How do you build on students' life experiences in your teaching?* To improve your responses to this prompt try to increase your knowledge about using learners' life experiences in teaching from books, colleagues and/or by attending courses. Develop skills to apply that knowledge and reflect on attitudes that will help you value the life experiences of others in your subject. Make sure that you record your findings in a diary, on audio tape or in self-development files.

Planning for action

Find actions that address the prompt questions. For example, decide what steps you can take *to build on students' life experience in your teaching.* Your reading, consulting and reflection may reveal the following ideas:

- Initiate new learning by encouraging students to reflect on their experiences in relation to the topic.
- Build student confidence by asking them to find experiences that match the learning they are doing.
- Relate stories from your own experiences to illustrate teaching points.
- Ask students to find stories from their own experiences that illustrate teaching topics.
- Ask students to match experiences to teaching points and principles.
- Set assignments that ask students to apply new learning to their life experiences.
- Teach students to record their life experiences.

Relating new learning to life experiences is a natural process that does not need much encouragement. It won't be long before students will use their experiences as learning tools without further prompting. At that point it is time to start a new self-development activity.

Monitoring progress

A self-developer who does not closely monitor progress is like a dieter without scales. A number of different monitoring 'scales' are available.

Diaries and reflective journals are very good. Used regularly they enable you to keep a close check on progress. Just note down details of what you planned, what happened, and what you learnt. Some people do this in two steps. They first write down everything that comes to mind on the topic. They write freely and instinctively. Then they analyse what they have written and draw lessons from it. It is important to record outcomes and planned changes.

If drawing comes more easily, use that instead of words. Tape recordings can also substitute for written reflective diaries and journals.

You can achieve the same detail in less time using checklists. Pre-record self-development activities on a piece of paper and check them off as you do them. Figure 1.3 offers a checklist for prompt four as an example. If my objective is *build on students' life experience,* my checklist could look like this:

Activity	Achieved		Notes
	Yes	No	
Initiate new learning by encouraging students to reflect on their experiences in relation to the topic.			
Relate stories from your own experience to illustrate points.			
Have students apply topic information to their own experiences.			
Have students identify experiences that illustrate topic points and principles.			
Set assignments that ask students to apply new learning to their life experiences.			

Figure 1.3. A checklist for recording and monitoring reflection

Critically reflective practice for change

Thinking about critical reflection

Although reflection on experiences is central to adult learning and teaching, it has been criticised. The following is a brief summary of some of these criticisms.

- Our memories of experiences vary. Every time we reflect on our experiences, they change in some way.
- When we reflect on our experiences we want to achieve specific purposes and may change conclusions drawn from these experiences according to that purpose. Consequently, reflection can never be trusted as accurate.
- In any learning situation, some of our experiences are more appropriate than others and we do not automatically reflect on the most appropriate experience.
- We accept individual reflection as a true account of experience. This has the effect of putting the individual on a pedestal and reducing the importance of the shared experiences of different groups such as Maori and women (see Chapters 5, 6 and 8 for ideas following up this criticism).
- Reflection is very inward looking. If we do not actively seek new experiences, we won't do any new learning.
- Individual experiences are defined by the experiences of groups we belong to such as socio-economic class, gender or culture. Membership of such a group may set boundaries on what we reflect on, and consequently on our learning.

Brookfield (2000) sorts these criticisms of reflection into four different traditions.

1. *Ideological critique.* This holds that certain belief systems, such as capitalism, impose one way of thinking on us. This creates inequities in education and society at large. Simple reflection does not look at the wider picture and so cannot identify and help us escape from dominating ideologies and the inequities they protect.
2. *The humanist psychology of adult learning.* According to this tradition, people want to develop themselves to their full potential. To achieve this, they must be able to critically examine their experiences. They can't do this using simple reflection.
3. *Philosophical.* This tradition argues that we do not learn effectively unless we know how to identify and refute false arguments. The focus of simple reflection is definitely not on logical fallacies and errors of fact.
4. *Social constructivism.* This holds knowledge to be constructed by different groups. Ethnic, socio-economic, gender and religious are examples of groups constructing views of the world that differ from the views of other groups. Simple reflection does not lead to an understanding of the social origins of knowledge.

All four traditions support the view that development cannot be based on reflection alone. To be an effective tool for self-development, reflection must be critical.

In the remainder of this section, I approach critical reflection. I try to clarify what 'being critical' means to you as a learner. I do this using two questions: 'What is being critical?' and 'How can I be critical?'. In answering the first question I will examine some meanings of 'being critical' and outline critical activities belonging to these. For the second question I propose the use of a simple tool.

What is 'being critical'?

In the light of the discussion above, I offer four meanings for 'being critical':

- Identify faulty facts or logic in the thinking and reflection of others.
- Recognise and challenge ideas that ensure the dominance of certain ideologies.
- Examine your own reflections and assumptions about the world in the light of how others explain theirs.
- Actively work to improve yourself so that you reach your potential.

The practical suggestions that follow pick up all of these meanings under two headings: 'criticising' and 'critiquing'. In 'criticising' we examine the factual and logical bases of meanings. When 'critiquing' we critically reflect on ideologies and our own assumptions. When taken together, 'criticising' and 'critiquing' tackle critical reflection for self-improvement.

Criticising

Criticising is finding fault. Being critical in this sense is to spot a problem with an idea, structure or action, to analyse and research the problem, to argue your findings.

Reflecting–Learning–Teaching

You may find an acceptable alternative idea to replace the faulty one. In general there are three ways to spot, analyse, research and argue faults in an idea.

- Problems with factual claims
  An idea uses problematic facts. These could range from incorrect use of statistics and questionable appeals to evidence, to unsupported generalisations. An example illustrating all three uses of problematic facts is found in the statement *adult learners are self-directed*. This idea implies the statistical concept of 'all'. This in common-sense terms alone is absurd. Moreover, it is a generalisation that assumes that the sentence is fact regardless of culture or gender. In being critical you will be sceptical about such facts.

- Problems with faulty logic
  An idea is based on wobbly reasoning. The facts may support a premise (assumption) but not the conclusion the author wants to draw from it. Take the statement *some adults are self-directed*. You may find on analysis that this claim is factually defensible. It can become the basis for an idea and the premise of an argument. But this premise may not support a conclusion an author wishes to reach. For example, it would not support a conclusion that lecturing to adult students is inappropriate. Self-directed learners may choose to be lectured. There is no logical bridge here between premise and conclusion. Try to spot unbridged rivers of logic.

- Problems with questionable assumptions
  Presented without specific evidence, the statement *adult learners are self-directed* is an assumption. Assumptions are often the focus of criticism. They may be unreasonable in that they run counter to facts, logic or our own experiences. *Adult learners are self-directed* is not a reasonable assumption when we have worked exclusively with students who just want us to give them the facts. Assumptions can also be criticised if they are inappropriate. The assumption *adult learners are self-directed* is inappropriate if it is used to underpin policies reducing funding for classroom learning.

Critiquing

For me criticism takes care of formal flaws in arguments. Critique enables me to recognise and challenge ideas that ensure the dominance of certain ideologies; to examine my own reflections and assumptions about the world in the light of how others explain theirs and to actively work to improve myself so that I reach my potential. Critique occurs from two conflicting viewpoints: distrust of universal truths and trust that a kind of truth will emerge as the result of critique. Both viewpoints are useful when 'being critical'.

- Truth busting
  It is not wise to accept sentences like *adult learners are self-directed* as true statements. This simple sentence carries many possible meanings. For example,

the word 'adult' does not describe a single identity. The precise meaning of adult depends on variables like age, gender, socio-economic status, culture, geographical location. Learning is a many-faceted activity. 'Self-directed' can apply to people who wish to learn alone, as well as to those who seek out learning groups. In short, a universally correct meaning is unattainable as each person considering the sentence interprets it differently. True, over time some interpretations, like those of Malcolm Knowles in this example, become privileged. Their versions, after all, are published as texts. But this fact does not make their interpretations true or protect them from your critique (Chapter 6 offers such a critique). With truth unattainable, your critique is important as it could contribute to new insights into the text *adult learners are self-directed*.

- Truth trusting
  This viewpoint holds that it is downright dangerous to leave ideas, structures and actions uncritiqued. *Adult learners are self-directed,* for example, can be used to exclude and oppress groups of people. Learners who don't want to be self-directed or cultures that value group over individualised learning can be oppressed by exclusion if such ideas are seen by a trusting majority as natural, preordained and for the good of society. Left uncritiqued, such ideas can be used by a powerful minority to impose processes serving their own interests. Money-saving 'student-directed learning' comes to mind as an example. Active critique, on the other hand, leads to dialogue that can reduce misunderstandings and that enables people to escape 'false' consciousness (assumptions) and achieve a kind of personal truth and emancipation.

How to be critical?

Being critical means questioning the validity of arguments, the nature of truth and the contexts which generate the arguments. In my view a major critical tool is *the question* that opens up for evaluation any idea encountered in learning. The following questions can be used as a starting point for the critical journey.

Factual claims
- How sensible are the numbers supporting the argument?
- How conclusive is the empirical (scientific) evidence provided?
- How well supported are the generalisations?
- How do the facts match personal experience/knowledge?
- What suggests that the facts should be distrusted in this argument?

Faulty logic
- What are the premises here?
- What other conclusions do the premises allow?

- What makes these premises sensible, sound?
- What is suspicious about the premises?
- What other premises does the conclusion allow?

Testing assumptions
- What are the assumptions here? Are there any hidden ones?
- What world-view/ideological standpoint do they have?
- How well do the assumptions match personal experience?
- Do I want to challenge any assumptions? In what way?
- If I can challenge any assumption, would the argument stand?

Truth busting
- What is my interpretation of the meaning of this?
- How does this differ from the author?
- What other interpretations are possible? How do they match my experience?
- What interpretations are privileged? Why? How?
- What other insights about the idea are possible?

Truth trusting
- Who will be oppressed if this idea is accepted?
- Who is currently oppressed by this idea?
- What needs to be changed in this idea?
- Who will help me get this idea challenged?
- Who should listen to my challenge?
- How can I achieve personal truth?

A question to finish this section: how critically reflective have you been about what I have written?

Revealing the unknown: Reflection beyond reason

Both reflection and critical reflection focus on one human attribute – rationality. Yet we are not just disconnected heads relying on reason to learn. There are other facets to being human. We are physical, emotive and spiritual beings as well as rational ones. Theories of learning originating in the East, with feminism and also with first peoples, such as Maori, have long recognised the holistic nature of learning. They suggest that we learn from all our experiences: physical, social, emotional and spiritual as well as mental. In adult education one aspect of holism, spirituality, has recently surfaced 'like dandelions in the spring' to balance its love affair with the rational (English and Gillen, 2000, p. 1). According to English and Gillen spirituality is not necessarily religious. They define it as "an awareness of something greater than ourselves, a sense that we are connected to all human beings and to all of creation" (p. 1). Such awareness can tempt us away from seeing learning as food for the intellect alone.

Meditation is a word often used to describe reflection focusing on the whole person and our connection to other humans and to all creation. It is often described as a holistic process involving relaxation, concentration and an opening of self to the world. The object of meditation is to achieve clarity beyond mere thought: to learn "that there is an awareness that exists independent of thought" (Chance, 2002, p. 2). Meditation is a process embedded in the practice of many religions and spiritual movements. In such traditions awareness beyond thought is associated with finding 'God', 'soul', 'the inner guide', 'peace' or 'enlightenment'. Many different techniques and practices have been published in books and presented on videotapes and film. My purpose for writing about meditation in this chapter is not to introduce you to the ways of a particular religion or spiritual movement or a particular community of practice but to complete my survey of reflection for self-development by introducing you to a reflective process which is beyond reason.

In doing so I feel a fraud. I don't belong to a community of practice myself and am struggling to develop my own meditative self. I liken my current practice of meditation to my understanding of cooking ethnic food. I know its ingredients, preparation and cooking processes, but I don't know the spiritual and cultural underpinnings and folkways that Indians, say, or Chinese or Thai infuse into their cooking. So I cook ethnic-tasting food, but not the authentic Indian or Chinese or Thai fare. I am relieved somewhat by Millman (1999), who assures me that meditation is not a special, higher spiritual practice, an elevated state of being or exclusively Eastern. Chance (2002, p. 3) believes that "there is no 'right' meditation technique .... The important thing is to find what works for you."

Meditation as reflective practice

Whereas reflection and critical reflection focus consciously on the development of a specific skill, idea, understanding or behaviour, meditation attempts to create a void. We use meditation techniques to help eliminate conscious thoughts from our mind so that we become aware of peacefulness, increased mental focus and clarity. Inner peace, focus and clarity enable us to develop our understanding of and sense of being in the world and therefore our learning and teaching. There are possibly hundreds of ways to meditate. I offer some general thoughts here, with the purpose of developing teaching and learning.

Relaxation

- Go to a familiar place. It does not have to be specially set aside or furnished for meditation. It could be your bedroom, a corner of the passage, your office, classroom or the bathroom. It could also be outdoors under a tree, beside a river or a favourite place in your garden.

- Get into a relaxing position. It does not have to be a yoga position. You could lie down, try to achieve balance through movement, or soak in a hot tub. I meditate as I run on the gymnasium treadmill.
- To achieve relaxation some people listen to music, chant a repetitive mantra, deep breathe or inhale fragrances. This works for some, but others do not require external help to relax. Find out what works for you.

Concentration

- Meditation involves intense concentration. You aim to ease random thoughts out of your consciousness.
- To assist your concentration, try focusing intensely on an object such as a candle, a flower, a picture or a physical movement.
- Some find music and mantra not only relaxing but useful in developing and maintaining concentration. Make the mantra meaningful, otherwise you may fall asleep. Others wait for an inner voice to speak to them.
- Concentration is hard work. Random thoughts are energetic beasts and can easily return once you have got rid of them. I seem to be able to clear my mind for a mini-second before it is re-infested. I am assured that with continued practice, I will get better at clearing my mind.

Timing

- How often should you meditate? Once a day is desirable. However, it is probably more useful to meditate irregularly and/or rarely than not meditate at all.
- It is difficult to say how long we should meditate. The textbooks I have consulted suggest between 15 and 30 minutes. I am aiming for 10 minutes.
- Morning seems to be a good time for many people to meditate. Some seem to do best when they first wake up, but there is no set time. Go with your bio-rhythms.

Insight meditation

Meditation as I have described here may not seem to lead to any specific improvements in teaching skills. Unlike reflection and critical reflection there seems no action plan, no payoff. True, there is no written action plan, no reflective journal; after all, the whole purpose of meditation is to reflect in ways not driven by our rational selves. But there are outcomes. "Insight meditation involves noticing (that is, becoming mindful of) everything that arises in your awareness" (Millman, 1999, p. 155). You notice events, emotions, behaviours – anything that arises in your awareness. You gain an understanding of it then let it go. Awareness, understanding and surrender are the outcomes of reflection offered by meditation.

I 'meditate' while exercising. I relax by 'listening' to my steps as I pound along on the treadmill in the gym. There comes a time when I am aware of nothing but my steps. Then there is nothing at all. This is not associated with any particular feeling of peace or happiness and, by my untested reckoning, probably lasts no more than a few seconds. Yet from this 'nothing', insight is born. In my case this has never yet been earthshaking. Often it is the solution to a practical problem I have been wrestling with in the conscious world. Sometimes it illuminates a corner of the *unknown* pane in the Johari Window. This morning I learnt how I might finish this chapter.

Developing reflective practice

I have explored three different ways to reflect. 'Simple' reflection enables us to learn from our experiences by constructing knowledge from them. It is a very rational process and I have emphasised this by offering some tightly structured methods as a guide to becoming a reflective practitioner. But reflection is an inward-looking process that neglects the outside world and can restrict our learning. Critical reflection focuses us on the outside world. It, too, is a rational process but one which recognises us as creators of intellectual and social change. Meditation is a reflective process that considers us to be spiritual and emotional as well as intellectual beings. Reflection occurs in a relaxed and intensely focused state and enables us to achieve insight about ourselves. Unlike the other forms of reflection, meditation does not necessarily lead directly to action.

In reading this chapter, we have only skimmed the surface of reflection. What are other aids to developing reflective practice? I finish by offering some ideas:

- Talk to others about how they reflect. Will their methods and techniques work for you?
- Read more books. Here are some suggestions in addition to the books cited in the *References* section:

    Brookfield, S. (1995). *Becoming a Critically Reflective Teacher.* San Francisco: Jossey Bass.
    Jackson, R., & Caffarella, R. (eds). (1994). *Experiential Learning: A New Approach.* San Francisco: Jossey-Bass.
    McKeever, S. (1997). *Learn to Meditate.* San Diego: McKeever Publishing.

- Design your own prompts for good practice. Be particularly careful to include prompts for critical reflection. Which of these prompts will illuminate the *unknown* pane of the Johari Window?
- Design your own self-development programme based on reflective techniques. Will you try meditation?
- Reflect with others and get feedback from others too. Reflecting alone is like cooking for yourself: tedious and without joy. Chapters 2, 3 and 8 delve much more closely into collaborative learning and teaching.

Glossary

Constructivism: describes a view of learning in which the learner takes an active part in making meaning of experiences.

Ideology: a set of ideas about social life based on tightly defined beliefs, values, sense of history and place in society.

References

Arlidge, J. (2000). Constructivism: Is anyone making meaning in New Zealand adult education? *New Zealand Journal of Adult Learning, 28* (1), 32–49.

Brookfield, S. (2000). The concept of critically reflective practice. A. Wilson, & E. Hayes (eds), *Handbook of Adult and Continuing Education*. San Francisco: Jossey Bass and the American Association for Adult and Continuing Education.

Chance, J. (2002). *An Approach to Spiritual Consciousness* [Web Page]. URL http://www.spiritweb.org.Spirit/meditation-faq.html [2002, March 6].

English, L. & Gillen, M. (2000). Addressing the spiritual dimensions of adult learning: What educators can do. *New Directions for Adult and Continuing Education, 85*. San Francisco: Jossey Bass Publishers.

Higher Education Research and Development Society (HERDSA) (1992). *Challenging Conceptions of Teaching: Some Prompts for Good Practice*. HERDSA.

Kolb, D. (1984). *Experiential Learning*. Englewood Cliffs, New Jersey: Prentice Hall.

Luft, J., & Ingham, H. (1955). *The Johari Window: A Graphic Model for Interpersonal Relations*. University of California Western Training Laboratory in Group Development.

Millman, D. (1999). *Everyday Enlightenment. The Twelve Gateways to Personal Growth*. Sydney: Hodder.

— Chapter 2 —

Collaborative Learning Using Reflective Storytelling

Maxine Alterio and Janice McDrury

Introduction

In this chapter we focus on the relationship between reflective learning and communicative action. To demonstrate how reflection and dialogue can enhance collaborative learning endeavours we:

- outline the theoretical constructs that underpin communicative action and link the associated dynamics of 'social interaction' and 'lifeworld' to reflective learning;
- explore communicative action as a process that involves engagement in critical discourse to develop awareness of, and insight into, our intentions, feelings and motivations;
- introduce a *Levels of Engagement Model* to show how past experiences and feelings influence our perspectives during storytelling sessions;
- describe a collaborative storytelling approach that emphasises the role of critical reflective dialogue in constructing new knowledge;
- conclude with some suggestions on how to develop a storytelling approach to learning.

Communicative action

The transformative nature of the learning process continues to interest theorists from a range of disciplines. Jürgen Habermas, a philosopher and sociologist, is influential in the area of adult learning. He contends that three areas of human interest – technical, practical and emancipatory – are involved in knowledge generation and that all are "grounded in our relationships to the environment, other people, and power, respectively" (Mezirow, 1991, p. 72). We offer an example of how these areas relate to learning and provide you with an opportunity to reflect on your practice and apply Habermas's approach to your particular context.

Areas of Human Interest (Mezirow, 1991)	An example	Your example
Technical (Telling or listening to a story)	What happened? I taught a maths session recently that I didn't feel happy with because the students seemed uninterested.	Think of an example from your practice.
Practical (Asking questions about a story to explore meaning and context)	What might have contributed to the students' lack of interest? It was after lunch on a hot Friday afternoon. I was showing them how to classify different objects and record the findings in a table. I asked them to take notes, which they did half-heartedly.	What might have contributed to your experience?
Emancipatory (Engaging in conversation to reveal new layers of meaning or reflecting on similar situations which had different outcomes)	What might I have done differently? I remembered a really good science session I did on a hot Friday afternoon last year. We went outside and collected materials, then came back into class where I got the students to work in small groups and decide for themselves how they could best report their findings. The students were really interested; they shared ideas and produced creative presentations to the rest of the class. Perhaps I could have engaged my maths class in a similar way. From now on I will include active learning strategies into this Friday afternoon session.	What might I have done differently?

Figure 2.1. **Examples of human interest**

Habermas (1989) suggests that the technical and practical areas of human interest can be separated into two different learning domains: instrumental and communicative. Instrumental learning is concerned with controlling and manipulating aspects of the environment, while communicative learning focuses on understanding ourselves and being understood by others. We include an example of these two modes of learning and provide you with the opportunity to reflect on your practice from both perspectives.

Instrumental learning Providing art students in a print-making session with a specific dye, material and frame.	*Think of an example from your practice.* *To what level did the students engage in this activity?*
Communicative learning Engaging students in a discussion about appropriate dyes, materials and frames and encouraging them to share the reasons behind their choices with the class.	*Think of an example from your practice.* *To what level did the students engage in this activity?*

Figure 2.2.   Learning domains

Communicative action takes place when we engage others in dialogue for the purpose of making sense of our experience and working together to achieve our respective aims. When we negotiate meanings and purposes, rather than passively accepting the social realities of others, we enhance our potential to construct new perspectives and bring about change to our practice.

Fundamental to this process are two interrelated dynamics:

- 'lifeworld', our culturally transmitted and socially generated perspectives, and
- 'social interaction', those we involve in our learning processes.

Two key learning skills are associated with these dynamics.

- participating in critical reflective dialogue where claims are made overt and examined
- assessing the validity of statements in relation to supporting evidence.

When reflection is focused in these ways, we can examine the assumptions and premises that underpin communicative action.

Critical reflection and storytelling

It is our contention that we can engage in critical reflective learning with others and, at the same time, recognise and challenge the "faulty assumptions and dominant ideologies" that Nick Zepke refers to in Chapter 1. In order to do so, we need to:

- draw on personal experience
- promote dialogue
- use creative group processes to surface multiple perspectives
- value feelings as integral to the learning process
- explore the impact of context (cultural, social, political, spiritual, etc.) on experience
- encourage the development of critical reflective approaches to learning.

We believe that when we reflect on experience, we frequently encounter complex and diverse situations; therefore, straightforward rational approaches are not sufficient. It is our contention that meaningful learning occurs when we critically reflect on experience using creative group processes such as storytelling. We believe a key factor in storytelling's success is that it involves others and can be formally structured to incorporate a range of critical reflective activities (McDrury & Alterio, 2001).

Reflection

Reflection is not only an individual process, something we do in private. Rather it is, as Moon (1999) believes, "an orientation to the activities of life" (p. 100). Her position lends support to Brookfield's (1995) claim that reflective activities frequently become more productive when others are involved. When we engage in opportunities to view experiences from different perspectives we create the potential for new learning.

Critical reflective dialogue plays a significant role in maximising these learning gains and revealing multiple perspectives, as demonstrated in Brockbank and McGill's (1998) observation:

> For us dialogue that is reflective, and enables critically reflective learning, engages the person at the edge of their current knowledge, their sense of self and the world as experienced by them. Thus their assumptions about knowledge, themselves and their world are challenged (p. 57).

An example of how critical reflective dialogue can reveal multiple perspectives is demonstrated in the following example. We invite you to reflect on a similar situation from your practice. (See Figure 2.3.)

To engage in critical reflection, we must genuinely believe in the value of embracing a reflective orientation to learning. It is not enough to think reflection is a good idea; we must give thoughtful consideration to why, how and when it can be used to bring about focused learning. Haigh (2000) suggests three factors are essential to effective reflection: "belief in the value of reflection, knowledge of what would be a worthwhile focus for reflection, and a rich repertoire of reflection skills" (p. 95).

Teacher's perspective	Student's perspective
Lee, a student in my geography class, failed to submit an assignment that had a three-week lead-in time and a clear process for applying for an extension. He didn't make any attempt to contact me or tell me that he hadn't completed the assignment. I had no alternative but to fail him.	I had been working really hard on my assignment when my grandmother got sick and had to come and stay with us. I was torn between needing to help look after my grandmother, who has been very good to me, and wanting to keep up with my school work. Every time I started on my assignment, my grandmother called me to help her. I felt really anxious about my assignment because I knew the teacher would be mad at me but I wanted to help my grandmother too and I didn't want to bother Mum because she was really busy.
Think of a similar situation from your practice.	*Think what the student's perspective in your story might have been.*
Mother's perspective	**Principal's perspective**
We've had a really tough time lately. Mum got sick and needed to come and stay. Both my husband and I were working different shifts so we had to rely on Lee to help look after Mum and the younger children. I know Mum is really demanding, always calling out for something so Lee's been under a lot of pressure. I hope his school work is not suffering.	When I reviewed the class results I noticed that Lee had failed a major assignment. According to his profile, he's usually conscientious and hands things in on time. I'm sure he talked to me about going to university. I wonder what's happened?
Think of what the parent's perspective in your story might have been.	*Think of what the principal's perspective in your story might have been.*

What do you think might have happened if all these perspectives were known?

How might you get to know these perspectives?

Figure 2.3. **Multiple perspectives**

We also stress the importance of context. Reflection as a social process, for example when storytelling is used as a learning tool, cannot be understood without reference to context. Critically and reflectively examining where, when and why events occurred is as important as processing who was involved, what happened and how the scenario was constructed. It is, therefore, necessary to ensure that contextual aspects are incorporated into storytelling processes.

Storytelling

In recent years, the reflective movement has promoted the idea that we each carry within us creative learning capabilities. Storytelling is one of those capabilities. When we critically reflect on our stories and process them in focused and thoughtful ways, learning is enhanced. Learning through storytelling provides us with opportunities to:

- work co-operatively
- encompass holistic perspectives
- value emotional realities
- link theory to practice
- stimulate critical thinking skills
- capture complexities of situations
- reveal multiple perspectives
- make sense of experience
- engage in self-review
- construct new knowledge.

We can also challenge faulty assumptions and question dominant ideologies as part of critical reflective processes. Each storytelling group can negotiate guidelines that enable them to work with their stories in ways which meet specific learning outcomes.

While there are many ways to work with and learn from stories, tellers and listeners always play key roles. Habermas (1989) classifies this aspect as 'social interaction'. The degree and type of interaction will depend on how storytelling groups work together and what outcomes they wish to achieve. Also relevant are the settings in which stories are told, and whether a *spontaneous* story, one that has not been through any previous form of reflection, is shared, or a *predetermined* one that has already undergone some reflective activity such as journalling (McDrury & Alterio, 2002).

Formal and informal storytelling settings

We distinguish between *informal* and *formal* storytelling settings because we think they serve different purposes. When we talk of *informal settings* we mean the places where we engage in casual conversations, such as stairways, lifts, staffrooms, corridors or car parks: the times we encounter a colleague, or a group of colleagues, and say something like, "You'll never guess what happened to me in class today", then unload the event and our associated feelings through a story. In these circumstances, outcomes tend to be primarily cathartic, in that they enable expression and release of emotions; however, while we may feel better, we rarely achieve a changed perspective.

When we use the term *formal settings* we refer to situations where space and time have been organised for specific storytelling sessions and where those involved have negotiated storytelling processes to meet their learning needs. Such formal arrangements have the expectation that while feelings and emotions are shared and valued, new learning or insight will also occur, and, as a consequence, practice will be examined and frequently changes actioned.

Storytelling and learning outcomes

Knowing what we want to achieve when we work with stories is crucial. In our earlier work, we discussed how selecting different storytelling pathways impacts on potential learning outcomes (McDrury & Alterio, 2001). While there are many ways in which stories can be defined, in this chapter we focus on eight. The initial four pathways tend to have greater cathartic outcomes. The latter four focus on higher levels of reflective learning.

1. Informal setting, single listener, spontaneous story.
2. Informal setting, single listener, predetermined story.
3. Informal setting, multiple listeners, spontaneous story.
4. Informal setting, multiple listeners, predetermined story.
5. Formal setting, single listener, spontaneous story.
6. Formal setting, single listener, predetermined story.
7. Formal setting, multiple listeners, spontaneous story.
8. Formal setting, multiple listeners, predetermined story.

While each pathway has a useful purpose, we recommend *formal setting/single or multiple listener* options when critical, reflective outcomes are desired. When a single listener and single teller are involved in a formal storytelling process, depth of reflection is present and two perspectives are available. Multiple listeners encourage breadth of reflection and offer multiple perspectives to a single teller. In both situations, assumptions and perspectives are likely to be challenged.

Each storytelling group will process their stories differently, depending on their focus and purpose. As Metzger (1986) explains:

> Stories go in circles. They do not go in straight lines. So it helps if you listen in circles because there are stories inside stories and stories between stories and finding your way through them is as easy and as hard as finding your way home. And part of the finding is getting lost. If you're lost you really start to look around and listen (p. 104).

To convey what we think might be happening under the surface, we have borrowed the scriptwriting term *backstory*. Backstory implies that another story (or stories) has

Collaborative Learning Using Reflective Storytelling   41

shaped the main story, the one currently being told. For example, in the story about multiple perspectives involving Lee, his parents, a teacher and a principal, the backstory about his grandmother being ill and coming to stay with the family was only available to Lee and his parents. In the following exercise, we invite you to identify a backstory. From a scriptwriting perspective, the backstory contains information needed for the main story to have a plausible context, authentic drama and complex directions that eventually lead to a credible resolution (Rubie, 1999). Scriptwriters use the phrase *pacing of information* to describe how they present this information, flashbacks being a commonly used technique (Rubie, 1999). If we think of our backstories as being informed by our past experiences, which include the contexts in which we operate, we begin to appreciate how they might shape our main stories.

Dramatic presentations of our main stories vary, according to the chronology or sequence of events we choose to share: for example, what information we reveal and what we leave out, how and when dramatic effects are applied, which aspects are accentuated and what themes we consciously or unconsciously use to underpin our stories. Crucial to the successful presentation of any story is how the question *why* is answered. *Why* did events unfold in a particular manner and *why* did those involved behave in certain ways. In other words, what are the backstories?

In the example you used to explore multiple perspectives, how might you have uncovered a backstory?

How would having knowledge of the backstory influence your decision-making process?

What happens when we tell and process stories in educational settings?

The concept of backstory appealed to us, so we explored how it might be adapted to convey what we think happens when we tell and process stories in educational settings. We suggest that along with backstories, two other influences contribute to our learning potential: what Habermas refers to as 'lifeworld' and 'social interaction'. As we stated earlier, 'lifeworld' encompasses our culturally transmitted and socially generated perspectives, which include our spiritual orientation, whereas social interaction refers to those whom we involve in our learning. Interaction helps us to articulate, explore and clarify details within our stories. Our feelings also shape what and how we learn. When we experience intense emotions in relation to particular stories, unresolved issues might be present. Perhaps we have felt the same way before, possibly in relation to similar situations. If we work with our emotions in positive ways they can assist our learning; however, if they overwhelm us or have a negative impact, the reverse may occur.

Through stories we can explore, with others, the significance of our backstories, 'lifeworlds' and feelings. To be successful as a learning tool, storytelling processes must incorporate critical, reflective dialogue and establish shared meanings that enable us to examine, explain and creatively reconstruct events.

Critical reflective dialogue is a key component in our Levels of Engagement Model (Figure 2.4). At each of the five stages of engagement, tellers and listeners are involved in communicative relationships. However, there will be variations in tellers' and listeners' perspectives, given their different backstories, 'lifeworlds' and emotional involvements. There will also be variations in learning for the same reasons.

Levels of engagement

We have identified five levels of engagement. While there are similarities in the way tellers and listeners engage in storytelling, there are also differences, given their perspectives and roles. We now outline these differences. We start by exploring what might be happening for tellers, then consider the same levels from a listener's perspective.

Tellers

Tellers operating at the first level, *connecting with context*, are initially involved in establishing rapport with listeners. Greetings may be exchanged, connections acknowledged and the physical layout of the room considered. Guidelines may be discussed and the storytelling process described. This is a time for orientation, shifting focus from previous activities to the current situation and setting. Reflection at this stage is unlikely.

At the second level, *telling the story*, focus is on the teller's representation. "Motives, ideas, words or events depict their point of view and are substantiated through tone of voice, points of emphasis, and gestures" (McDrury & Alterio, 2001, p. 64). Tellers choose, consciously or unconsciously, which elements will be included and excluded, whether they will tell their stories as comedies or dramas and whether or not to identify winners or losers. Tellers also determine what level of affective involvement they will reveal. Reflection still tends to be minimal at this stage.

The third level involves *clarifying events*. Tellers may backtrack after making a statement or comment or follow it with a retraction or further substantiation.

Collaborative Learning Using Reflective Storytelling

Social Interaction

Teller's Perspective — Listener's Perspective

- Lifeworlds
- Past Experience
- Feelings

Main Story

↓

Back Stories

↓

Connecting with context

↓

Telling/Listening to story

↓

Clarifying events

↓

Engaging in critical reflective dialogue

↓

Constructing new knowledge

↓

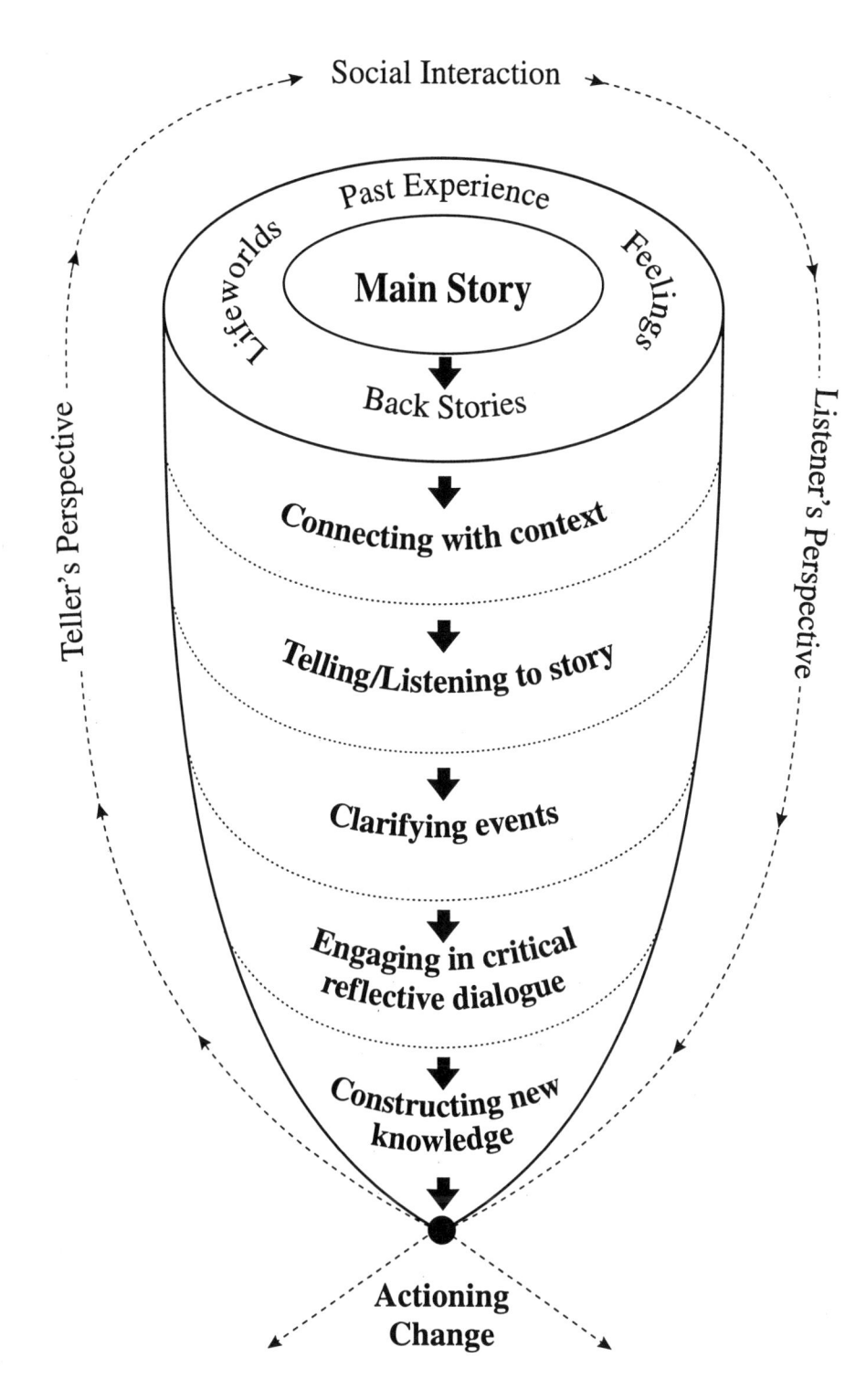

Actioning Change

Figure 2.4.   Levels of engagement

Listeners might ask questions or seek clarification over particular aspects and tellers will respond accordingly. At all times it is essential for tellers to retain control of their stories. They can "confirm, elaborate, explain, clarify or refute aspects raised by listeners" (McDrury & Alterio, 2001, p. 64). Tellers are also listeners to their own stories. They may hear their story in a new way or be aware that something they say is not quite right or clear and rectify it. Tellers also remember additional aspects about their situations as they tell their stories. Reflection starts to play an important role in the storytelling process as tellers and listeners engage in dialogue to uncover previously unconscious connections or to question assumptions. Aspects relating to context and 'lifeworld' may also be revealed during this stage.

It is our contention that only after tellers feel comfortable operating at these three levels will they venture into the realm of *engaging in critical reflective dialogue*, the fourth stage. This stage is particularly important to the learning process because when tellers actively involve listeners in processing their stories, opportunities are created to acknowledge and value feelings, make links between present situations and past experiences and critically explore relevant aspects. Being open to alternative perspectives and willing to challenge existing assumptions and dominant ideologies indicates a critical orientation. Shifts in thinking are now possible and critical reflection is evident.

The fifth level, *constructing new knowledge*, may enhance understanding, expand possibilities or result in changed perspectives. Tellers may view their situations and themselves, or the worlds in which they operate, differently. When tellers reach this final stage, they frequently demonstrate the ability to critically reflect on their experiences from multiple perspectives and are able to critically evaluate a range of possible resolutions and solutions. Implications for self and practice are also thoughtfully considered before any change is actioned. Evidence of critical reflection is apparent throughout this level.

Listeners

While tellers are managing their storytelling roles, listeners are also working. At the first level of engagement they are *connecting with context,* which includes establishing relationships with the teller and others in the group. They are also actively involved in negotiations regarding processes and guidelines and may suggest changes to room layouts. However, as with tellers, there is little evidence of reflection at this stage.

During the second level, the role of listeners is *focusing on* and *listening to the teller's story*. They may note the teller's tone of voice, points of emphasis and gestures. They may wonder about particular aspects or ponder over why the teller chooses to tell their story in a particular way: for example, as a comedy rather than a drama. While they may identify their own feelings as they listen, it is important for listeners to remain focused on the primary story rather than recalling one of their own, even if it has a similar theme. It is also useful for listeners to note any emotions they see or hear the teller express. Although such aspects may be noted, reflection still tends to be minimal at this stage.

When listeners enter the third level of engagement they are checking details or

Collaborative Learning Using Reflective Storytelling

clarifying events and may ask the teller questions to fill in any gaps. Alternatively, listeners might provide their own answers through internal cognitive processing, a clear example of their own backstories influencing their understanding and perception of the current story. While it is appropriate for listeners to seek clarification about aspects of the teller's experience, it is not useful for them to make judgements or give opinions about actions taken or not taken. Again, reflection is minimal at this stage. Focus is on establishing a clear description of the experience.

The fourth level, characterised by *engaging in critical reflective dialogue*, will, as with all levels, be shaped by the listeners' understanding of the teller's situation. Also, the way and degree to which listeners engage the teller in critical reflective questioning influences what they learn themselves. At this stage, it is crucial for listeners to *present* other possibilities as discussion points, to *ponder* over key aspects and perhaps *wonder* about the role of current assumptions and dominant ideologies. The purpose for listeners is to engage the teller in critically reflective conversations and to identify alternative perspectives. While focus is on shifts in the teller's thinking, listeners can also make significant cognitive movement. Reflection, at this level, is critically orientated.

Listeners may also reach the fifth level, *constructing new knowledge*, and bring about change to their practice as a result of involvement with the teller's story. Some listeners may have experienced a similar situation to the teller. Being able to step back from personal situations and listen to the teller's story, and later evaluate possible resolutions and solutions, can provide listeners with enough distance to consider their own concerns from different perspectives.

As stated, the learning that occurs for tellers and listeners may differ, which is appropriate given their different backstories, 'lifeworlds' and associated feelings. What remains consistent is that learning occurs when we use storytelling in critically reflective ways. As we noted earlier, although our experiences can be storied differently, there will always be some commonalities because when we tell stories we are describing aspects of the human condition. Perhaps it is because of these commonalities that we can, on occasions, come to shared understandings.

To summarise, we believe that the key to successful learning through storytelling rests on:

- where we choose to tell our stories
- what type of stories we tell
- which storytelling process we use
- who we involve in the process
- how the process is managed
- what level and degree of critical, reflective dialogue we engage in
- which outcomes we wish to achieve.

When thoughtful consideration is given to these aspects, and negotiated processes are established, learning is maximised. This is particularly true if we consider and address other key issues as part of our initial co-negotiations.

What issues do we need to consider?

It is prudent before engaging in storytelling sessions to consider and address a range of issues such as whether any aspects will be assessed, how ethical issues will be managed and what principles best underpin the processes we use. Although we will briefly address each issue in turn, for a more in-depth discussion on assessment and ethical issues in relation to storytelling, we refer you to 'Ethical and Assessment Considerations' (McDrury & Alterio, 2002, Chapter 10).

Assessment issues

We take the position that assessing the telling and processing of stories during a storytelling session is not useful because it changes the nature of the storytelling process in the same way that assessing journal entries alters students' writing styles and content. We prefer to use exemplars, which, from our perspective, are creative pieces of work based on experiences. When used in relation to storytelling, exemplars involve "documenting the whole or parts of a story or stories in particular ways for specific purposes (McDrury & Alterio, 2002, p. 103). We prefer this approach for several reasons. First, successful stories are those tellers share that are unhindered by assessment requirements. Focus remains on the telling, not the evaluation. Second, having a period of time between telling our stories and writing about our learning enables us to participate in an additional reflective phase. In our experience, additional learning frequently surfaces during this extra phase. Finally, exemplars can be structured so the focus remains on key learning points. We recommend that everyone involved co-negotiates criteria for each exemplar.

Ethical issues

Storytelling, like any learning tool that draws on experience, can be challenging because it raises several ethical issues. This is particularly true when we tell stories about our work experiences. Stories that emerge from practice often contain a range of feelings, concerns and uncertainties and we may experience some distress when we share them. For this reason we recommend that experienced facilitators with sound communication and group skills are used to manage storytelling sessions. We also suggest that appropriate forms of support are made available to those who participate in storytelling activities, such as counselling or one-to-one sessions with an appropriate person.

As with any sharing of sensitive information, regardless of whether it is in pairs or groups, it is also prudent for tellers and listeners to establish co-negotiated ground-rules or guidelines. Such precautions ensure that a safe environment that is conducive to learning is provided and that issues such as projection, confidentiality, anonymity and ownership are safely managed (McDrury & Alterio, 2002).

Another key contributor to the success of storytelling is to establish, as part of the co-negotiated ground-rules or guidelines, a set of principles for each process. These principles then provide a worthwhile focus for reflection.

Storytelling principles

Three principles underpin the group storytelling process that we are about to outline:

1. Value the range and intensity of feelings expressed.
2. Explore the story from multiple perspectives.
3. Consider alternative responses, resolutions and solutions.

Group storytelling process

With this process, which has one teller and between six and eight listeners, and takes place in a formal setting, we follow several key steps that link to the Levels of Engagement Model (Figure 2.4) and the storytelling principles described above. We recommend that a skilled facilitator is used and that everyone involved co-negotiates guidelines prior to the storytelling session. We now outline each stage.

Deciding on a story

This stage begins with the facilitator inviting the group to think about a recent work situation. Questions may be posed to facilitate focused responses. Examples are:

- Is there some aspect that you are still thinking about?
- What concerned, intrigued or challenged you?
- Which aspect would you to like to work with?

It may take time for a story to emerge but eventually one always does. With most groups the problem is not finding a story but deciding which story to work with when several are offered. We suggest that each group establish some way of managing untold stories. One strategy is to provide everyone with a story folder in which they keep their story fragments, Post-it notes or other jottings. These can be used later as the beginning point for an exemplar, or as story triggers for other sessions.

Telling the story

Once a story has been found, it is told from the teller's perspective, and without interruption. Focus at this stage is on the story itself. It is useful if listeners focus on content, which includes the context in which the experience occurred. They should also note any feelings the teller expresses or they themselves experience.

Clarifying aspects of the story

Characterised by making meaning of an experience told in story form, this stage provides opportunities for listeners to ask the teller to clarify any aspects, including feelings, and to expand on other elements which the listeners regard as essential to their understanding of the story. The teller also has time to recall forgotten aspects. It is not uncommon during this stage for both listeners and tellers to link aspects of the story to their existing knowledge and past experiences which encompass their backstories. Emphasis, however, is on *why* events occurred as they did and *why* those involved behaved in particular ways.

Critically reflecting on the story

Critical reflective dialogue is the key to this stage because it enables the teller and listeners to work with the meaning of the story. Through dialogue or communicative action, multiple perspectives emerge, assumptions and ideologies are challenged and the impact of context is explored. The ways in which listeners and tellers engage each other in critical reflective dialogue influences what each learns. If this interaction is robust and rigorous, tellers and listeners often become aware of how past experiences have influenced their actions; therefore, both groups frequently gain insights. It is also useful during this stage for listeners to acknowledge and value the teller's feelings and to describe any emotions they experienced themselves as they listened to the story. Listeners' feelings may differ from those expressed by the teller, which highlights the range of possible emotions and perceptions experienced during any given event. This is further evidence of how backstories and 'lifeworlds' influence perspectives.

Reconstructing the story from multiple perspectives

This stage has a critical emphasis because it involves exploring the teller's story from different perspectives. The facilitator begins by asking those involved to identify who they thought were the key-players in the story. It is prudent to refer to people by role, not name: teacher, student, supervisor, parent. To move beyond obvious key-players, it is useful to engage in a brainstorming exercise. Sometimes a friend or a counsellor, who initially appeared to have peripheral involvement, takes on more significance. This exercise also provides the teller with an opportunity to provide additional details about key-players and to describe their significance to the story. A heightened or new awareness of the contextual elements within a story may also become apparent.

After key-players are identified, the facilitator asks the teller and listeners to decide who they think are the most significant. It is essential to match the number of key-players with the number in the group. The role of each key-player is then written on a piece of card, for example:

Teacher	*Friend*	*Supervisor*
Counsellor	*Parent*	*Student*

Collaborative Learning Using Reflective Storytelling — 49

These cards are shuffled and placed face-down on a central table. The facilitator asks each person to select a card. The role written on the chosen card is the one the person will play in this reconstructed version of the story. It is useful to allow a few minutes for everyone to think about their role before telling the story from their key-player's perspective. This simple but effective reconstruction shifts the story from a single perspective to multiple views. The aim is to provide the teller with a range of alternative ways to examine their story.

Debriefing

It is essential to debrief those involved so they can come out of the role and explore any insights they have gained. It is important for these listeners-turned-tellers to *wonder* rather than offer opinions to the owner of the story, the original teller. Rather than say, 'If I was you, I would have done … ', it is more helpful to start with, 'If I was in a similar situation, I *wonder* if I might … '. It is, however, helpful to acknowledge evidence of good practice or insight. At the end of this process the original teller is given time to comment on any aspect of the role reconstructions they witnessed. The final task for the teller is to consider alternative approaches that may provide them with a solution or resolution to their particular situation. While the teller retains ownership of their story and outcome(s), viewing their situation from multiple perspectives enables them to learn from their own and others' reconstructions.

Reflecting with others

When we use creative processes to reflect with and learn from others, opportunities to make sense of experience are enhanced. In the process, we often develop insight into our intentions, feelings and motivations. Using storytelling in thoughtful and formalised ways increases our potential to construct new knowledge. When we construct new knowledge, we learn about others and ourselves in ways that enable us to critically reflect on, and critique, our experiences, and to examine what shaped our perspectives. Existing assumptions and dominant ideologies influence these perspectives. Formalised storytelling processes enable us to challenge and critique them in safe environments. Storytelling also provides us with a tool to action change in constructive ways.

Preparing for a storytelling approach to learning

We have explored a creative approach to reflect on experience and, in the process, learn in collaborative ways. The storytelling approach we described shifts the focus from inward reflective activities to active participation in a critically reflective group process. If you want to develop a storytelling approach to learning, how can you prepare? We end this chapter with some suggestions for activities.

- In a small group, identify three ways in which you could use storytelling in your teaching practice.
- Select and read a text from the book list and reflect on why and how you might implement two storytelling strategies.
- Talk to colleagues already working with stories and find out what types of stories they use and how they introduce them into their learning contexts.
- Participate in storytelling sessions with colleagues and write your reflections in a journal.
- Tell stories to demonstrate teaching points and seek feedback from students to ascertain their usefulness as a learning tool.
- Select proven storytelling activities and tell a colleague why you selected them and how you will construct appropriate learning outcomes.
- Design, evaluate and critique your own storytelling activities in conjunction with others.

Further reading

Bage, G. (1999). *Narrative Matters: Teaching and learning history through story*. London: Falmer Press.

Bishop, R., & Glynn, T. (1999). *Culture Counts: Changing power relations in Education*. Palmerston North: Dunmore Press.

Brookfield, S., & Preskill, S. (1999). *Discussion as a Way of Teaching*. Buckingham: Society for Research into Higher Education and Open University Press.

McEwan, H., & Egan, K. (1995). *Narrative in Teaching, Learning and Research*. New York: Teachers College, Columbia University.

Schön, D. (1991). *The Reflective Turn: Case studies in and on educational practice*. New York: Teachers College Press.

Witherell, C., & Noddings, N. (eds). (1991). *Stories Lives Tell: Narrative and dialogue in education*. New York: Teachers College Press.

Glossary

Backstory: A background story that shapes and influences the main story.

Communicative learning: Learning that is aimed at understanding ourselves and being understood by others through dialogue.

Critical discourse: Dialogue that involves robust reflective examination of content, context and process.

Instrumental learning: Learning that controls and manipulates aspects of the environment.

Lifeworld: Our social and cultural background.

Social interaction: Who we involve in our learning process.

Storytelling perspectives: Different views of the same story from different people.

References

Brockbank, A., & McGill, I. (1998). *Facilitating Reflective Learning in Higher Education*. Buckingham: Society for Research into Higher Education and Open University Press.

Brookfield, S. (1995). *Becoming a Critically Reflective Teacher*. San Francisco: Jossey Bass.

Habermas, J. (1989). *The Theory of Communicative Action, Volume 2*. Cambridge: Polity Press.

Haigh, N. (2000). Teaching Teachers about Reflection and Ways of Reflecting. *Waikato Journal of Education* (6), 87–98.

McDrury, J., & Alterio, M. G. (2001). Achieving Reflective Learning Using Storytelling Pathways. *Innovations in Education and Training International, 38* (1), 63–73.

McDrury, J., & Alterio, M. G. (2002). *Learning through Storytelling: Using reflection and experience in higher education contexts*. Palmerston North: Dunmore Press.

Metzger, D. (1986). Circles of Stories. *Parabola, IV* (4).

Mezirow, J. (1991). *Transformative Dimensions of Adult Learning*. San Francisco: Jossey Bass.

Moon, J. (1999). *Reflection in Learning and Professional Development*. London: Kogan Page.

Rubie, P. (1999). *The Elements of Storytelling*. New York: John Wiley & Sons.

— Chapter 3 —

Action Research Transforming Practice

Pip Bruce-Ferguson (with Anne O'Brien Kennington)

Introduction

Have you ever faced a situation in your teaching practice that challenged or baffled you, or that you felt you wanted to investigate and change in some way? Action research is a good approach to use. It can help you to identify a situation in your practice that you want to change or a new technique that you want to try. You can systematically investigate how the change might be brought about, how the new technique might improve your practice, and 'tweak' aspects of the improvement until it gets to the point where you're satisfied. Lots of teachers, both here and overseas, use the action research approach to resolve problems, extend practice and understand their environments better.

In this chapter I shall explain, using a case study, how the approach might work. I will use the perspectives of several writers in the field. The chapter will include the following:

- a brief consideration of the history of action research in the US, the UK and Australasia
- an examination of three different ways of carrying out action research
- an examination of how Habermas's critical theory perspectives have been incorporated into technical, practical and emancipatory uses of action research
- a consideration of the issue of carrying out solitary action research when almost all writers stress the need for collaboration.

Through the whole chapter, the case of one of my action research students (a fellow teacher, Anne O'Brien Kennington) will be used to illustrate how practising teachers use the approach.

Coming to grips with action research

Anne was challenged and puzzled. She taught second-chance students who were enrolled in a twelve-week 'bridging course' designed to assist them back into formal study and/or paid work. Her concern, as one who taught literacy skills with the aid of computers, was that students seemed to find writing original work very difficult, if not impossible. They would happily transcribe the writing of others into their word processing documents, but write their own original stories? No way! How could she move her students past this blockage? How could she help them to develop the confidence in self-expression that would assist them in further study or paid work? At this point, Anne enrolled in my action research course and began to find ways to investigate her situation. In order to understand Anne's options for using action research, it is useful to survey the history of the method.

A brief history of action research

The US experience

Action research has an interesting history. Some writers ascribe its origins to the work of the Austrian J. L. Moreno, who used action methods in group facilitation through psychodrama, sociodrama and role play from the 1920s onwards (see, for example, McTaggart, 1991). Most, however, describe Lewin's work in the US as the origin of action research – Lewin used the process to improve productivity in factories through "democratic participation rather than autocratic coercion" (Adelman, 1993, p. 7). The US uses of action research were rooted in the work of Lewin in the late 1930s. This also related to action by Stephen Corey, who used the method in education "to improve the rate of curriculum change in schools and to reduce the gap between research knowledge and instructional practices in classrooms" (in Zeichner & Noffke, 1998, p. 7).

However, where Lewin had used a cyclical process of planning, action, observation and reflection, Corey followed a more linear series of steps, reinforced in later work by Hilda Taba. This development reduced the potential of the method being used as a way of teachers producing knowledge. Instead, it became more a systematised way of carrying out in-service teacher education.

> *Activity*: How does this account make you wary of the possibility of any 'prescribed method' becoming subverted from initially liberating purposes?

The method fell out of favour in the US for the best part of 30 years, although recent writers (e.g. in Reason & Bradbury, 2001) have described its resurgence there.

The UK experience

In the UK, action research gained prominence in the 1960s when, according to Elliott (1997), there was dissatisfaction with the secondary modern schools and teachers sought ways of restructuring the curriculum. Others, however, attribute the first usage of action research described in the UK to the much earlier work of the Tavistock Institute of Human Relations, set up in 1947 to "deal with problems of human relations and group dynamics in industrial settings" (Zeichner & Noffke, 1998, p. 9). Lawrence Stenhouse, who was influenced by work at Tavistock, coined the term 'teacher as researcher'. He encouraged the idea of practitioner inquiry as a form of curriculum development (Stenhouse, 1975). This idea of teachers working to change their own practices has continued throughout the development of the movement in the UK.

The UK action research tradition has continued, with Stenhouse, Somekh and Elliott being strong proponents in the East Anglia area, particularly through the establishment of the Collaborative Action Research Network (CARN), which has an excellent website where you can read of the work of UK action researchers. In another part of the UK, McNiff, Laidlaw and Whitehead have been active advocates through collaborative work at the University of Bath. Their book, *Creating a Good Social Order Through Action Research* (1992), describes their action research practice as a way of helping teachers to see how values can be enacted in practice. Jack Whitehead's website is another lively site of action research practical reports. Jean McNiff has also promoted action research through a series of books, both individually authored and through her work with Una Collins in Ireland through the Marino Institute (see McNiff, 1994). Peter Reason and Judi Marshall, at the University of Bath, have also been users of the action research approach, with Reason having a particular concern about the impact of human activity in isolation from its effects on the planet. Reason has recently (2001) co-authored the latest *Handbook of Action Research* with Hilary Bradbury.

> *Activity:* How does this UK-based work raise questions for you, as a teacher, about what your values might be and how they might be worked out in your teaching practice?

The Australasian experience

The approach reached Australia through the work of Stephen Kemmis, who was familiar with the work of Elliott and the East Anglian action researchers. He found receptive colleagues in Robin McTaggart and Shirley Grundy at Deakin University, and the group has argued strongly for grassroots involvement in decision-making and in educational practice. This argument is echoed in Ernie Stringer's work, drawing on wide experience of both educational and community action research. Both Stringer and McTaggart have worked closely with various Aboriginal groups and recommend sensitive use of the action research approach with these communities.

A formal ALARPM (Action Learning, Action Research and Process Management) network exists. It has organised several World Congresses in active methods of research. It is based in Australia but has strong links throughout the world (US, UK, New Guinea, South Africa and New Zealand are currently represented on the Executive). It aims to encourage users of the action research approach to share and extend their knowledge of the methods. The New Zealand Action Research Network holds conferences once a year at which New Zealand action research projects are described and understanding of the approach is broadened.

> *Activity*: Can you see how globalisation has acted for a positive purpose here, with Internet developments and ease of travel enabling action researchers to 'spread the word' to other places? What benefits might this development have in terms of keeping the method dynamic and flexible? (See Chapters 10 and 11 for discussions of globalisation.)

Is there such a thing as a standard action research approach?

When Anne joined my action research course I introduced her and her fellow students to the history of the approach, as described above, then showed them several models of how people use it in practice.

I used Carr and Kemmis's (1986) definition to help them understand the approach, as it stresses:

- the need for a social practice to be investigated with the aim of bringing about improvement
- the following of a standard plan–act–observe–reflect sequence which proceeds in a spiral of cycles
- involvement of those responsible for the practice, collaborating in its improvement
- widening the project gradually to involve others affected by the changes (see Carr & Kemmis, 1986, p. 165–6).

Some writers (Jean McNiff is one of these) prefer to leave methods as open-ended as possible, in order to avoid prescribing 'best' ways forward for individual practitioners. She says that there is "no such thing as Action Research but there are action researchers" (McNiff, Whitehead & Laidlaw, 1992, p. ix).

McNiff has gone on to challenge UK action researchers about the dangers of being too prescriptive:

> Are we not then in danger of providing an élitist group within CARN that is actually going to start setting clear parameters as to what constitutes quality action research, or what constitutes action research itself? ... Some eminent action researchers – I

certainly don't share this view – are quite specific about the kind of criteria they lay down as to what counts as action research (McNiff, 1994, p. 19).

While McNiff allows for the usual 'spiral' process of planning, action, observation and reflection as a way of taking researchers forward, she also describes the 'side spirals' that can occur during an investigation (McNiff, 1988). Sometimes these side spirals can prove to be more rewarding than the initial research question, and may be followed either alongside or instead of the first question.

A third action research writer, Ernie Stringer, describes his use of the approach in the mainly educational and community-based work he carries out in Australia. His way of using action research covers the routine 'Look, Think, Act'.

In the 'look' stage, participants gather relevant information (data) and build a picture (define and describe the situation). In the 'think' stage, they explore and analyse (possibly hypothesise) then interpret and explore (theorise the practice). Finally, they 'act' – plan (report), implement changes and evaluate the success of the initiative. Stringer's model collapses the usual 'plan, act' stages into the one 'act'. 'Look' is the same as 'observe' in the Carr and Kemmis sequence, and 'think' has the same meaning as 'reflect'.

One other point I make with my action research students is that the cycle can be entered at any stage (see the work of Kolb (1984), on whose reflective cycle the action research four-step model is based). Nick Zepke talked about this cycle in Chapter 1.

A working example

Anne's work was based most closely on the Carr and Kemmis action research cycle, but I shall explain how she could have used McNiff's and Stringer's approaches also, had she wished to do so. Being a whiz on the computer, she presented her action research project in a series of graphical depictions of each of the three action research cycles she followed.

The first cycle

Anne started her work at the reflection stage of the cycle. Her work in Cycle One involved *reflecting* on the students' reluctance to write, their lack of knowledge of grammar, and their limited vocabulary. Her *planning* showed how she tried to engage her students in what *they* thought would improve their writing skills and how she gained permission from her Head of Department and fellow staff with regard to proceeding with the research. Her *action* involved getting students' consent forms (ethics of research), collecting samples of their written work, allowing 'free writing' time during literacy sessions, and teaching basic grammar. *Observation* showed that one of the reasons 'free writing' was difficult was that students felt they had few positive life experiences to draw on, and also that the basic grammar they were being taught was not being incorporated into their written work.

What can I do to encourage the development of writing skills in Cal students?
(format amended from Anne's diagrams – originals no longer available)

Initial Reflection:

Observation shows me that the Cal students are reluctant to write.

Their knowledge of sentence structure, spelling and grammar is limited.

They have a limited vocabulary.

What could I do to help develop their skills?

Observation:

1. Free writing is difficult for students with few positive life experiences to call on.
2. Basic grammar is not being internalized and transferred to original work.

Planning:

1. Question students as to what they think will help improve their writing skills.
2. Prepare consent form for students.
3. Plan lessons in basic grammar.
4. Liaise with HOD and fellow staff re research.

Act:

1. Advise students of research and distribute consent forms.
2. Collect samples of written work.
3. Allow free writing time during literary sessions.
4. Teach basic grammar in group sessions and individually using GG programme.

Figure 3.1.   **Action Research Planner – initial spiral**

The second cycle

Anne's second cycle *reflected* that progress was slow, that students needed more support and that they were still not transferring grammar skills to writing, which they still hated. So she *planned* to develop some mini-assignments where answers were self-contained (therefore providing immediate reinforcement). She also *planned* to organise some positive experiences about which students might be motivated to write. Her *action* at this stage was to work through the new assignments, showing students how to find the answers. She also took her students to the Agricultural Field Days held in Hamilton. Her *observation* at the end of this cycle was that sentence structure was improving (written work from the Field Days was great) and that the group writing assignments were taking the pressure off individuals.

What can I do to encourage the development of writing skills in Cal students?

Second Reflection:
Little progress is being made. It is not enough to ask the students to write something original and think I can teach from their own work. They need more support. They are not transferring their skills or knowledge. They still hate writing.

Observation:
1. Sentence structure is improving.
2. Written work from the Field Days was great.
3. Modelled writing and group writing sessions are taking the pressure of individuals.

Planning:
1. Develop some mini assignments where the answers are self-contained.
2. Plan some modelled writing sessions.
3. Organise some positive experiences.

Act:
1. Work through weekly assignments with students showing how to take the first part of the answer from the question and the second part from the info supplied.
2. Take the students to the Field Days.
3. Give modelled writing sessions.

Figure 3.2. Action Research Planner – second spiral

The third cycle

Not content with this improvement, however, Anne then extended the class and her own practice by carrying out a further cycle of action research. She noted in her *reflection* that sentence structure was improving, but stories remained "just a collection of sentences" (O'Brien, in Bruce-Ferguson, 1999: Appendix B). She used her computer skills to *plan* a Power Point presentation on paragraphing, and involved her students in *planning* a further field trip.

Fortunately, Nelson Mandela was to visit a local marae (ceremonial meeting place) around this time, so the students, many of whom were Maori, opted to visit the marae for his welcome and speech. Part of Anne's *planning*, too, involved using expertise on site to introduce students to the Internet, and to expand their knowledge of writing to include bibliographies and footnotes. *Action* involved students surfing the net for information on Nelson Mandela, from which they wrote an essay using focus questions,

What can I do to encourage the development of writing skills in Cal students?

Third Reflection:
Sentence structure is improving, but their stories are just a collection of sentences. I need to introduce the students to the format of a tertiary level essay.

Observation:
1. At last ... an essay that looks like an essay.
2. Still very reliant on being fed information. But they are willing to write original comments if it is part of the factual essay.
3. Plagiarism is rampant!

Planning:
1. Use Power Point to make a presentation on paragraphing.
2. Plan Mandela visit.
3. Organise with Stephen to show the students Internet.
4. Liaise with Jenny to introduce students to a bibliography and footnotes.

Act:
1. Students learn to surf the net for information.
2. Use info from the net on Mandela to write an essay. Use focus questions.
3. Take the students to Mandela marae visit.
4. Jen teaches session on bibliographies and footnotes.

Figure 3.3.   Action Research Planner – third spiral

engaging in a session on bibliographies and footnotes, and finally visiting the marae. Her *observation* was triumphant: "At last ... an essay that looks like an essay". But ongoing development was needed – they were still reliant on being fed information. They *were* willing to write original comments based on the marae visit, which had obviously been very powerful for them, but "plagiarism is rampant!". Having discovered the research possibilities of the Internet, students were now downloading entire sections and "dumping them" in their essays without referencing.

Anne ceased formally recording her action research at this point, in order to write up her report and pass the course, but the work continued.

Activity: Can you see how similar this action research process is to the way you may currently operate as a reflective practitioner?

The first chapter in this book should assist you to make these connections if you were not initially familiar with the reflective practitioner approach. I have written about the connections between action research and reflective practice elsewhere (Bruce-Ferguson, 1999, p. 25ff.). Anne's work provides a good case study of how action research is used in practice by busy teachers, trying to find solutions to the challenges they face. While her use of the method most closely parallels the Carr and Kemmis model, I shall briefly explain how it could have been presented by using either McNiff's or Stringer's approaches.

Alternative approaches to presentation

You can see (above) how Anne carried forward three separate issues in her work. These were:

1. the problem of students not producing original work (perhaps because of a difficult life experience, previous negative classroom experiences, or a lack of motivation);
2. the problem of their not knowing how to construct written work in formal settings (hence Anne's comments about sentence structure, grammar, bibliographies and footnotes);
3. the problem of not knowing how to access materials to support their study.

If Anne had written this up using McNiff's model, she could have followed a main question (overcoming students' reluctance to write original work) as a series of cycles. Instead, she kept the 'side spirals' of cycles involving academic work on the one hand and accessing materials using the Internet and library on the other. As it was, she chose to investigate all three problems (diagrammatically at least) simultaneously, using the Carr and Kemmis model. This is much easier to depict graphically than using McNiff's side spirals. It is difficult to depict graphically how a multi-level investigation is carried out. The advantage of McNiff's model is that it better captures the 'messy' nature of action research in practice, which doesn't always proceed forwards in the straightforward plan–act–observe–reflect way that most models indicate.

If you like things 'cut and dried', you might need to adjust your expectations when using action research. It can be quite 'evolutionary'. Stringer admits to the method's potential messiness in his writing:

> As experience will show, action research is not a neat, orderly activity that allows participants to proceed step by step to the end of the process. People will find themselves working backward through the routines, repeating processes, revising procedures, rethinking interpretations, leapfrogging steps or stages, and sometimes making radical changes in direction (Stringer, 1996, p. 17).

So even though Stringer's model of 'look, think and act' seems linear, he agrees with McNiff that variation must be possible. Had Anne chosen to use his model to present her work:

- her 'look' stage would have included the observations of her students' abilities and disabilities academically;
- her 'think' stage would have included her reflections on these abilities and disabilities and how to encourage ongoing development;
- her 'act' stage would have included the planning processes she went through and the actions and evaluations she carried out.

Using Stringer's model she probably would have needed, still, to go through three cycles of action research, and would have continued to present each of her three problems simultaneously. The advantage of Stringer's model is that it lends itself well to presentation and encouragement with groups who are familiar with traditional research processes – he uses words like 'hypothesise' and 'theorise' which will strike chords with those used to traditional research processes. He presents action research as a method with *some* similarities to the way groups may have been used to working, while still explaining, as the initial quotation in this paragraph shows, that variation is not only possible but likely.

Habermas and critical theory

There are two other aspects of action research practice that I wish to engage with in this chapter. I shall continue to refer to Anne's work in explaining these, to help you to understand how they might operate, and to continue to build on the excellent work that Anne did with her students. Habermas, whose philosophy underpins much of the work in this book, described three ways of engaging in education.

- The first involves largely instrumental or practical work, the aim of which is to control or manipulate situations or people in order to bring about change of some description, usually determined by the 'researcher'.
- The second involves communicative action, the aim of which is to understand situations or people by collaborating closely with them.
- The third is to transform or emancipate situations or people, usually by engaging with them in systematic and committed action.

Habermas's project aimed to break down the grip that 'scientism' (the standard scientific method) has had for the past couple of centuries over the production and use of knowledge. 'Scientism' has become the norm. As Carr (1998, p. 114) puts it, "Instead of accepting that science has to justify its knowledge claims against epistemological standards derived from philosophy, it is now assumed that epistemology has to be judged against standards laid down by science". This means that a possibly inappropriate ruler gets used to judge the worth of what we count as sound knowledge. It can result in our curricula being distorted and not meeting the actual needs and interests of our students, particularly where they may come from cultures whose notions of science differ from Western models.

Carr and Habermas are not the only critics of scientism. McNiff and Collins (1994,

p. 16) also recognise the effect that this scientific domination has had, not only over knowledge production and use, but over what may count as valid research. "As teachers we tend to get brainwashed by the social scientific view of empirical research as the only valid form of doing research." Even Sandra Harding, who is trained in the methods of science, criticises scientific approaches as leaving out women's perspectives (Harding, 1986). She argues that the standard scientific method is based on male, rather than female, ways of thinking and exploring issues, and on male values.

Action researchers have sought, in various ways, to challenge the hegemony of scientism in the ways they encourage teachers to investigate their *own* practice, using methods that make the most sense in what are often very particular situations. Maguire (2001), for example, writes of how she uses action research from her feminist perspective. Habermas's three-layer approach was included in action research development by writers like Grundy (1988), and Carr and Kemmis (1986). I like to use the latters' explanation (Bruce-Ferguson, 1999, p. 22ff.):

- *Technical action research* happens when an outside facilitator persuades practitioners to test findings from external research in their own practice. An example is a teacher being persuaded to try out a hands-off approach to classroom management on the basis of research which shows that this approach might work better with a particular group. The aim of the research is to add to external research literatures. Any improvement in the teacher's own situation is secondary. Anne's research was obviously not based on technical action research.
- *Practical action research* happens when "outside facilitators form co-operative relationships with practitioners, helping them to articulate their own concerns, plan strategic action for change, monitor the problems and effects of changes and reflect on the value and consequences of the changes actually achieved" (Carr & Kemmis, 1986, p. 203). This is what happened with the work Anne and I conducted. I helped her with the theory and practice of action research, but the questions and actions were entirely hers, and it was her practice that benefited. Contributions to an external research literature (such as this book) were coincidental.
- *Emancipatory action research* is the final level of action research, corresponding to Habermas's work. Carr and Kemmis claim that this happens when a practitioner group takes joint responsibility to change and improve practice, aiming to "explore the problems and effects of group policies and individual practices" (ibid., pp. 203–4).

Anne's work was not designed as emancipatory action research. She *could* have moved into this area had she and her students chosen to investigate *why* so many students leave the education system unable to write properly, what social and ethnic backgrounds of these students are, and what the education and political systems in New Zealand could or should be doing about the situation. Chapters 5, 6, 10 and 11 investigate such questions, although not necessarily from an action research perspective.

Carr and Kemmis are unapologetic promoters of emancipatory action research. The quotation from McNiff and Collins shows that they are also critics of oppressive research definitions, and Stringer quotes Foucault in advocating that "people should cultivate and enhance planning and decision-making at the local level, resisting techniques and practices that are oppressive in one way or another" (Stringer, 1996, p. 152). It is fair to say, however, that many action research writers do not make the distinction between technical, practical and emancipatory work, and examples in the literature are often focused on technical or practical aims.

> *Activity*: Is there one of these approaches that feels 'comfortable' for you? Would you rather work on a specific practical classroom challenge than take on the power structures of your organisation?

Can you do action research alone?

One final issue that I wish to present is the issue of collaboration. I have not given a formal 'definition' of action research here, bearing McNiff's caution in mind! However, all definitions I have encountered stress the importance of collaboration. For example:

- Carr and Kemmis (1986, pp. 165–6) mention the involvement of "those responsible for the practice ... includ[ing] others affected by the practice and maintaining collaborative control".
- The World Congress definition, put together by a range of international action researchers, stresses "Participation (in problem-posing and in answering questions) in decision-making ... Collaboration among members of the group as a 'critical community'" (Altrichter, Kemmis, McTaggart & Zuber-Skerritt, 1990, p. 119).
- In the first chapter of their *Handbook of Action Research*, Reason and Bradbury describe action research as "a participatory, democratic process concerned with developing practical knowing in the pursuit of worthwhile human purposes, grounded in a participatory worldview" (2001, p. 1).

Given this common emphasis on collaboration, backed up even more strongly by Kemmis & McTaggart's (1988, p. 15) they claim that:

> Activities where an individual goes through cycles of planning, action, observation and reflection cannot be regarded as action research. Action research is not individualistic.

How can Anne's work be called action research? Can people do action research *on their own?*
 Habermas warns of the difficulties of this.

> The self-reflection of a lone subject ... requires a quite paradoxical achievement: one part of the self must be split off from the other part in such a manner that the

subject can be in a position to render aid to itself ... in the act of self-reflection the subject can deceive itself (Habermas, 1974, p. 29).

I recognised this tendency to distortion in my own, 'solitary', action research (see Bruce-Ferguson, 1999, p. 217). It is easy, as Nick Zepke says in Chapter 1, to 'reflect' without critical insight into your own logical shortcomings or personality quirks.

But sometimes, despite your intention to be collaborative and inclusive, the way you express your question or invitation to peers, or their workloads, can work against gaining their participation. I recognised in my own work that the way I had set up the action research course, with students deciding on their question before going back to their departments to try to involve colleagues, had worked against collaboration and was a flaw in my design (ibid., p. 254ff.). Anne tried to include her colleagues in her action research, but felt that time pressures or lack of inclination prevented collaboration. She attempted with some success to include her students as co-researchers (ibid., p. 225).

If you find yourself in a situation where you want to carry out action research into some aspect of your practice, consider the categories described above. Is your action research likely to aim for *practical* outcomes, such as improving your own classroom practice (in which case solitary action research might work for you) or *emancipatory* action research, where you try to influence wider social contexts? If the latter, then I would strongly advise working collaboratively with others to design the question, decide on strategies and support each other as you carry out the work.

You *can* use what action research writers (e.g. Laidlaw, 1997) call 'critical friends': people prepared to act as sounding-boards to give positive and critical comment on your work as it progresses and to call into question your assumptions and methods. If you have to continue on your own, be aware that there are writers who *do* admit that action research can be conducted in solitary ways. As Webb (1996, p. 62) stated, "The example provided by Jack Whitehead may be argued as a challenge to the privileging of group over individual. He has shown how an action research approach may be applied to an individual, in fact, to oneself". Quite a number of the action research papers and theses that you can look at on Whitehead's website are examples of solitary action research.

Can you use the approach in your practice?

I hope you can see from this chapter what a powerful tool action research can be in supporting reflective teachers in their search to improve their practice. You can find action research courses offered in a number of polytechnics and universities around New Zealand, and of course you could seek further support by attending the New Zealand Action Research Network conferences held each year. These would help you to hear ways in which many different action research activities are carried out, in a diversity of educational and community contexts. The method seeks to improve practice, to liberate researchers from slavish adherence to 'traditional' research methods that may not be relevant in specific situations, and to develop research skills in practitioners.

Are you now ready to begin an action research topic? If you would like further information first, try to sample some of the following readings.

Further reading

Alcorn, N. (1986). Action Research: A Tool for School Development. *Delta*, 37, pp. 33–44.
   Noeline Alcorn describes early work done in schools in New Zealand using the action research approach. Noeline is currently Dean in the School of Education, The University of Waikato.

CARN website: see http://www.uea.ac.uk/care/carn/
   The CARN group is very active, and from their website you can locate many papers describing action research work in various areas around the UK, but particularly in East Anglia.

Elliott, J. (1997). School-based curriculum development and action research in the United Kingdom. In S. Hollingsworth (ed.), *International Action Research: A casebook for educational reform.* London: Falmer Press.
   John Elliot's work is well worth looking at; he has been an influential writer in the field for decades.

Kolb, D. (1984). *Experiential Learning.* New Jersey: Prentice-Hall.
   Kolb's work was instrumental in specifying the plan, act, observe, reflect sequence commonly used in action research but also in experiential learning methods.

Peters, M., & Robinson, V. (1984). The Origins and Status of Action Research. *The Journal of Applied Behavioral Science*, Vol. 20, No. 2, pp. 113–124.
   These two New Zealand writers have both been active in encouraging others in their research and offer sound critical perspectives on a range of ways of conducting research.

Piggot-Irvine, E. (2001). Appraisal: Reducing control – enhancing effectiveness. Unpublished PhD thesis, Palmerston North: Massey University.
   Eileen Piggot-Irvine's work demonstrates how she worked with staff engaged in appraisal processes to promote ongoing development and effectiveness rather than the appraisal process being construed as purely an exercise in control.

Robertson, J. (1995). Principals' partnerships: An action research study of the professional development of New Zealand School Leaders. Unpublished PhD thesis, Hamilton: The University of Waikato.
   Jan Robertson describes her work in assisting with the leadership development of staff in schools, using a range of action research approaches. Jan now heads the Leadership Development Centre at the University of Waikato.

Strachan, J. (1997). Feminist educational leadership in a "new right" context in Aotearoa/ New Zealand. Unpublished DPhil. thesis, Hamilton: The University of Waikato.
   Jane Strachan used action research in investigating women's development as educational leaders.

Whitehead, J. Website: http://www.bath.ac.uk/~edsajw/
   Jack Whitehead's site, like the CARN site, will give you access to papers, discussion, theses and other action research-related websites around the globe.

Glossary

Curriculum (plural: curricula): a combination of teaching topics and methods of study for a given programme.

Emancipatory: intending to liberate (e.g. from bondage or restraint).

Empirical research: research that is carried out using experiment and observation rather than theory.

Epistemology: the theory of knowledge, especially the critical study of its validity, methods and scope.

Hegemony: power or dominance in a specific area, e.g. of one group over another in an organisation or political arena.

Idiosyncratic: particular ways of behaving that are specific to an individual.

Marae: a traditional Maori ceremonial meeting place.

Practitioner inquiry: a type of self-development carried out by those involved in the practice rather than by outside researchers.

Reflective practitioner: a person who constantly inquires into their own practice with the intention of improving it.

Research culture: perhaps best described as "the way we do (or don't do) research around here". Depends on resources, support, staff attitudes, etc.

Side spirals: the kinds of issues that emerge in an action research project that are not the main question being investigated but add significantly to it (and may well become more interesting than the original idea).

References

Adelman, C. (1993). Kurt Lewin and the Origins of Action Research. *Educational Action Research, 1* (1), 7–24.

Alcorn, N. (1986). Action Research: A tool for school development. *Delta* (37), 33–44.

Altrichter, H., Kemmis, S., McTaggart, R., & Zuber-Skerritt, O. (1990). Defining, Confining or Refining Action Research. In O. Zuber-Skerrit (ed.), *Action Research for Change and Development*. Brisbane: Centre for the Advancement of Learning and Teaching: Griffith University.

Bruce-Ferguson, P. (1999). Developing a research culture in a polytechnic: An action research case study. Unpublished PhD thesis, University of Waikato.

CARN website. URL http://www.uea.ac.uk/care/carn/

Carr, W. (1998). *For Education: Towards critical educational inquiry*. Buckingham: Open University Press.

Carr, W., & Kemmis, S. (1986). *Becoming Critical: Education, knowledge and action research*. London: Falmer Press.

Elliott, J. (1997). School-based Curriculum Development and Action Research in the United Kingdom. In S. Hollingsworth (ed.), *International Action Research: A casebook for educational reform*. London: Falmer Press.

Grundy, S. (1988). Three Modes of Action Research. In S. Kemmis, & R. McTaggart (eds.), *The Action Research Reader* (3rd ed., pp. 353–364). Deakin, Australia: Deakin University Press.

Habermas, J. (1974). *Theory and Practice*. London: Heinemann.

Harding, S. (1986). *The Science Question and Feminism*. Ithaca: Cornell University Press.

Kemmis, S., & McTaggart, R. (1988). *The Action Research Planners*. Geelong, Victoria: Deakin University Press.

Kolb, D. (1984). *Experiential Learning*. Englewood Cliffs, New Jersey: Prentice Hall.

Laidlaw, M. (1997). How can I create my own living educational theory as I offer you an account of my educational development? Unpublished PhD thesis, University of Bath, UK.

Maguire, P. (2001). Uneven Ground: Feminisms and Action Research, pp. 59–69 in Reason, P., & Bradbury, H. (2001). *Handbook of Action Research: Participatory Inquiry and Practice*. London: Sage Publications Ltd.

McNiff, J. (1988). *Action Research: Principles and practice*. Hampshire: Macmillan Education Ltd.

McNiff, J. (1994). Conversations with Action Researchers. *Action Researchers*, (1), 18–19.

McNiff, J., & Collins, U. (1994). *A New Approach to In-Career Development for Teachers in Ireland*. Bournemouth, Dorset: Hyde Publications.

McNiff, J., Whitehead, J., & Laidlaw, M. (1992). *Creating a Good Social Order Through Action Research*. Poole, Dorset: Hyde Publications.

McTaggart, R. (1991). Point and Counterpoint. *Curriculum Perspectives, 11* (4), 43–65.

Melrose, M. (1995). Development and evaluation of the certificate in educational leadership. An investigation of the context and the perceptions about a programme for polytechnic staff. Unpublished PhD thesis, The University of Auckland.

Peters, M., & Robinson V. (1984). The Origins and Status of Action Research. *The Journal of Applied Behavioral Science, 20* (2), 113–124.

Reason, P., & Bradbury, H. (2001). *Handbook of Action Research: Participative inquiry & practice*. London: Sage Publications Ltd.

Robertson, J. (1995). Principals' partnerships: An action research study of the professional development of New Zealand school leaders. Unpublished PhD thesis, The University of Waikato.

Stenhouse, L. (1975). *An Introduction to Curriculum Research and Development*. London: Heinemann Educational Books.

Strachan, J. (1997). Feminist educational leadership in a "new right" context in Aotearoa/New Zealand. Unpublished DPhil thesis, The University of Waikato.

Stringer, E. (1996). *Action Research: a Handbook for Practitioners*. Thousand Oaks, Calif: Sage Publications Ltd.

Webb, G. (1996). Theories of Staff Development: Progress and Power. *International Journal of Academic Development, 1* (2), 59–66.

Whitehead, J. URL http://www.bath.ac.uk/~edsajw/ [2002, March 20].

Zeichner, K., & Noffke, S. (1998). Practitioner Research. *Handbook of Research on Teaching* (4th ed.). Washington, DC: American Educational Research Association.

— PART II —

Working with Learners

Overview

In Part II we examine practical aspects of teaching practice. Here we put the spotlight on how you could work with students, and provide both a parachute for those jumping into teaching for the first time, and a glider for those wishing to discover what lies behind the first line of skills. The three chapters offer a learner-centred viewpoint. The first explores interactions between learners and teachers. It gives down-to-earth accounts of working with learners. The second examines ways of dealing with difference – how to be an inclusive teacher. The third explores the transformation from independence to interdependence.

Teaching is a very personal activity and in Chapter 4 Dean Nugent gives a personal account of how he works with students. He explores his own motivation, then outlines his approach to managing learning activities. He takes us through the first sessions, from introducing ourselves and developing rapport to creating and managing an effective learning environment. Dean also outlines his personal approach to lecturing and teaching on-line, with practical examples of how good communication skills underlie everything he does. Indeed, in many ways Dean's chapter is a treatise on how teaching for learning is good communication.

The challenge of good communications also underpins Chapter 5, which examines the challenges posed by learner differences. Nick Zepke identifies two kinds of difference. One concerns individual differences: different learning intentions, intelligences and learning styles. Nick offers seven practical approaches to dealing with such differences. The other notion of difference sees the classroom as a community in which different social groups come together to learn. He argues that groups based on ethnic, gender and class differences must compete for attention. Nick suggests that negotiation skills and a multi-layered approach to meaning-making help us create a more inclusive classroom.

The politics of teaching for learning is further examined in Chapter 6. Linda Leach argues that a feature of Western-style education is an emphasis on the individual. Drawing on key adult education literature, she shows how the autonomous learner has become an ideal to aim for. Linda suggests that such an ideal is mistaken. Many social groups, such as some ethnic groups and women, value a more communal approach to learning. She suggests, therefore, that a transformation from independence to interdependence is called for. Linda backs up her contention with some practical ways that such a transformation can be achieved in the classroom.

— Chapter 4 —

Teaching for Learning

Dean Nugent

Introduction

In this chapter I describe my present approach to teaching, with the beginning teacher as well as the experienced teacher in mind. I outline some fundamental understandings that help inform my teaching and I provide reasons for my particular approach. I do not wish to imply that my practice will necessarily suit your teaching situation. Rather, I invite you to consider my approach and to compare and contrast it with your practice.

The chapter is structured round five headings:

- A context for my own motivation
- Managing learning activities
- Creating an effective learning environment
- Teaching effectively (with special reference to lecturing and on-line teaching)
- Evaluating the learning situation.

A context for my own motivation

I consider teaching to be helping others to:

- recognise new possibilities for growth
- develop critical insight
- participate creatively in the times and circumstances into which they are born.

The teaching strategies I describe in this chapter are informed by a number of adult learning theories and principles. I am particularly interested in the ideas of experiential learning, reflective practice, self-directed learning and co-operative learning, as well as the exploration of learning potential.

I believe that all my teaching–learning encounters occur in an experiential learning framework (Jackson & Caffarella, 1994). Everything that occurs is an experience that can be felt emotionally and perceptually and considered conceptually. I create opportunities for learners to reflect on and express their own thoughts and feelings and consider those of others. I want to provide learning environments where everyone experiences safety and trust and where there is a balance between activity and reflective time. I endeavour to establish an environment of co-operation where we practise dialogue and negotiate differences.

I therefore find the concept of *facilitator* useful. I understand *facilitator* to be someone who *guides or guards the learning process*. There are different aspects of process to which we can be attentive. Each individual is a process and the collective of individuals is a process: the entire planet is a complex, interrelated process. I need to have some idea of how human processes function. Besides observing myself and others, I have found it useful to be informed by a wide range of human knowledge in addition to the theory of adult education. Earlier interests in philosophy, literature, psychology, physical sciences, linguistics, futurism, sociology, history, anthropology and politics have extended in later years to the wisdom-teachings of the world's religions and my own spiritual practice.

I remain aware of the limits to learning placed on us by objective constraints, such as cultural, political and economic circumstances, and by our subjective limitations such as doubts, beliefs, self-suppression and fear. Now, in the context of spiritual and religious studies, I am exploring the limits to our thinking about the purpose of existence and the nature of reality. I will speak of teaching from a spiritual perspective in Chapter 12.

In particular, I am keen to explore the various 'relationships' involved in the teaching–learning situation: the relationship between teacher and learner, obviously, but also relationships between colleagues, among learners, to the subject being learnt, to learning activities, to knowledge in general, to the institution, to society, to the planet and universe, to reality altogether.

Managing learning activities

There are numerous teaching and training methods to choose from. I try and use something new in every course I teach. I consult books to get ideas and borrow ideas from other teachers. I consider my work 'learning-centred' and find it useful to view 'teaching methods' as 'learning activities'. From my point of view, learning activities in the formal learning situation work best when they are well managed. If the discussion group 'didn't work' it doesn't mean that discussions 'aren't any good'. I need to pay attention to how I managed it.

An important principle when considering my management of a learning activity is to ask what decisions and choices are available to the learner. Vella (2000) puts it in the form of a question: "Who is deciding what on behalf of whom?". Am I making decisions that learners are quite capable of making for themselves? Am I stealing learning opportunities from learners by making decisions for them?

The challenge is to facilitate as full an experience as possible. This makes my role as a communicator and a builder of relationships central to the learning process. For me, the success of any teaching strategy depends upon these functions. Within these considerations I use a variety of learning activities:

- lectures, guided reading of texts, guided question and answer exercises, demonstrations, instruction and guide sheets, text books, visiting 'experts' and written exercises
- structured experiences, videos, audio recordings, field trips and visits
- pair discussions, small group discussions, peer teaching, project work, action research
- learning contracts, case studies, practical exercises, Internet research, library research, action learning, role play, simulations, games, self-paced packages.

Although I am speaking here in the context of face-to-face meetings between learners and teachers, the facilitator role applies equally well in the context of on-line learning. There are important differences, of course. For instance, in the virtual world we do not see the body language that usually guides our face-to-face communication, and to help facilitate a cyber learning community requires us to develop different protocols and rituals (Collison *et al.*, 2000). You might consider other differences as you read the various topic headings I use here.

First meetings and beginnings

In this section I consider the first meeting with a new group of learners and the first session of a new topic and course. I also consider teaching a topic for the first time and how to resume and link learning and teaching from session to session.

For learners, a first class may be looked at differently. They may be anxious about whether they will be capable of learning the subject, making new relationships and relating to the instructor. I aim to have them leave their first class feeling confident that they can learn this subject, having made some new acquaintances, and feeling at ease with me as their teacher.

I always find the meeting with a new group of learners an enjoyable challenge. Although I now have many years' experience of meeting with new groups, every occasion is unique and I always give considerable thought as to how I might go about establishing, from the beginning, an effective working relationship (also see Chapter 7).

From the very beginning, then, I like to take the opportunity to learn about the participants and to give them the opportunity to learn about each other and me. I try to create a situation that is:

- supportive
- co-operative
- friendly
- sensitive
- relaxed
- efficient
- well organised
- well informed
- challenging.

I try, in other words, to create a situation that is at once welcoming and embracing of everyone, and yet also presents a demand and a challenge. Growth and learning requires both aspects – nurture as well as demand.

Establishing personal goals and course objectives

Even before looking at any 'official' course prescriptions I like to work with the knowledge that already exists in the group. One way is to ask them to consider what they envision themselves *able to do* at the end of their course. They discuss this in pairs and maybe then in groups of four. They may write on sheets of paper we can display or I might quickly compile on the whiteboard the knowledge, skills and attitudes they have been considering. Only after compiling the group understandings do I then suggest we look at the 'official' syllabus. We ask "Is there something we need to add to our compiled list from the set course prescription or is there anything we can add from the group's list to the course prescription?".

Then I ask participants to do some self-assessment. "Considering the list of course objectives, identify those you think you are competent in and those you think you need to give special attention to". Often I will also ask them to draw (using colour pens or paints) a picture of themselves at the end of the course. This reinforces the goals they have been setting for themselves. With longer courses, we can come back to re-consider these goals at different times. Individuals may choose to refine or make other changes to their original ideas. I usually get each member of the group to show their drawings and summarise their self-assessment to the whole group.

At this first meeting I stay 'light' and with appropriate humour. I am asking people to be vulnerable to each other and this needs to be done with a delicate touch. Similarly, I have to model that vulnerability myself. I don't ask them to say or do anything I would not do myself. Right from the beginning I try to encourage a degree of intimacy and trust with one another.

I suggest that we consider our classes together as a kind of laboratory where we can feel free to explore and experiment and make mistakes. We should feel free to question (and test) anything – our own beliefs and presumptions as well as the viewpoints of the received knowledge from so-called experts or authorities.

Encouraging a learning community

I like to help create and sustain a learning community. The idea of 'vulnerability' is critical to the idea of 'community'. Peck (1990) suggests that when true community occurs, members speak from deep parts of themselves, there is a deep vulnerability, there is no uneasiness in the silences, there is no attempt to 'convert' someone else to your point of view. There is a healing and an integrity that occurs. People feel free to be and express themselves without feeling judged by others. I take every opportunity to encourage free expression and exploration and to stay alert to signs that members of the group are not participating as freely as they might (also see Chapter 8).

Working with a sense of agreement

I like to work with a sense of agreement. This is also an important element of 'community'. Indeed, one definition of adult behaviour is the ability to make agreements with others and be accountable for them.

In the beginning, then, I am looking for a sharing of expectations with each other, leading to some agreement on what it is we are doing here together. This agreement should then lead to a commitment to the work to be done. Figure 4.1. shows the progression.

Sharing of expectations
↓
Making agreements
↓
Commitment
↓
Learning

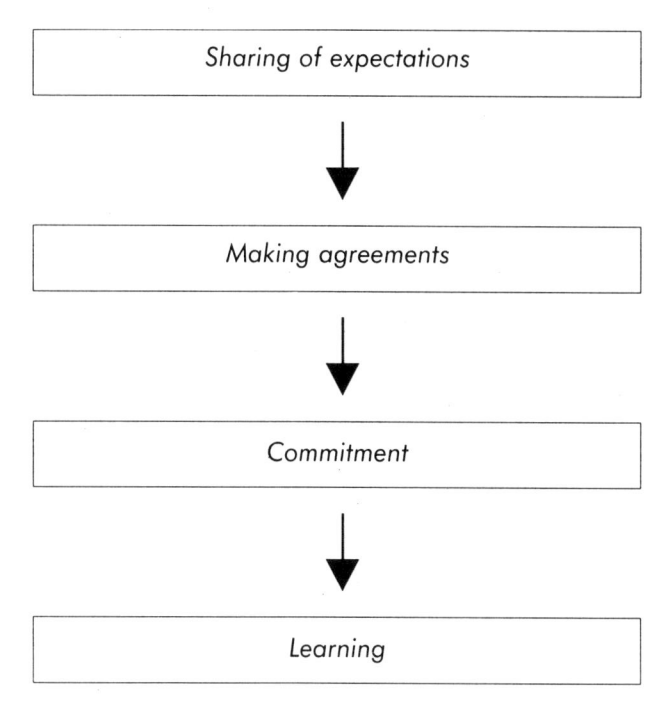

Figure 4.1. A learning sequence

I find this a very useful sequence. If I am not clear at any time about what may be going on, I reconsider the agreements and expectations. We may have to re-negotiate our agreements. For instance, if we agreed to take a 30-minute lunch break and most start returning after 40 or 45 minutes, I can return us to our original agreement and ask if we need to reconsider it. Younger adults are often not so assured in making agreements and we may need to return to them fairly regularly.

We can make agreements about many things, for example:

- what knowledge, skills and attitude outcomes learners and teachers expect from a course;
- what sorts of behaviours and experience are necessary to achieve intended outcomes
- what topics, what teaching methods, what human resources and physical resources are needed;
- what forms of assessment and continuous and final evaluations of the course are required.

An important way of establishing trust with others is to make small agreements and keep to them. Without agreements relationships can break down, often disastrously.

Teaching institutions usually consider that they have clear agreements with their students. However, these 'agreements' can take the form of bureaucratic rules that have not been examined and considered with the individual learner. As teachers and facilitators, however, we can practise dialogue and negotiation with our learners, relative to agreements with each other (see Chapter 5 on negotiations).

There are many components to the learning process and relative to each of them we can ask, "Who is deciding what about whom?". I am advocating much more learner and teacher collaboration in decision-making. This extends to assessment. As Heron (1988) points out, assessment is the most political of all educational processes for it is the area where issues of power are most at stake. If there is no teacher–learner collaboration on assessment, then the teachers exert a stranglehold that inhibits the development of collaboration with respect to all other processes. I consider this point to be very important for all teachers to consider. Our real values as teachers are reflected in the way assessments are decided and conducted. How does our espousal of learning-centredness measure up against our actual assessment processes (see Chapter 9.)?

Beginning a new session

It may be some hours or days since I was with the group. I have observed that every time I meet with the group it is a new beginning. I like to review in some way the learning from our last session together. For instance, I might give a brief summary myself; "Remember last time we looked at Chomsky's notion of 'manufactured consent'. Today we were going to apply this to …". Or I might elicit key points from the learners; "What are the key elements to Chomsky's argument regarding 'manufactured consent'?". I often repeat the responses so that everyone hears. Or I may quickly note them on the whiteboard. Or I start with a visual on the board, for example:

Teaching for Learning

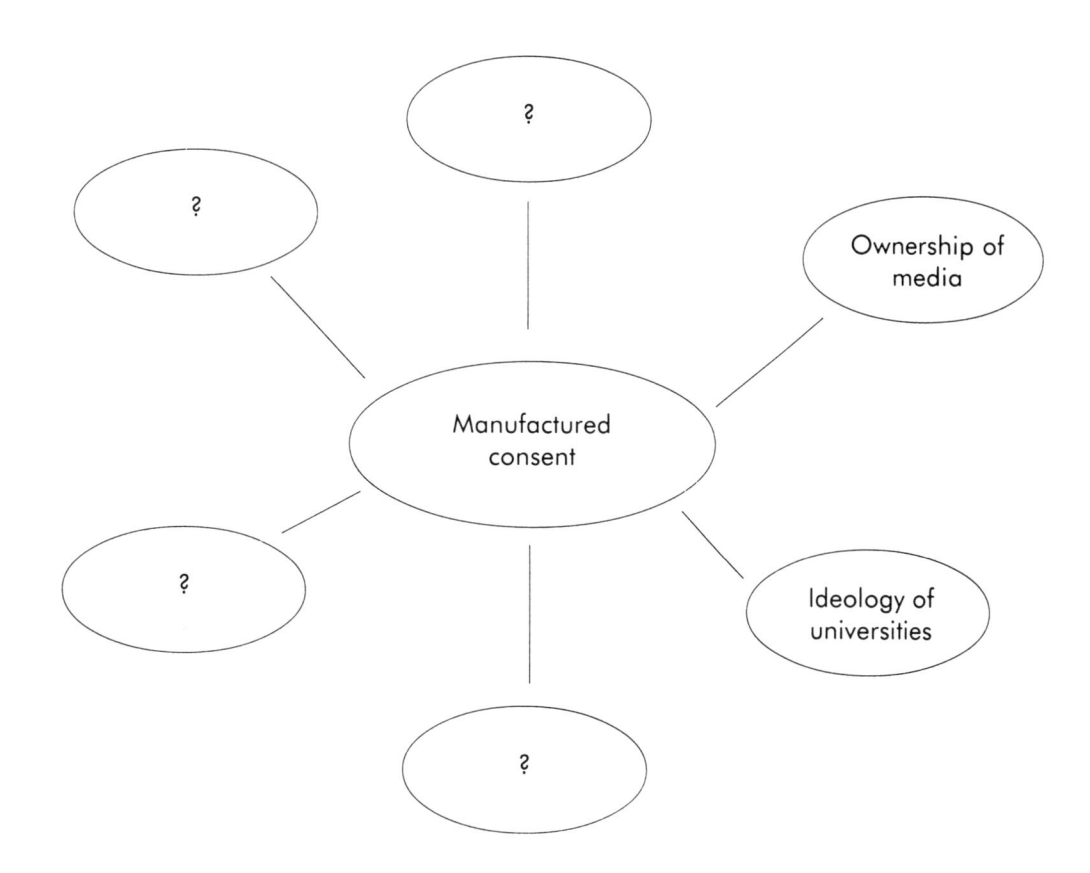

```
        ( ? )
         |
( ? )    |              ( Ownership of
   \     |             /    media    )
    \    |            /
     ( Manufactured )
     (   consent    )
    /    |            \
   /     |             \
( ? )    |              ( Ideology of
         |                universities )
        ( ? )
```

I like to encourage learner interaction:

> "Before we start today's topic, I'd like you to turn to the person next to you and check that you both know the important elements of Chomsky's 'manufactured consent'. A couple of minutes". After a couple of minutes, I ask: "Any comments or questions?" (This gives a chance to clear up any confusion.)

Another approach to learner interaction might be:

> "Before we start today's topic, I'd like you, in pairs, to tell each other what you learned in the last session, if anything. A couple of minutes." "Any comments?"

Such pair discussions are useful because:

- Less confident learners are encouraged to ask questions.
- Learners are helped to 'arrive': to begin focusing on the learning.

For such activities it is useful to give the participants an idea of how much time they've got. I use pair discussions frequently. With only two people involved there is a good chance that each will have fairly equal 'airtime'.

Communicating learning outcomes

Another way of helping learners to focus is to consider what the learning outcomes for the session might be. The formal writing down of learning outcomes is a useful planning tool for the teacher: "At the end of the session, the learner will be able to …".

Some teachers like to give their learners the outcomes in formal language. I tend to opt for a more informal tone:

- "In today's session, we'll be looking at …" (must knows)
- "And if we have time, we can examine …" (should knows)

You may want to write the outcomes up on the whiteboard and leave them there throughout the session. I usually plan my use of board space beforehand. For instance: A more interesting strategy is to develop the learning outcomes with the learners. For instance, "Today we're looking at how the requirements of capitalist modernisation have affected social and educational policy" (write on board). "What kinds of things do you think we need to know?" I have found I often elicit all the aspects I had in mind and some extra things I hadn't thought of.

Schedule for today's session Learning outcomes	Workspace	Key ideas

Setting standards

Because it is vital that learners understand what they have to know or be able to do, I can:

- tell them
- show them
- give them a copy of the competencies or levels of achievement required

- discuss their work with them, encouraging them to reflect on and assess the quality of their own work
- give them an opportunity to assess each other's work. I am looking for very specific assessment, however, and I usually have to teach them how to do it. What, *specifically*, is 'good'? What, *specifically*, is 'not so good' and how could it be improved?

Creating an effective learning environment

This section focuses on how to create an emotionally healthy climate in which everyone works together safely and productively.

The emotional environment

When considering the emotional aspects of the learning environment, it is important to contract for 'ways of working together'. I look for a set of protocols or guidelines to help us work together. It is useful to spend some time discussing them. I only look for three or four. We can change them or add some later if we need to. The following can be included:

- Confidentiality.
- Starting and finishing on time.
- Taking responsibility for expressing own insights, questions, disappointments and needs.
- Full participation and commitment.
- Check that everyone's name is known.
- Use learner's names (pronounced correctly).
- Feel comfortable with allowing learners the space and time to 'arrive'.
- Encourage and be comfortable with silence.
- Give non-verbal encouragement to speakers. For instance, eye contact, smile, nod, acknowledgement with hand gesture – open hand, palm upward.
- Maintain a relaxed voice level.
- Supportively interrupt unnecessary challenges or other 'attacks' from learners on other learners.
- Take frequent breaks: For instance, two or three minutes every 20 minutes.
- Use open-ended questions.
- Vary the pace.
- Express feelings about the group's co-operation and participation. For instance, "I feel uncomfortable that some are not participating in all activities. Can we discuss it?".
- Get feedback on your teaching and facilitation.
- Encourage learners to speak for themselves and be specific in what they're saying.
- When learners appear to be speaking for others, check it out.
- Watch and listen for non-verbal cues that someone wants to speak – for instance, a leaning forward, an intake of breath.

- Use opportunities for pair and small group activities. Ensure, however, that it is a real, useful learning activity. Learners can be told the reason for the activity.
- Remember points made by learners that can be referred to in later sessions. For instance, "As John said last week ...".

All learning involves emotions and feelings. Boud and Walker (1993) emphasise attending to the feelings that accompany an experience of learning. When we re-evaluate our knowledge, understanding, or point of view as a consequence of a particular learning experience, it is useful to be aware of our emotional state or reaction to the experience. Our emotions may be clouding our understanding. I stay alert to signs of strong feelings and check them out. I can't change someone else's feelings but I can give them 'space' to express their feelings and perhaps discover what they'd like to do.

Goal-setting

I encourage learners to set their own goals, to keep their own learning journals, to note down what they understand about a particular topic, or what skills they consider they have, and then to contract with themselves their own learning goals. I discuss with them how it's going – whether they have achieved the goals and what they may yet have to do. Sometimes, of course, students will modify their goals.

Anticipating difficulties

It helps to keep brief notes of 'what could be improved'. Sometimes I discuss things with a sympathetic colleague. He or she may help me clarify things and find ways of making the improvement.

There are difficulties that I have learnt to anticipate, for instance:

- I need more time to explain new concepts.
- The equipment isn't available or doesn't work.
- The layout of furniture doesn't suit me.
- There is a wide range of differences in learner abilities and learning skills (do I require note-taking, note-making, discussion skills, numeracy and literacy, listening skills?).
- Can the learners quickly get into small groups for tasks or pair work (what if there's an uneven number of participants)?
- Is there enough variety of learning activities?
- How will I handle different learner expectations?

I can take action to ease some of these difficulties, for instance:

- In organising furniture and layout I know the numbers of learners. I can arrive early enough to check out and perhaps change the layout and seating, try and get

everybody grouped in one area rather than have isolated pockets of learners scattered round the room.
- With lighting and ventilation, I can check with the group.
- In organising equipment, I can have a checklist as part of my session plan, give myself enough time to organise and ensure the equipment is working.
- In organising time, I can commit to start and finish on time and negotiate any changes with the participants.
- Maintaining a workable noise level is a matter of discussing with the group. This can be particularly important if other classes nearby are affected by the noise that we make with our activities.

Working co-operatively

It is useful to discuss with learners how they feel about working together. Identify with them what skills are needed. For instance, there may be a need for goal-setting, communication, negotiation, decision-making, evaluation and leadership skills.

Learning in groups

Because I like to develop cooperative learning, I need to understand something of group behaviour. Here are some considerations that have helped me. They are based on the work of Auvine *et al.* (1978, 1981).

The 'ideal' group size is whatever number the participants feel happy with. I'm always prepared to listen to the participants' views on the size of the group.

Be clear about what is negotiable. Vella (1995) writes that you need to be clear on the distinction between the consultative (suggestion) voice and deliberative (decision-making) voice. Heron (1988) similarly points out that the facilitator needs to be clear on what is negotiable and what is not.

Placing a high value on co-operation does not mean that I am looking to eliminate conflict. Groups with some conflict are often more creative and productive than groups without.

Any time a group engages in difficult or prolonged activities, someone will emerge as informal leader. Leaders play important and diverse roles: they may serve as a model or example for the group, help the group solve problems, provide interpersonal smoothing between members and make decisions for the group. If the leader seems too dominant, ask the group how suitable the leader's decisions or actions are. For example, "Does that suggestion seem OK to you all?" "Does anyone else have any ideas?".

Sometimes leaders are not so obvious. To detect them look for these clues.

- Who talks the most?
- Whose suggestions are most often accepted by the group?
- Which person do group members look at the most when they are talking?

- To whom are suggestions referred to when they come up? Who is the final arbiter on decisions?
- Who takes the most responsibility?

Sometimes a group will blame a particular person for group problems. The scapegoat is often someone who has broken the informal rules or norms of the group. Avoid focusing blame on individuals. Have the group discuss the offending behaviour instead. Ask the group to suggest changed behaviour.

Sometimes the group may unite in scapegoating an issue or a situation. A favoured target is the 'system'. Blaming 'them', though, freezes people into a very simple viewpoint and discourages action. Again, discuss what is going on and help the group to see issues without blame. Encourage them to suggest actions to change the situation.

Encouraging learner responses

Questions encourage learner involvement. I ask questions for at least three purposes.

- to establish learners' knowledge and understanding
- to clarify information
- to elaborate on and link information and ideas.

To ascertain learners' knowledge my questions will mainly begin with words like 'what', 'how', 'where', 'when', 'which', and are intended to elicit specific information. For instance, "How do you justify that ...?", "What relevance does that have in ...?", "What qualities do these have in common ...?", "How does that connect with ...?".

Some examples of clarifying questions are "What do you mean by ...?", "Can you give me an example?".

To help learners express themselves more fully, both in thought and in feeling, I can ask elaborating questions. For instance, "Can you tell us more?", "Can you be more specific?", "Could you elaborate on that?", "Uhhuh, what else?", "How do you feel about that?", "How did it seem to you?".

Questioning needs to be meaningful.

- Adjust your questions to the way learners are responding rather than thinking up 'good' questions beforehand.
- Avoid playing the game "guess what's on my mind". If you have a favourite solution to a problem try and draw out a range of possible answers from learners first and invite a discussion of their merits. You may then reveal your own favourite for comparison.
- Once you have asked a question, be prepared to wait for an answer. It can take a little while for someone to think about the question and formulate a reply. Reflective learners, in particular, take time to come up with answers.
- If you did not get the answer you were looking for perhaps you asked the wrong question.

Giving constructive feedback

Making feedback specific is important. For instance, I don't just say, "That's very good". I state the specific things that are 'good'. Likewise, be specific about what can be improved. Invite learners to be specific in their self-assessments and in the feedback they give to each other. I invite suggestions from learners and encourage comparisons with my own. It seems important for learners to be able to rectify their 'incompetence'. Check that the learners understand what they must do to improve and then provide the opportunity to do so.

Arranging the physical space

It is important to create appropriate learning environments. Check the temperature and flow of fresh air. Remove any useless items from walls and any rubbish that may be left around. At least for the first meeting, I'll arrange the room how I'd like it. After that, when the space has also become the participants', I will consult with them as to how we can best arrange the room.

Teaching effectively

The ideas so far in this chapter focus on communication and relationship building. My approach to teaching is based on the idea that good communication and good relationships are essential to good teaching. These ideas underpin this section in which I discuss my approaches to the more formal side of teaching, lecturing and on-line teaching.

Myths about 'good' communications

Jensen (1988) offers many tools to improve our communications. His description of three communication myths is particularly useful when we consider teaching.

The first myth is that "It's up to the learners to get the message". He suggests that if we want to be effective, we must pretend and believe that it is all up to us as teachers to communicate. It is the responsibility of the sender to make sure that the meaning of the message is received. This means that the sender must do whatever it takes to get through to the receiver. The only way that the sender will know whether or not the message got through is from the reaction of the receiver. Believe that the meaning of your communication is the response that you get, he says, and your results will go up dramatically.

The second myth is that "Communication is primarily with words". In fact, it is something like 7 per cent verbal (words), 38 per cent vocal (volume, pitch, tonality, rhythm), and 55 per cent body movements (posture, gestures, face).

The third myth is that "Communication is a natural process". Rather, he says, it is a complex process that requires accurate skills that teachers must learn and practise.

I now turn to describe how communication affects my more formal teaching.

Lecturing logically and clearly

I use the term 'lecture' here to describe any prepared teacher talk with pre-set objectives. The talk can be for the familiar 50 minutes in a lecture theatre to an 'audience of hundreds' or it can consist of a 10-minute burst with your normal group of, say, 15. Race (2002) suggests that good planning is vital, regardless of the lecture's duration or audience. He suggests that preparation can take up to 10 times longer than the duration of your eventual lecture.

The following are some of the principles I bear in mind when putting my lectures together.

- When planning, I look closely at the learning objectives. Are they clear? If not, how can I clarify them? My most important challenge is to ensure that the structure of the lecture covers the objectives.
- I apply the KISS (Keep It Strictly Simple) formula. Check your lecture plan for unnecessary complications in how you have structured it and how you develop ideas. If it isn't clear and logical to you, it won't be for others. If necessary, check the clarity and logic with a colleague. However, I am not suggesting you oversimplify. Some ideas are complex and this needs to be taken on board.
- When planning I sometimes have a block. To remove it, I brainstorm on a sheet of paper what I know. Then I leave it a while, before trying to break it down into *must* know, *should* know and *could* know.
- This triplet of *must know*, *should know* and *could know* is excellent for sorting out *what is* from *what is not* absolutely crucial to achieve learning objectives.
- Plan to use supporting materials. Handouts are very useful, particularly if they are interactive and invite learners to respond to them. More formal lectures often require a computer-generated 'Power Point' presentation these days. Reprint the slides of your presentation on a handout and include space for note-making.
- Get familiar with the room/lecture theatre before the learners arrive. I am particularly keen to check out technology before I use it.
- Think in terms of 20-minute slots. Talk for that time and then plan a brief break or have a pair activity. Concentration spans are limited and it is useful to energise learners with a break.
- Lecturing is a performance. How we present ourselves is important. But the performance need not be solo. Involve learners by setting them small activities.
- Learners will have had some experiences that they can call on to make sense of my words, so I draw on this in activities for pairs or fours. People remember what they participate in! (See Chapter 8 for further practical ideas.)
- I start with an *attention grabber*. It could be a provocative question, a prop, or a surprising fact. (For instance, "Since World War Two, there have been 150 major wars. Twenty-three million people have been killed and 90 per cent of all these casualties were civilians. In this lecture I will be presenting some facts about the militarisation of the planet, identifying the main protagonists, and suggesting what needs to be done to avoid even worse catastrophes.")

- My lectures have a *beginning* (where I tell them what I'm going to tell them), a *middle* (where I tell them) and an *end* (where I tell them what I've told them).
- I use verbal cues. "There are *three* main causes of death. *Firstly*, there are the various forms of cancer. *Secondly*, heart diseases. And *thirdly*, doctors." Using *number cues* like this helps the listener and note-taker. Often I illustrate key concepts using diagrams or mind-maps. Even a confusing diagram will give birth to a feeling of curiosity.
- During my presentation I make general eye contact with everyone (we often favour one side of the room) and try to stay alert to looks of puzzlement or someone wanting to say something.
- I summarise using verbal cues. "So, remember, four fundamental aspects …", or "Can someone tell me then, the four important …".
- In my planning I also try and anticipate problems, for instance with jargon and concepts, and to identify what understanding I am assuming and should check. For example, I've got a video to show. Are there any concepts or principles I should pre-teach? Should I produce a worksheet? Can I stop it at any place and have the learners, in pairs, discuss questions? Can I turn the volume down and work only with the visuals?

Teaching on-line

Boehm (1992) has suggested that a paradigm shift is occurring in teaching that changes the role of the teacher. I agree with this. My teaching certainly is becoming more holistic and collaborative. For many teachers paradigm change means going on-line. Their teaching is mediated by the computer. Zepke (2002) suggests that within five years most of us will be teaching in this way to some extent. As I teach on-line I want to keep the values and beliefs that sustain my teaching face-to-face. I want to focus on:

- learning-centredness
- learner experiences as a basis for learning
- positive relationships leading to mutual trust
- clear and interactive communications.

I am working on developing approaches to on-line teaching that achieve this vision. In some ways, computer-mediated teaching is little different to face-to-face teaching. I need to:

- know something about learners
- try to engage their interests
- recognise differences
- negotiate objectives and course structure and assess fairly
- ensure learning is active, problem solving and communicative
- provide focused and well-organised input.

However, in some ways teaching on-line is different. It is communicative in a different way. I must learn a whole new language in place of body language. Remember, this makes up 55 per cent of communication, according to Jensen (1988). I must develop 'netiquette' – behaviour that is acceptable on the Internet. For example, feedback in writing has to be carefully framed. Holding discussions in a 'chat room' has different rules to chatting in the classroom.

It is difficult to set up common experiences for learning. So I must take care to set up learning that is authentic for everyone as well as active. By authentic I mean experiences that are immediately relevant to learners and that they can apply in their lives. By 'active' I mean learning that is centered on projects that ask learners to address problems that are authentic to them.

I need to feel comfortable with the technology. Not only must I learn to think and communicate effectively in new ways, I must teach learners to use the technology to good effect. I must acquire the skills and attitudes to surf the net and negotiate in chat rooms and by e-mail. I must press the right buttons.

Listening to learners

Whether I facilitate groups, give a lecture or teach on-line, I constantly check on whether I really am 'listening' to the responses a learner is making.

- Non-verbal signs that we are listening include looking in the general direction of the speaker (although maintaining direct eye contact is not always culturally appropriate); leaning forward; nodding; and moving our body forward with warm gestures at the appropriate moment.
- Verbal signs include "Uh-huh", "Mmhmm", "Yeah"; a simple restatement of the learner's last statement; repetition of one or two key words in the learner's reply; asking an elaborating question ("Can you be more specific?"); asking a clarifying question ("How come?" "What do you mean …?"); and giving a short paraphrase of what has been said to check you've understood ("Are you saying …?"). Repeating what a learner has said can ensure that everyone has heard the response. If I want to avoid a long conversation with one learner I can repeat the learner's question and invite the group to offer their responses. If one learner tends to dominate 'air time', I can suggest, "Thank-you, John. Can we hear what others think about this …?".
- On-line signs include prompt answers to e-mails, answering all the questions in the e-mail or the chat room and answering appropriately. On-line listening includes checking out whether I have the right end of the stick.

Evaluating the learning situation

The ongoing evaluation of the learning situation involves examining my personal performance, listening to the learners, and acting to maintain learner commitment.

One way of evaluating my performance as a teacher is to isolate and examine the things that I do. I can devise or find a list of competencies. I can use the kinds of competencies that are identified in this book, for instance in Chapter 1.

I check off those that I am strong at and those that I'd like to improve. How am I going to assess my development? It can be helpful to have someone observe my teaching and provide feedback. I may ask a colleague, the local professional development staff or my manager. It is important that the person I ask has some understanding of what I'm trying to do in my teaching: someone who is on my 'wavelength'. Having asked someone to observe my teaching it is important, also, to agree on a procedure or set of rules on how I'd like to receive the feedback.

Conclusion and next steps

Learning is about the personal construction of meanings and the sharing of them with others. The teacher isn't the sole fount of experience and knowledge. This idea is central to my practice. It leads to teaching that builds relationships, communicates openly and challenges and supports learners.

Reflecting on the following questions may help you to further develop your teaching for learning.

- What steps do you take to extend the range of learning activities that you draw upon in your teaching?
- How do you allow for learners preferring to learn and participate in different ways?
- How do you encourage questions from learners and respond in a way that facilitates their learning?
- How do you respond when learners indicate difficulties with content, pace, emphasis or style?
- If necessary, how do you find out about the causes of disruptive behaviour and remedy them?
- How do you frame questions to help learners learn effectively?
- What 'golden rules' do you adopt when lecturing or teaching on-line?

Keep a diary to help you answer these questions over time. The following readings may also help you answer the questions.

Further reading

Biggs, J. (1999). *Teaching for Quality Learning at University.* Buckingham: SRHE and Open University Press.
Brookfield, S., & Preskill, S. (1999). *Discussion as a Way of Teaching.* Buckingham: SRHE and Open University Press.
Brown, S., & Race, P. (2002). *Lecturing: A practical guide.* London: Kogan Page.
Heron, J. (1993). *Group Facilitation.* London: Kogan Page.

Jolliffe, A., Ritter, J., & Stevens, D. (2001). *The Online Learning Handbook. Developing and Using Web-Based Learning.* London: Kogan Page.

Silberman, M. (1996). *Active Learning.* Boston, Massachusetts: Allyn and Bacon.

References

Auvine, B., Densmore, B., Extrom, M., Poole, S., & Shanklin, M. (1978). *A Manual for Group Facilitators.* USA: The Centre for Conflict Resolution.

Auvine, B., Densmore, B., Extrom, M., Poole, S., & Shanklin, M. (1981). *Building United Judgement.* USA: The Centre for Conflict Resolution.

Boehm, D. (1992). Writing depends on "point of view". *Writing Notebook: Visions for Learning,* 10, (1), 10–11.

Boud, D., & Walker, D. (1993). Barriers to Reflection on Experience. In D. Boud, R. Cohen, & D. Walker (eds), *Using Experience for Learning.* Buckingham, UK: SRHE and Open University Press.

Collison, G., Elbaum, B., Haavind, S., & Tinker, R. (2000). *Facilitating Online Learning.* Madison: Atwood Publishing.

Heron, J. (1988). Assessment Revisited. In D. Boud (ed.), *Developing Student Autonomy in Learning.* London: Kogan Page.

Jackson, R., & Caffarella, R. (1994). *Experiental Learning: A new approach.* San Francisco: Jossey Bass Publishers.

Jensen, E. (1988). *Superteaching.* Del Mar: Turning Point for Teachers.

Peck, M. (1990). *The Different Drum.* London: Arrow Books.

Race, P. (2002). *Notes on Lecturing* [Web Page] URL: http://www.lgu.ac.uk/deliberations/lecturing/content.html [2002, August 28].

Vella, J. (1994). *Learning to Listen, Learning to Teach.* San Francisco: Jossey Bass.

Vella, J. (1995). *Training through Dialogue.* San Francisco: Jossey Bass.

Vella, J. (2000). *Taking Learning to Task.* San Francisco: Jossey Bass.

Zepke, N. (2002). *Computer Mediated Learning in Post-school Education and Training.* Wellington: Massey University Study Guide.

— Chapter 5 —

Inclusive Teaching: Making Space for Difference

Nick Zepke

Introduction

I was introduced to learner differences by a sociogram. This is a map showing relationships within groups (Sherman, 2002). A colleague introduced me to it in my early years of teaching and I continued to use it for a time. I told students to imagine we were going on a bus trip. I asked them to name two classmates they would most like to sit beside, then two they definitely would not want to travel with. I mapped their choices on a piece of paper. The people regarded most positively by their classmates were placed in the centre of the map showing their relationships to others. The least popular I placed on the margins of the map. Every year, there were well-connected students clustered in the middle and others who were outliers.

After a while I discovered a pattern. Students for whom the classroom was a comfortable space held the centre ground of acceptance. Those who felt uncomfortable or who were noticeably different in some ways to their peers ended up on the margins. Sometimes women were outliers in male-dominated classes; sometimes quiet or very loud students; sometimes Maori in a Pakeha (European) class; sometimes working class or upper-class people. Often student outliers turned out to have learning difficulties. In short, I found that 'difference' pushed people to the margins and that marginalised people had trouble connecting with their peers and my teaching. I decided that it was my job to try to include people at the margins into classroom society.

This was more easily said than done. As we can be different from others in so many ways, people are at the margins for a variety of reasons. People also have different responses to being at the margin. Some put themselves there deliberately. Some are not aware of their position. Others are aware but feel powerless to change it, while a few take the initiative to move to the centre. I found what worked in one situation did not work in another. I finally set out on two different pathways to become an inclusive teacher. One is made of a variety of teaching approaches that enable practical, emotional, spiritual as well as intellectual learning to take place. The other is political. It recognises that confinement to the margins often results from a lack of power and that how power operates in a class is something to be negotiated. Together, the pathways seek to make space for learners to be different and for their voices to be heard (Sheared & Sissel, 2001).

This chapter explores these pathways.

- It first addresses the question, "What can I, as a teacher, do to enable individuals who are different to feel comfortable in the classroom and so enable them to learn better?". This section outlines teaching approaches that help individual learners learn better.
- In the second part of the chapter I ask a different question, "What can I do to better meet the needs of groups of learners who feel powerless?". This is a much more radical question and implies that we, as teachers, can do something to change what, to some people, are oppressive structures.

Mapping difference

The two pathways suggest that there are at least two notions of 'difference' in classrooms. One focuses on the individual and considers the way people learn and what we, as teachers, can do to help them do it their way. It deals with how we work with different ways of being, multiple intelligences and varied learning styles.

The other notion understands the classroom as a society in which quite different social groups come together. 'Diverse' is the term often used to describe classrooms with cultural dissimilarities (Wlodkowski & Ginsberg, 1995). I think diversity goes far beyond ethnic culture. It also includes gender, socio-economic class (wealth and status), age, sexual orientation and disability, among others.

Dealing with individual difference is a challenge, not a problem. I don't for one moment think that to be different is bad or that diversity makes teaching difficult. Quite the contrary. People can be very proud of their differences; they can be a spur, an inspiration to learn. By adopting inclusive and power-sharing teaching methods, we can make it so.

Valuing different ways of being and learning

Individual differences in people are like grains of sand on a beach. They cannot satisfactorily be identified, listed or described. Many attempts have been made to group them by category. So, over time, difference in who we are, our different ways of being, has been linked to factors such as our gender, race, upbringing, social and economic position, state of health, personality and sexuality (Tisdell, 1998). For learning, such differences have been refined to consideration of factors like intelligence, learning styles and learning intentions. But these are differences associated with cognitive processes (thinking). Emotional, spiritual and value factors also seem to play their part. The range of differences is well captured by learner comments reported

Inclusive Teaching: Making Space for Difference

in research studies. Leach (2000), in research on self-directed learning, for example, spotlighted just some of the many different views on learning.

- Some learners wanted the teacher to control the learning process. Others didn't care or wanted control of their own learning. For example:

  I like to be controlled ... I think, as a learner, I like to be controlled (p. 162).

  I would actively look for somewhere else (to learn) ... (if I am not given opportunities to have some control) (p. 166).

  I think that learning is part of my life. And it doesn't actually matter how it happens, it's going to happen anyway (p. 155).

- Some learners like to learn for learning's sake. Others expect it to be practical and relevant.

  I do find learning very pleasurable. I love it. I love the challenge. I love the stimulation. I love just finding out something that I didn't know before (p. 194).

  (I) want to be given the class. I want to gain some of the knowledge and I want to go away again. I don't want to be willy-wollying around ... I'd just rather get it done (p. 195).

  Unless it's something I can really see the relevance, that I want to use, then I'm not bothered with it (p. 191).

- Some learners are confident in wanting to work with others. Others suffer from severe self-doubt.

  I feel that there must be peer contact. If you have no contact and you're working by yourself, you don't have ideas to bounce off, you don't have other people to actually, to compare what you're dealing with (p. 140).

  This year's probably been one of my hardest with self-doubt coming through ... I've just been self-fighting all year. And the cost of that is no study (p. 189).

- The very learning process seems to vary. Flannery and Hayes (2001) revealed their quite different ways of learning.
  First, Daniele Flannery:

  I learn through feelings, experiences, and information incubating within me for a while ... When it finally 'feels right', 'I know'. To people who make sense of things the way I do, I don't have to use many words, complete thoughts, or logical sentences to share what I have learned ... We judge the authenticity of the knowing and what is known, that is the learning, from what 'feels' right (pp. 29–30).

Then, Elisabeth Hayes:

> I rely on logic and rationality in most of my learning, and I approach most new situations by trying to make 'sense' of them intellectually. I love to analyze ideas and concepts. However, when it comes to something that requires 'embodied' knowing I have a hard time (p. 30).

Three windows on difference

These examples represent mere grains of sand, not the beach. There are many more differences in learning. Indeed, every classroom has a different mix of differences. To help us make sense of the profusion of learning differences we can sort them into categories. They open windows to help us recognise and understand learning differences. The following three categories can be useful when planning to teach our diverse classes.

Learning intentions

Learners come to learning with different intentions (Entwhistle, 1998). Some merely want to acquire the skills, knowledge and attitudes necessary to achieve a goal. They want to pass an exam, master skills, gain a qualification needed to, say, get a job. The learning is not the primary goal. The outcome is. The approach to learning is governed by that external outcome. It is likely to be based on memorising, gaining superficial understandings and reproducing the teacher's words and meanings without analysis. This approach has been called *surface learning*.

Other learners' intention is to engage fully with the knowledge on offer. They want to understand not only what they need to know, but also what concepts underpin knowledge, skills and attitudes. Passing exams, mastering skills and gaining qualifications are not the primary aims. The learning itself is. Such learners will dig deeply and travel widely for their understanding. Rather than memorising necessary facts, they seek to remember and reinforce their understanding from beyond the curriculum. This approach has been called *deep learning*.

Recently a third learning intention has emerged. From a teacher's point of view, learners with this intention could be ideal learners. They exhibit the same practical outcome orientation as surface learners but also seek to understand fully the knowledge on offer. They honour the teacher's knowledge and meanings but are able to do something different, something original. This approach has been called achievement learning. I prefer to call it *strategic learning*.

Multiple intelligences

I won't win any prizes for claiming that your students have different forms of intelligence. I don't mean that some of your students are less intelligent than others. What I do mean is that there are many different kinds of intelligence in your classroom and that this affects how students learn. Howard Gardner identified eight different

Inclusive Teaching: Making Space for Difference

kinds of intelligence or 'smarts' (Roberts, 1996), although there could be more. The eight kinds of smart are:

- **Word Smart**: the ability to use words to express yourself effectively, orally and in writing, to understand how language is constructed and used, to use a wide range of words and expressions to inspire and convince others, to explain concepts and ideas.
- **Space Smart**: the ability to see the world with your mind's eye, to visualise, to use pictures and graphic design to show complex ideas, to work accurately from a map or other visual media, to orientate ourselves in strange situations.
- **Music Smart**: the ability to sing accurately and tunefully, to be sensitive to beat, pitch or melody and tone colour of music, to have an intuitive understanding of music, to understand and to use technical knowledge to read and compose music.
- **Logic Smart**: the ability to use numbers effectively and to reason logically, to be sensitive to logical patterns, relationships, arguments, use categories, inferences, generalisations and calculations to solve complex problems, analyse and explain concepts in using symbols.
- **Body Smart**: the ability to use the body to express feelings and ideas as do actors, dancers, athletes; use our hands to make things such as a crafter, sculptor or surgeon; to use physical skills such as balance, dexterity, flexibility and speed.
- **People Smart**: the ability to see, feel and understand others' intentions, motivations and feelings, to recognise many different kinds of interpersonal cues such as gestures, facial expressions, tone of voice, to respond effectively to those cues in some practical way.
- **Self Smart**: the ability to understand ourselves and to act on the basis of that understanding, to have a useful picture of our strengths and limitations, to be aware of our moods, intentions, motivations and desires and the consequences they may have for us.
- **Nature Smart**: the ability to observe, understand and organise patterns in the natural environment, to care for natural specimens such as plants, animals, rivers and mountains, developing strategies for protecting endangered species and putting such plans into action.

Multiple Intelligence theory is useful in identifying possible learning strengths of our students. It is also dangerous. It can tempt us into wrapping students into neat parcels and labelling them as having or lacking any particular kind of intelligence. We command all to some extent and probably can develop those we might now be weaker in. Moreover, I am not convinced that these eight are the only intelligences we have. I suggest at least another two.

- **Intuition Smart**: the ability to recognise and value our feelings, to use them to decide what is a right decision or path for us and to have the trust to follow the feelings, but also to know when to support our feelings with our other intelligences.

- **Spiritual Smart**: the ability to recognise that we are but a part of something greater than ourselves, that we are connected to all other beings, including our ancestors, our pasts, our environment, indeed all creation.

Learning styles

Another window on how students' learning differs is opened by Learning Styles theory. This focuses on how individuals usually organise and process information. It turns out that each person has distinct and individual ways of dealing with information and concepts. To manage such diversity, learning styles are usually described in sets of opposing characteristics. Over 21 different style sets have been identified, so there are many learning styles we could choose from. To illustrate the concept, I describe only two learning style sets here.

- ### Groupers and stringers (Roberts, 1996)

    Groupers like to get the big picture of a subject first and then build towards a full understanding of that picture. They like to relate one topic to as many other areas of knowledge as possible. Groupers learn best in unstructured situations and do less well if knowledge is presented within a rigid framework.

    Stringers like to begin with examples and details and string these details together to make a meaningful whole. A very structured learning process works best for these learners, as they must master many details.

- ### Activists, reflectors, theorists and pragmatists

    Another learning style set was produced by Honey and Mumford (1992), who based their four learning styles on research by David Kolb (see Chapter 1).

    - **Activists** involve themselves fully in new experiences. They are open-minded, not sceptical. They tend to be enthusiastic about anything new and so their philosophy is "I'll try anything once".
    - **Reflectors** like to stand back and ponder on experiences, observing them from many perspectives. They are great data collectors but take their time to come to conclusions.
    - **Theorists** think problems through in a step-by-step logical way. They are keen on basic assumptions, principles, theories, models and systems thinking. Subjective judgements are not for them.
    - **Pragmatists** are keen to try out ideas, theories and techniques to see if they work in practice. They are down-to-earth learners who like to solve practical problems.

    Many learning style sets come with inventories (questionnaires) that you can administer to pinpoint your students' learning styles. I am not keen on learning style inventories. They only ever capture one set of multiple possibilities and their results often box people into a very narrow understanding of how they learn. Like learning intentions and Multiple Intelligences, Learning Styles open a window on the diversity that is your classroom.

Dealing with difference

It is impractical to even try to cater for every learning intention, intelligence and style present in your classroom. Trying to be everything to everyone all of the time ends in nervous collapse. All you can expect to do is to *vary* your teaching enough so that students feel that their individual learning preferences are recognised and addressed *some* of the time. To do this, develop a toolkit of teaching approaches. Consider these seven:

Take the pulse

I don't recommend attacking your students with sundry inventories and questionnaires to identify learning differences. You can establish the range of differences in less intrusive ways. Talk to your students. Ask them informally why they are taking your class and what they want to get out of it. Even with big classes a few minutes per lecture spent in dialogue can reveal much. Invent tasks that illuminate how students think and what kind of intelligence they prefer to use. Observe how students react to different kinds of learning activities. Identify those learners that like structure and also those that don't. Reflect on your efforts. Keep a diary and use the entries to plan and evaluate your own teaching.

Use the learning cycle

Organise learning experiences to involve a full range of activities. For example:

- Provide a memorable experience. Experiences are the basis for all learning (see Chapter 1), but good educational experiences are memorable and engage the whole person including our rational and intuitive selves.
- Provide space for reflecting on experiences. This involves learners describing the meaning of the experience. Again, reflection can be analytical or intuitive, involve discussion and debate, journal keeping or even reflective silences.
- Give opportunity for learners to connect the underlying assumptions, explanations or conclusions arising from the experience with other learning. Such theorising enables learners to transfer knowledge.
- Enable learners to plan new learning experiences that will test their reflections and theories. Teach skills so learners can learn more effectively from their experiences.

Stimulate the brain

Challenge your learners. Provide them with peaks to climb without endangering their confidence. Rose and Nicholl (1997) advance a six-point plan to achieve a balance between challenge and security.

- Create a low stress environment – where expectations are high but mistakes are welcomed.
- Ensure the subject matter is relevant. Learners want to learn when they see the point.
- Make learning emotionally positive. Have learners work with others, foster humour, give breaks and provide enthusiastic support.
- Involve all the senses. Seeing and doing are just as important as hearing. Feeling is on a par with thinking. Creative thinking is as valuable as logical thinking.
- Engage as many intelligences as are relevant.
- Enable consolidation of what is learnt. Give space for reflection and review.

Engage more than mind

Learning is more than thinking. Every learning experience has an emotional dimension that offers opportunity for further learning. You can encourage such learning by including it in the learning cycle, by creating an emotional climate that enables learners to speak about their feelings to others. Even in the most objective science lesson you can ask, "What do you feel about that?" For many, learning is also a spiritual process. First Peoples, like Maori for example, like to include spiritual matters in their learning. They like to invite ancestors into their midst. Provide learners with opportunities to engage with their spiritual selves. For example, open your sessions with a minute's silence so that the spirit can arrive in the classroom.

Enable learner construction of knowledge

Chapters 6, 8 and 11 deal more fully with constructivism. Here I note that most learners don't just absorb the information you or textbooks provide. As the learning cycle suggests, they must do something with the information in order to turn it into knowledge: turn experience into learning. To help learners construct knowledge:

- Emphasise reflection. Teach learners how to reflect constructively (see Chapter 1 for some ideas).
- Encourage questioning (Chapter 1 again).
- Set real-life problems or projects for learners to solve. Listen to students' interests and life experiences to settle on suitable problems/projects.
- Use group work to enable students to question the material and to answer questions for themselves. Even in a filled lecture theatre learners can work in pairs or fours.
- Teach students techniques and skills helpful in knowledge construction – questioning, mind-mapping and brainstorming, for example.

Make learning authentic

Authentic learning is learning that students can relate to and apply to their own lives. Try to think up examples and set problems or projects that have personal meaning. To get good at that you will have to listen to student conversations, to their questions and their answers. One way to keep the learning authentic is to ask various students to come up with examples and even set problems.

Provide choice

If you always treat the class as one group you are stifling difference. If, on the other hand, you involve learners in making and taking responsibility for decisions about their learning, you strike a blow for inclusiveness. So:

- Look critically at what you are doing. Are there learning matters that you control now that could be shared with students? What skills must you teach students to take greater responsibility for their own learning?
- Plan your teaching so that learners have some choice about what and how they learn. In tightly structured courses that may be limited to framing learning activities around authentic tasks over which learners have some control.
- Base your teaching on questions, problems and projects. You can be sure that students will tackle them in many different ways.
- Lay the ground-work for independent and interdependent learning. Take time to hear sundry students tell of their ways of solving problems. Praise different approaches even when they lead to wrong solutions. Learners will trust their own decisions more if you constantly show that you value difference.

The politics of difference

So far we have discussed difference as something affecting the individual. I have outlined some teaching approaches that can address many differences in our classrooms. A number of these approaches have even involved sharing power with students by giving them space to be themselves and make decisions about their own learning. Indeed an underlying, yet unstated, assumption of this chapter is that teaching is about power; that it is political.

Power, politics and the 'other'

Some of you might find this hard to accept; but consider this. Should I treat every student the same? If I do, I assume that all students should conform to some norm I have in my mind. The norm is shaped by what I consider to be normal attitudes to learning, normal behaviour, normal standards of work. Every student must conform to these norms. Take an example. Say I like students to be compliant learners. Those who do things my way behave in certain approved ways and meet my norms.

They like working with me, are praised and achieve good outcomes. They are privileged.

Learners who don't do things my way are not 'normal' students in my own mind. They are 'other': immature, dumb, lazy, disruptive, absent or irresponsible. They become underprivileged learners. Every time they ignore my preferences they are seen to challenge my norms and my power as a teacher.

So, when the 'other' approaches me to ask to be heard, power is used. When students misbehave, mentally and emotionally detach themselves or stay away from classes altogether, more power is used. When there is a threat to complain to my boss, more power still is used. In the face of this kind of power I might have to give in. The whole process is political because students and I struggle for the power to decide how learning should occur in my classroom.

Ah, you might say, struggles are rarely as open as that. True. Some students are silenced by our power as teachers while others just leave. We also work hard to smooth over differences. When we set out to accommodate differences by being inclusive we further reduce the chance of conflict. But we never eliminate the subtle interplay of the political entirely. In the end, teaching and learning are political acts.

The political is personal, practical and structural

Cervero and Wilson (2001, p. 4) would suggest that up to this point I have merely been "romancing the adult learner". The political here is *personal*, with learning seen in purely individual terms. They claim that this view has been the dominant view in adult education, but argue that it is only a partial view. They add two other ways in which politics affects teaching and learning. One they call *practical*. This is the ability to get things done: to get resourcing for projects, to negotiate learning processes and to get permission to deal with individual differences in a preferred way. The other they call *structural*. This is about redistributing power relations in the classroom.

Structural politics concerns conflicts of interest among different groupings active in the classroom. Such groupings can consist of any collection or set of like-minded people. Often they are identified by labels such as gender, ethnicity, culture, sexual preference, age, disability. In terms of the politics of difference, conflicts of interest occur usually in response to certain classroom practices. For example, where a teacher imposes a regime of autonomous learning, this may conflict with the interests of groups who prefer communal practices, for example Maori and possibly women. Were the shoe on the other foot and communal learning the norm, the interests of other groups would be crossed, possibly those of some European men. I hope you have noticed that I use the words 'may' and 'possibly' here. While group interests do clash in classrooms, they can't usually be defined as easily as is suggested in my example.

Structural politics, then, assumes that certain teaching practices rule in classrooms, to the exclusion of others. Cervero and Wilson call such practices hegemonic. Sensible people take them for granted, as natural, as common sense, as simply right. Examples of such educational common sense include:

Inclusive Teaching: Making Space for Difference

- educate the brain, ignore the emotions and the spirit
- reproduce what you learn from teachers and books in examinations
- never reproduce without acknowledgement
- prepare yourself for jobs in the marketplace
- learn useful skills, knowledge, and above all learn to fit in
- achievement is personal and individual
- learn the subject, forget about the people
- meet the standards set by disciplines, professions and society at large
- hear the points of view only of people who matter
- learn to critique the 'other', but leave sensible people and ideas alone
- express all your ideas in well-constructed language.

This picture of current hegemonic practices may be a bit extreme and certainly does not apply to all classrooms. I use it here as a stalking horse to suggest that in any classroom there will be groups who do not buy into this form of educational 'common sense'. They challenge the hegemony and engage in structural politics. If we wish to be inclusive teachers we must deal with the structural politics in our classrooms.

Dealing with structural politics

My attempts at dealing with structural politics centre on the idea that difference and diversity are to be valued. Although sometimes valuing is difficult to translate into practice, I give it my best shot. I always remember that there are no certainties. Inclusive teaching involves high levels of communication and interpretation.

Win–win negotiations

Negotiating is one key element in balancing structural power differences. It offers a constructive way to solve problems. I try to use a tried and true process first developed by Fisher and Ury (1986).

- Negotiation is a process involving people. Try to remove from your mind problems you have had with them in the past. Think of them as partners with whom you will resolve difficult issues. For example, a group of women/men have accused you of discriminating against them in the way you mark work. Nasty for you. But you need their help to recreate a positive learning atmosphere.
- Focus on interests, not positions. Ignore the fact that you are the powerful teacher and they are troublesome students. Instead, list your objectives and clarify the reasons for them. Try to identify with their interests in this matter as well. Tell the students your objectives and listen to theirs.
- Together brainstorm some options. It is rare that one possible solution to the problem emerges that will satisfy both parties, so be creative, flexible, and show goodwill as you brainstorm options. Don't close your mind to their suggestions. Look for solutions that will support both sets of objectives.

- Agree on some criteria to select a suitable option. For example, where women/men in your class feel you discriminate against them, you may identify complete re-marking by you or another staff member and moderation as possible solutions. Decide on criteria that will highlight the option that best delivers a win–win solution.

It pays to remember that you have the structural power and that it takes time to establish the trust needed to enter an equitable process.

Sometimes we are not a party to negotiations needed to deal with structural politics in our classrooms. For example, power issues divided the men and women in one of my classes. I introduced them to the process and gave them space in class time to use it. After some false starts, the groups did negotiate a win–win outcome.

An inclusive approach to teaching

In the end, how we teach determines how successful we are in dealing with structural differences. A colleague and I (Zepke & Leach, 2002) have developed a three-layered approach to learning (meaning-making) based on the following goals:

- provide a wide array of learning experiences
- foster reflective practice
- develop critically reflective practice to examine power relations, hegemonic practices and respect differences
- enable learners to get in touch with their emotional and spiritual sides
- treat our classes as communities with both common and diverse interests
- identify views and ideas not usually represented in classrooms
- recognise and appreciate different ways of learning and being.

The three layers have the following features:

- One layer concerns the exposed and immediate experiences of a group. Here experiences are shared, analysed and questioned. Learning emerges out of this shared discussion. The views of different groups in the class form part of this open forum.
- A second layer explores the hidden meanings that inform and shape learners' immediate experiences. Here groups bring out the unstated beliefs, values, emotions and attitudes that influence individual and group learning.
- A third layer, also hidden, consists of the multiple and complex experiences of 'unheard voices'. These are groups, perspectives and knowledge constructions not represented in the class. For example, in New Zealand, Maori, rural, working-class, differently-abled and Pacific Nations people, among others, are under-represented in higher education. As a result their voices remain unheard.

In the first layer, learners construct their own meanings from readings, discussions (e-mail, audio-conferences and web pages for distance students) and media exposure.

Inclusive Teaching: Making Space for Difference

Through discussion a variety of meanings are exposed and made accessible to all members of the group who process these and integrate them, as they will, with their own. Critical questioning of all meanings is part of the process. Some kind of shared meaning emerges and is summarised, usually by one of us but not infrequently by one of the learners. One such discussion concerned theories of learning. Group members presented views from a variety of sources and in discussion made different meanings from these. After much debate most of the group arrived at a hard-won, shared meaning, while one member rejected it.

In our second layer we try to uncover cognitive, emotional and spiritual hidden meanings so that they become available to the whole class. For example, many Maori bring a strong spiritual quality to their learning, often demonstrated in karakia (prayer) before learning starts and at its end. They are often reluctant to surface this cultural practice in our Western classes. We now ask them whether they would like karakia and, if they do, invite them to lead it. The reasons behind this practice are hidden from many learners and are not always acceptable to them. In trying to expose such hidden meanings, we must also try to bring to the surface opposing views. For example, one learner constructed an entirely negative meaning from karakia. When asked, he volunteered his belief that, as a Christian, he was uncomfortable with what he considered to be pagan practices. This exposed to the group a different interpretation of Christianity as well as of cultural differences. These meanings had not been available before and influenced the meanings constructed by the group.

In our teaching we are aware of how selective we are in choosing authorities, ideas, opinions and theories, particularly for our distance learners. We want to build in the capacity to call unheard voices into group meaning-making. On one level this is orthodox academic thinking. Everywhere, learners are given bibliographies and invited to read widely. But we want more than this. We want to invite people from groups not represented, to brainstorm the identity of voices not included, and to construct meanings that do include them. A frequently unheard voice is that of the gay community. To include these voices, we scheduled sexuality as a content area in the course, and invited a gay person to address the group to facilitate the meaning-making process so the class could construct meanings from assumed gay perspectives.

Ensuring that all the layers are explored is our job as teachers. As the most experienced in the subject matter, we play a vital part in both social and individual meaning-making. But all the things that make us who we are – our gender, social status, age, power, values, emotions, ethnicity, sexuality – influence how we deal with meaning-making (Tisdell, 1998). To avoid us becoming unduly dominating, we too must try to surface our underlying meanings and expose them to critique. As the facilitators of learning we create an environment in which members of the group can learn. We enable learners to share and critically reflect on experiences and their meanings; we ensure that groups delve into the hidden connections made by group members and identify where they came from; and we encourage voices not represented in the group to be identified, heard and considered.

Summary and beginnings

I have offered you a two-pronged tool to deal with difference. One prong explores individual learning differences and offers some ideas for catering for them. The other looks at differences that result from power imbalances between groups in your classroom. It probes and offers ways of working with the politics of difference. In the end the central argument in this chapter holds that difference is a political issue that as a teacher you must deal with. The suggestions made are designed to give you ideas to create an inclusive classroom. To help you to progress your own understanding of the politics of difference, I offer the following suggestions:

- Try a sociogram with one of your classes. Better still, keep a diary of conversations you have had with your students on the first two occasions you have met. Note some details that:
    - enable you to devise authentic learning activities or assessments, for example something about their families, hobbies, life histories, jobs;
    - reveal something about the groups they identify with;
    - give you clues about their learning intentions, intelligences and learning styles;
    - tell you something about their general attitude to teaching.
- Negotiate the content and process of one session. Reflect on the result. Decide on future action.
- Read more widely about power and politics, for example:

    Apple, M. (1995). *Cultural Politics and Education*. New York: Teachers College Press.
    Foucault, M. (1996). Clarifications on the Question of Power. In S. Lotringer (ed.), *Foucault Live. Collected Interviews, 1961–1984* (pp. 255–263). New York: Seiotext (E).
    Hooks, B. (1994). *Teaching to Transgress: Education as the Practice of Freedom*. New York: Routledge.
    Shor, I. (1996). *When Students Have Power. Negotiating Authority in a Critical Pedagogy*. Chicago: The University of Chicago Press.
    Welton, M. (ed.) (1995). *In Defence of the Lifeworld: Critical Perspectives on Adult Learning*. Albany: State University of New York Press.

- Talk to three colleagues you know and respect.
    - Ask them to tell you how they deal with difference in their classrooms.
    - Discuss their approach to inclusive teaching.
    - Reflect on this information and incorporate your reflections into your own practice.

- Read more widely about individual differences, for example:

    Armstrong, T. (1994). *Multiple Intelligences in the Classroom*. Alexandria, Virginia: ASCD.

Bowser, B., Auletta, G., & Jones, T. (1993). *Confronting Diversity Issues on Campus.* Newbury Park: Sage Publications.

Fleming, N. (2001). *Teaching and Learning Styles: VARK strategies.* Christchurch, New Zealand: Fleming. Also at http://www.vark-learn.com

Honey, P., & Mumford, A. (1992). *Using Your Learning Styles.* Maidenhead: Peter Honey.

Marton, F., & Booth, S. (1997). *Learning and Awareness.* Mahwah, New Jersey: Lawrence Erlbaum.

Rose, C. (2000). *Master it Faster: How to Learn Faster, Make Good Decisions and Think Creatively.* Stylus Learning Systems.

Glossary

Brainstorm: a rapid-fire burst to generate ideas to solve a problem, make a plan, record what is already known. It is absolutely non-critical and is different from evaluation of ideas, a second stage in the generation of ideas.

Constructivism: describes a view of learning in which the learner takes an active part in making meaning of past experiences.

Mind-map: a form of note-making that organises ideas in a visual way. It is designed to clarify concepts and ideas logically for the mind-mapper.

References

Cervero, R., & Wilson, A. (2001). At the Heart of Practice: The Struggle for Knowledge and Power. R. Cervero & L. Wilson (eds), *Power in Practice. Adult Education and the Struggle for Knowledge and Power in Society* (pp. 1–20). San Francisco: Jossey Bass.

Entwistle, N. (1998). Approaches to Learning and Forms of Understanding. B. Dart, & G. Boulton-Lewis (eds), *Teaching and Learning in Higher Education* (pp.72–101). Melbourne: ACER Press.

Fisher, R., & Ury, W. (1986). *Getting to Yes. Negotiating Agreement without Giving In.* London: Business Books.

Flannery, D., & Hayes, E. (2001). Challenging Adult Learning: A Feminist Perspective. V. Sheared, & P. Sissel (eds), *Making Space: Merging Theory and Practice in Adult Education.* Westport, Connecticut: Bergin and Garvey.

Honey, P., & Mumford, A. (1992). *The Manual of Learning Styles.* Maidenhead: Peter Honey.

Leach, L. (2000). Self-Directed Learning: Theory and Practice. Unpublished PhD thesis, University of Technology, Sydney.

Roberts, C. (1996). Developing Teaching Skills. N. Zepke, D. Nugent, & C. Roberts (eds), *The New Self Help Book for Teachers.* Wellington: WP Press.

Rose, C., & Nicholl, M. (1997). *Accelerated Learning for the 21st Century.* New York: Dell Trade Paperback.

Sheared, V., & Sissel, P. (2001). Opening the Gates: Reflections on Power, Hegemony, Language and the Status Quo. V. Sheared, & P. Sissel (eds), *Making Space: Merging Theory and Practice in Adult Education* (pp. 3–14). Westport, Connecticut: Bergin & Garvey.

Sherman, L. (2002). *Sociometry in the Classroom* [Web Page].URL http://www.users.muohio.edu/shemalw/sociometryfiles/socio_introduction.html [2002, August 22].

Tisdell, E. (1998). Poststructural Feminist Pedagogies: The Possibilities and Limitations of Feminist Emancipatory Adult Learning Theory and Practice. *Adult Education Quarterly, 48* (3), 139–156.

Wlodkowski, R., & Ginsberg, M. (1995). *Diversity and Motivation. Culturally Responsive Teaching*. San Francisco: Jossey Bass.

Zepke, N., & Leach, L. (2002).Contextualized Meaning Making: One Way of Rethinking Experiential Learning and Self-Directed Learning? *Studies in Continuing Education, 24* (2), pp. 205–217.

— Chapter 6 —

Beyond Independence

Linda Leach

Introduction

Like most adult educators today you are probably using some form of independent learning: timetabled self-directed learning time, self-directed projects or individual learning agreements. You may be doing this willingly, because you believe it is a good way to work with adults. You may be using this approach reluctantly because some funding agency requires it. You are not alone! Embedded in adult education today is the idea that adults prefer to be independent, self-directed learners. Many of the (Western) theories about adult development identify independence from others as a key attribute of adulthood. This idea features in much of the writing about adult learning and surfaces particularly in theories about self-directed learning. In this chapter I discuss some of these ideas about independence in adult learning. I do this in four sections:

- I outline some of the key ideas about independent learning.
- I critique these ideas.
- I focus on interdependence as an alternative to the dominant view of self-directed learning.
- I offer some ideas for practice.

Independence in adult learning

Adults, of course, have been learning since time began, and self-directed learning has been recognised for thousands of years. But there has been an upsurge in theories about adult learning and self-direction since the 1960s. Malcolm Knowles became a central figure in this process. He used existing educational knowledge to develop a set of assumptions about adult learners and a set of principles for adult learning called andragogy – the art and science of helping adults learn. He contrasted these assumptions with pedagogy, which, he argued, applied to children.

Knowles' six assumptions about adult learners:

- The need to know: adults need to know why they need to learn something before learning it.
- The learners' self-concept: adults have a self-concept of being responsible for making decisions about their own lives. Once they have arrived at that self-concept they have a deep psychological need to be self-directed.
- The role of the learners' experience: adults have a greater volume of and a different quality of experience from youths.
- Readiness to learn: adults become ready to learn the things they need to know and be able to do in order to cope effectively with their real-life situations.
- Orientation to learning: adults are motivated to learn something when they see that it will help them perform tasks or deal with problems they confront in their life situations. Children are subject-centred.
- Motivation: while adults respond to some external motivators (e.g. better jobs, promotions, higher salaries), the best motivators are internal pressures (e.g. increased job satisfaction, self-esteem, quality of life). (Adapted from Knowles, 1990, pp. 57–63.)

Knowles' seven principles for an andragogical (adult-focused) style of instruction:

- Set the climate. The physical and psychological climate should encourage learning.
- Involve the learners in mutual planning. People will be more committed to decisions if they have had a role in making them.
- Involve participants in diagnosing their learning needs. Allow people some say in deciding what they need to learn.
- Involve learners in writing their learning objectives.
- Involve learners in designing learning plans.
- Help learners carry out their learning plans. Use a learning contract to turn learning needs into learning objectives, identify resources, specify evidence that will be used to judge how well the objectives have been met.
- Involve learners in evaluating learning. Learners are to be involved in assessing their own achievement and in judging the quality and worth of the training programme. (Adapted from Feuer & Geber, 1988, p. 33.)

The individual, independence and self-direction are central to Knowles' assumptions and principles. Adult learners are expected to be self-directed and to take high levels of control over their own learning, in formal as well as non-formal contexts. Self-directed learning is understood as an issue of autonomy – adult learners are in charge of their learning. The teacher's role changes. Teachers become facilitators, helping individuals to learn what they want to learn. Individual needs are identified and met. As a result, self-directed learning often involves individually negotiated learning contracts, independent projects and learning 'on your own'. Knowles' ideas struck such a chord with adult educators that they have become widely accepted. We see this today, for example, in New Zealand education policy documents, Skill New Zealand directives and New Zealand Qualifications Authority documents which promote self-directed learning. Your own practice may well be shaped by some of these policies and directives. Later, Knowles conceded that andragogy and pedagogy were on a continuum; that andragogy could be used successfully with children and pedagogy with adults. However, this change in his view is often overlooked.

I think there are two reasons why Knowles' ideas remain widely accepted – educational and political. Educationally, his ideas fitted with a shift in thinking about learning and teaching. Previously, a traditional view of learning held that knowledge exists 'out there' and that it can be passed from one person (the teacher) to other people (the learners) essentially unchanged. The teacher was seen as the fount of knowledge, the transmitter of information and the person in control of all aspects of this transmission process. The learner was a passive recipient whose main task was to memorise the information provided by the teacher and to regurgitate it in exams. You may have experienced this form of learning yourself. But this view is challenged. Learning is now seen as an active process. According to the constructivist view of learning, learners engage actively in learning, direct their own processes and work to create their understanding of ideas – they construct their own knowledge (Arlidge, 2000). Teachers become facilitators of learning rather than transmitters of information. There is a close fit between this approach to learning and Knowles' ideas about andragogy.

Politically, the 1990s environment in many Western countries ensured that the time was right for andragogy and self-directed learning. It fitted very well with the predominant ideas that emphasised the individual, personal responsibility and people's ability to control their own lives. Self-directed learning also helped address an economic problem. Funding per student in tertiary education dropped during the decade, so institutions had to find ways of doing more with less money. Staffing is a high proportion of their expenditure, so cutting staff costs was an obvious option. Because there was an educational rationale that adults are self-directed learners, institutions had a perfect argument to reduce staff contact time and save money: enrol students, take their fees, tell them that adults are expected to be self-directed and send them off to do a lot of their learning themselves. This approach has been called COFO learning – clear off and find out learning (Harris, in Hall, 1996). During the decade many institutions reduced staff contact time, replacing it with timetabled 'self-directed learning time', which essentially meant students were left to learn on their own.

Questioning independence in adult learning

I have shown that independence, in the form of andragogy and self-directed learning, has been central to adult learning for some time. Because it is so widely accepted, questions that have been raised about it have often been ignored. We must consider those questions. I will look first at the way changing ideas about learning, society and adult development affect these assumptions of independence. Then I will outline four criticisms commonly made about independent, self-directed learning.

Changing ideas about learning, society and adult development

Ideas about learning and society change constantly. They are influenced by new knowledge and by changing attitudes and values. Independence and self-directed learning belong to an era when ideas about learning were influenced by psychology and the focus was on the individual. Recent theories about learning come more from sociology and focus on context. They argue that individuals cannot be separated from the environment in which they live, learn and work. They cannot be entirely independent. They are influenced by, and influence, the people and circumstances around them. For example, if a young woman stops attending your course, the reasons may be complex – a lack of support from her partner, difficulties with childcare, the death of her mother rather than/as well as her concern about failing or her lack of motivation. The contextual issues need to be explored as well as the individual ones. How can this woman be independent when she is in relationship with so many other people, heavily influenced by her context? She has multiple roles and responsibilities, only one of which is learner. The interaction between them is complex.

This idea of multiple roles and responsibilities also connects with some ideas about adult learning that are called postmodern. Whereas humanist psychology views people as having a single identity that is developed over time, many postmodernists suggest that we have multiple identities. You may be, for example, a woman, partner, mother, daughter, sister, friend, Samoan, sportswoman, club secretary, teacher, learner, church member and belong to the working class. These identities interact in complex ways and with other people's identities in different contexts. There is a focus now on valuing difference and diversity and being inclusive rather than on assuming similarity and being exclusive (see Chapter 5 for more on this).

New ideas about adult development also influence theories of adult learning. Whereas earlier theories of development assumed that the goal of human development was independence and autonomy, more recent theorists argue that we move beyond independence to interdependence – being connected to, and in relationship with others (Bee & Bjorklund, 2000). First we become independent, and establish our own identity. Then we become interdependent. Independence precedes interdependence. Interestingly, the notion of interdependence is not limited to adult development theorists. People like Covey (1989), writing for a business context, also argue that our personal and interpersonal effectiveness develops along a continuum from dependence to independence then interdependence. Kegan (1982) argued that people want to be both connected (in relationship with others) and independent (differentiated from others). So we constantly seek some kind of balance between the two. We are at once independent and interdependent.

Common criticisms of independence

Independence is an attribute valued in white, middle-class, North American, male society. As most of the theorists who developed ideas about adult learning were white, middle-class, North American males, they assumed that what they valued would be valued by other people. Their assumption results in these values being accepted as 'normal' and in what has been called 'universalism' – in this case the assumption that all people would prize independence, self-direction and personal autonomy. However, this is not the case. Let us explore some reasons for this.

Cultural differences

The first critique, using a cultural analysis, argues that the notion of independence is Western. The individual is usually placed at the centre of the value system and the group is relegated to second place. Other cultural groups, for example Maori, Pacific Nations, Asian and Native American, value the community before the individual and find individualised, independent, self-directed learning foreign to their lived culture. For them it is often more important to work to benefit the community and the whanau (family) rather than yourself, to work together rather than to strive alone. Some writers (e.g. Flannery, 1994) claim that it is racist in these contexts to promote learning theories that focus on individual achievement. Others argue that self-directed learning is not necessarily a 'natural' state for adults; that we are more likely to become independent, self-directed learners if we are born into a culture that nurtures it (Joblin, 1988).

In New Zealand at the beginning of the twenty-first century, we have to ask "Is self-directed learning culturally appropriate?". For some learners it may not be. More and more adult learners here are Maori and people from Pacific Nations and Asia. Expecting, even requiring, them to be independent, self-directed learners may be inappropriate. Writers from collectivist/community cultures challenge the assumptions made by the likes of Knowles. Johnson-Bailey & Cervero (2000) have even claimed that Knowles' principles cannot work for people with community-based cultural values because it is inappropriate for them to share personal ideas and concerns in a classroom. As adult educators we have constantly to ask ourselves, "Is independent self-directed learning appropriate for these learners, in this context? How could I use interdependent, collaborative learning strategies that may be more appropriate for these people?".

But we must also be wary of making generalisations about people based on their cultural heritage. A white, middle-class, Pakeha male will not necessarily be an independent learner; neither will a Maori or Pacific Nations man necessarily be an interdependent one. Recently I had a white male student who asked me to provide him with a clear learning pathway – "Tell me what to do and when to do it by and I'll do it", he said. What happens to his learning if I require him to be self-directed, refuse to support and guide him and send him off to work on his own? What other solutions are there in this situation?

Gender differences

The second criticism of independence uses a gender-based analysis. Research done into women's learning has shown that many value connection with others – interdependence, affiliation, relationship and communion – over independence. They like to learn with others, talk together, feel welcomed and part of the group, to share ideas and experiences. They often value feelings, spirituality and intuition rather than thinking, 'common sense' knowledge rather than 'book' knowledge, and connected knowing rather than separate knowing. They may also learn a great deal through life experience. This is in direct contrast to the independent self: self-directed, autonomous, responsible and driven by reason rather than emotion. Two examples spring to mind. In a review I did recently on one of our programmes I noticed the number of women who said they found extramural learning difficult because they did not have the opportunity to talk their ideas over, to connect with and establish relationships with others. They felt isolated, alone and separate. I have run classes for small groups of women because it was clear that they wanted to learn with others rather than become extramural students. In such an all-women class this year I noticed that their emotions (fears in this case) surfaced spontaneously in the first session and that they were relieved to discover that others held similar fears.

But we must not fall into the trap of seeing all women as the same, of making generalisations about women (universalising). Feminist writers like Flannery and Hayes (2001) argue that women are different too, depending on their race, class and past experiences. We also need to be wary of trying to create a them/us division between men and women. Hayes and Flannery (2000) make it clear that, while their focus is women's learning, men may learn in similar ways to the women they write about. Men too can be interdependent, value emotion and connectedness. There is a growing acceptance that autonomy must be coupled with interdependence and interconnectedness as necessary attributes of adult learners – for both women and men (Chickering & Reisser, 1993).

Class differences and social justice

The third criticism questions independence from a class perspective, claiming it is a middle-class value that does not reflect the values of working-class people. Welton (1987, p. 52) even argued that it is a form of class oppression that "injures the self-concept of working class people". Discussions of classism are now appearing alongside those of racism, sexism and ageism. Writers are exploring working-class issues, describing ways in which people from working-class backgrounds feel in adult education contexts where the values are so different from their own. As they progress through the education system they often feel they don't belong – neither to their own community, nor to the academic world. So self-directed learning may not be appropriate for working-class learners either.

Independent, self-directed learning has also been criticised for its emphasis on the individual and its lack of attention to social issues. If we each, the argument goes, attend to our own needs and disregard the needs of wider society, major injustices and inequalities go unchallenged and unchanged. So self-directed learning has the potential to develop nations of self-centred, self-serving people, to block emancipatory learning.

Grace summarised many of the criticisms this way:

> Andragogy has tended to contract self-directed learning to concerns with the individual and technical, sidelining concerns with the social and cultural. Knowles ... appeared more concerned with individualistic learning and survival, with maintenance and conformity, than with resistance and transformation in social and cultural spaces. He failed to see adult learning spaces as sites to build social vision or resist the status quo ... He also failed to focus on learning in community as a social engagement where history, culture and politics matter in processes of making meaning and planning action as reflective, informed activities (Grace, 2001, p. 264).

If we are interdependent as well as independent we would be interested in the well-being of others and in wider society generally. We would work to improve society not just ourselves. We would be engaged in emancipatory rather than reproductive education. Clearly, we need to rethink the promotion of self-directed learning in New Zealand today.

Beyond independence in adult learning

In this section I consider two different ways to understand independent, self-directed learning. I suggest it may also be understood as learning 'with others' as well as learning 'on our own', and as 'making meaning' as well as 'taking control of learning'.

While there are many ways of understanding self-directed learning, it is often seen as a solitary activity – as learning in isolation, 'on your own'. I question this view. How much of our learning is really done 'on our own'? Even when we sit quietly by ourselves and read a book, we are engaging with the ideas of another person and our learning is coloured by what they write. When we listen to others' ideas and discuss issues with them we are learning 'with others'. When we learn from watching a programme on TV, a movie or a play, from observing other people, from seeing a work of art, we have been influenced by others' ideas. Yes, there are times when we learn something 'on our own', but I suggest the majority of our learning is done in association with others in some way.

Learning 'with others' can be understood as self-directed learning. If you want to learn something, and decide that the best way to learn it is to work with a friend who already knows what you want, you are self-directed. If I go to a word-processing class because I want to use my computer more effectively, I am not a dependent learner. I am, just like you, an independent, self-directed learner making the best use of learning resources available to me.

Indeed, there are some disadvantages with learning 'on our own'. Learning independently, in isolation, can be limiting. It restricts us to what we already know and to what we can work out on our own, narrowing our views and confining us within our existing knowledge, values and beliefs. We lose the opportunity to draw on the knowledge and experience of others. We are more likely to stay within our comfort zone, unchallenged, instead of reconsidering, even changing, some of our ideas. Some people I talked to about self-directed learning understood it as learning 'with others' and described the benefits they gained from learning this way (Leach, 2000). For example:

> I feel that there must be peer contact. If you have no contact and you're working by yourself you don't have ideas to bounce off, you don't have other people to compare what you're doing with (Leach, 2000, p. 140).

Some people (social constructivists) support these views and argue that learning is a social, collaborative activity, an interdependent rather than an independent, isolated one (e.g. Daniels, 1996). They draw on the work of people like Vygotsky (Doolittle, 1997) who said that we have a zone of proximal development (ZPD). This zone reflects our potential for learning. According to Vygotsky, what we can learn on our own is less than what we can learn in association with others who know more than us or whose knowledge is different from ours. So, while we might develop ideas for ourselves, we need to discuss them with others, exposing our views to their critique. Through communication with others, through collaborative activity, we build our understandings, our knowledge; we verify and justify it. And through this interdependent process we open the way for emancipatory education – working together to change the world, to remove oppression and injustice. Let us get beyond thinking of learning 'on our own' as the 'one best way' for adult learners. Let us take into account the learner and their circumstances. Let us accept that a learner who decides what is best for them in their circumstances is being self-directed. Let us rethink self-directed learning. Let us include 'learning with others' as self-directed learning.

There is a second way of rethinking self-directed learning. Since Knowles first wrote about andragogy, self-directed learning has been understood as an issue of control, of managing learning. This has been called an *external* dimension of self-directed learning. The control of learning shifts from the teacher to the learner. Adult learners are expected to be both willing and able to take control of, and responsibility for, their own learning. Instead, we could focus on an *internal* dimension, a dimension that concerns making meaning. In this interpretation, self-directed learning becomes 'making meaning' for ourselves, an active process of constructing our own understanding rather than passively receiving information from someone else. This rethinking also draws on ideas from social constructivism that I outlined above, particularly when the meaning-making process is a collaborative, interdependent one.

This understanding of self-directed learning as making meaning also appeared in the conversations I had. People used a number of expressions to talk about this idea:

'thinking about it for myself'; 'solving my own problems'; ideas 'sinking in'; 'making sense'; 'thinking'; 'developing my own ideas'; and 'understanding'. One person described what they were trying to do in one learning situation in these words:

> And so I deliberately made a choice to try and find as many perspectives as I can, to try and come to a sensible point of view ... it is giving me sufficient information to make my own (*meaning*), giving me a viewpoint on it (Leach, 2000, p. 125).

Garrison (1992, 1997) has brought together these two dimensions of self-directed learning. He argues that the ideal self-directed learning situation is one in which learners "assume responsibility for making meaning while sharing control of the educational process" (Garrison, 1992, p. 146). It seems to me that this view has much to offer our rethinking of independent, self-directed adult learning. It draws on but goes beyond Knowles' ideas, and sits more comfortably with current ideas about people, learning and society. Let us rethink self-directed learning as both learning on our own and with others, as making meaning and taking control of our learning. This expanded view offers us new opportunities for our practice.

Some suggestions for practice

If we are to go beyond independence, to go beyond the current understanding of self-directed learning as learning 'on our own', taking control of and being responsible for our own learning, then how do we work with learners in our classes? In this section I offer some suggestions for you to consider. Have a look at Chapter 8 too. There you will find some suggestions for collaborative learning strategies that will also foster interdependence.

First, I think we need to take into account the rethinking of self-directed learning. This means that we need to understand self-directed learning as learning interdependently with others to make meaning and as sharing control of the learning process with others, including the teacher. We need to take into account the diversity of learners in our groups, cater appropriately for them and not impose on them a version of self-directed learning that requires them to learn on their own and take control of their own learning. These ideas underpin the suggestions I make.

Negotiation

For me the starting point with any group of learners is consultation and negotiation – an empowering process for learners.

- We can start by discussing options with learners. Try asking them how much control they like to have of their learning and what form they like this control to take; how they like to work – together and/or alone; what they expect to learn; and what they expect of you, the teacher.

- Explain to them your views of learning and teaching, of the course content and how you might work together. Discuss differences and agree on how you will work together, at least for a trial period. This approach gives learners opportunities to express their views and to have some say in the learning/teaching process. It shares the control of learning between learner and teacher. You may find that, for a start, you have to be more directive than you would like to be because that is what these adult learners expect.
- Throughout the course consult and negotiate with learners, making changes whenever appropriate. Even young, reluctant adult learners usually respond positively to being listened to and to having their learning needs addressed. Note, however, that this does not mean that you, the teacher, do what learners want. You have your views on learning and teaching and they may be different to the views of the learners. You will also be constrained by the institution, by funding agencies' requirements and by quality assurance processes. Explain these constraints too and find ways to meet learners' needs, your own needs and the institutional requirements as best you can. (See Chapter 5 for more ideas on negotiation.)

The learning environment

Another aspect to attend to is the learning environment (also see Chapter 4). The emotional environment is particularly important. If we want people to feel safe enough to share their ideas, feelings and experiences with others, we need to create an environment that respects and values each of them and fosters interdependence. If we want to challenge attitudes, values and ideas held within the group, to engage in transformative or emancipatory education, the environment must be supportive. This is particularly important when we venture beyond the intellectual into emotional and spiritual realms.

These environmental factors are particularly relevant when we think of self-directed learning as making meaning. We will not see ourselves as the sole holders of knowledge, to be transmitted to learners through long lectures. Rather we will see everyone in the group as a knowledge holder. We will encourage learners to:

- actively engage with ideas in discussion with us and with one another
- hear different views on subjects rather than memorise 'correct' information
- actively create their own understandings
- make meaning for themselves by drawing on the thinking of others as well as their own.

To do this we create a learning environment that encourages and supports questioning, discussion, debate and challenge. In such an environment people may feel able to express views that would otherwise remain unspoken, hidden and therefore not available for meaning-making within the group. In such an environment, interdependence flourishes, fostering the meaning-making of individuals, including the teacher and the group. Individuals are actively engaged in their own learning and contribute to the learning of others – both independent and interdependent. In such an environment lies potential for emancipatory learning, too.

Specific strategies

Now let us consider some specific strategies that are appropriate in an interdependent, self-directed adult learning context.

Collaborative learning

Obviously collaborative learning will be one. Discussions and projects that encourage learners to engage with one another, to rely on one another and to work together to create meaning will be relevant. However, as teachers we need to ensure that any group work we initiate is not simply 'busy work'. There needs to be a carefully thought through purpose for the activities, a purpose which will foster interdependence and meaning-making. Some suggestions for collaborative learning strategies are discussed in Chapter 8 of this book.

Group work and discussion ideally will go beyond thinking. As we saw in the culture-and gender-based questioning of self-directed learning, Western education is criticised because it focuses on thinking and ignores, for example, the emotional, spiritual and intuitive skills. An interdependent adult learning context will be inclusive of the wholeness of people, not just their cognitive dimension: wairua (spiritual), hinengaro (intellectual), tinana (physical) and whatumanawa (emotional) (Tangaere, 1996). Group work that we plan should be designed for this wholeness.

Group assessment

Group assessment goes hand-in-hand with group work and discussion strategies. If we aim to develop interdependence through group work it is important that we find ways to assess the learning done in these groups. Currently, while group assessment is possible, there is still much opposition to it because it disguises the contributions made by individuals. Here again we see the Western focus on the individual. The fear is that 'undeserving' individuals will be awarded credentials they have not earned, or that an 'outstanding' individual will be awarded a lower grade because others in the group were not up to their standard. There are strategies for assessing group work. What we have to do is convince the system and wider society that group assessments are appropriate. Certainly group assessment is likely to be more relevant for collectivist cultures.

Class discussions

Organised class discussions also encourage interdependent meaning-making. If they are well planned and monitored, open discussions about topics – particularly controversial topics – provide opportunities for learners to hear views that are different to their own. This may mean individuals' current meanings and assumptions are challenged. New meanings may be constructed or new arguments created to support existing meanings. Learners try out developing understandings with others in the class and reshape them in response to others' views. In the same way, case studies, problem-based learning and project work can also be used to enhance learner interdependence.

On-line interdependence

Interdependence can also be fostered across time and space. Developments in communications technologies have made it possible to create synchronous and asynchronous learning relationships via the Internet, for example. We can go beyond the image of the individual learner locked onto the computer screen day and night as she or he searches for information alone. We can instead create learning situations that link learners across locations, including countries, to share, discuss and debate ideas as they develop their understandings both of one another and the topic.

Peer teaching and assessment

In peer tutoring one learner, who understands the content, works alongside another learner who has not yet understood. Both benefit from this interaction. The 'more knowledgeable' peer tutor reinforces their learning because they have to think through the meanings they have made and explain them clearly to another person. The learner makes additional meaning from the interaction and develops their understanding of the topic. It is important that the interactive nature of peer tutoring is explained to learners, particularly to the ones being tutored. Otherwise they may see themselves as 'dumb' or 'stupid', relying on a 'brighter' peer to help them understand. Peer tutoring need not be a permanent arrangement. From time to time a brief period of peer tutoring can be arranged. Learning Support Centres frequently arrange for senior students to become peer tutors for new students.

Peer assessment is another strategy that can develop interdependence in meaning-making. Peers learn to assess one another's work using criteria that are developed with the group. They provide both positive feedback and constructive comment on what the person could have done differently. This requires each learner to think about the criteria and what they represent, to compare the qualities evident in another's work with the criteria and to communicate their judgement to another person. In doing this they learn a great deal about their own understanding of the knowledge or skills being assessed.

It will be apparent to you that some of Knowles' ideas about self-directed learning remain in these strategies. Let us use those ideas that fit with our changed understanding. Be assured, too, that there is still a role for the teacher. We are members of interdependent groups of learners. We have knowledge, understanding, skills and ideas to be shared with learners – in lectures, even! We are guides, mentors, support

Beyond Independence

people, there to assist in ways we see as appropriate for each group. And we are interdependent learners ourselves, constantly constructing meanings from our interactions with learners and colleagues.

Conclusion and development

It is time for us to think beyond the Western emphasis on individualism and independence, time for us to recognise and value the whole person and the interrelationships between people, time to promote a view of self-directed learning that is interdependent, concerns learning with others for the benefit of others as well as of individuals, and has, as its prime focus, meaning-making rather than transmission of information. We will need to convince colleagues, learners, institutions and systems that we must go beyond independence for the benefit of our society as a whole. And our personal challenge is to change our practice so we foster the development of interdependent, self-directed people who construct their own meanings through interaction with others.

Of course, no chapter can ever fully cover all the possible perspectives that can be explored on a topic. This one serves only to introduce you to some of the ideas about independence and interdependence in learning. You may now want to examine the ideas of others, to travel more widely and/or deeply in the literature and to try out some ideas in your practice. Some suggestions for reading and activities to try are listed below.

Further reading

Bishop, R., & Glynn, T. (1999). *Culture Counts: Changing Power Relations in Education*. Palmerston North: Dunmore Press.

Knowles, M., Holton, E., & Swanson, R. A. (1998). *The Adult Learner: The Definitive Classic in Adult Education and Human Resource Development*. Houston, Texas: Gulf Publishing Company.

Pere, R. (1994). *Ako: Concepts and Learning in the Maori Tradition*. Wellington: Te Kohanga Reo National Trust Board.

Sheared, V., & Sissel, P. (2001). *Making Space: Merging Theory and Practice in Adult Education*. Westport, Connecticut: Bergin & Garvey.

Wilson, A., & Hayes, E. (2000). *Handbook of Adult and Continuing Education* (New Edition). San Francisco: Jossey Bass.

Suggested activities

- Think about your own teaching. To what extent do you focus on independent self-directed learning? What are your reasons for this?
- To what extent do you foster interdependence in learning? Why do you do this?
- Identify at least two ways you could go beyond independence in your teaching. Try them out and reflect on what happens.

- Talk to colleagues about fostering interdependence in learning. What are they doing in their practice that you could try in yours?
- Talk to learners in your groups. What are their views of independence and interdependence in learning? How would they like you to work with them?
- Include a discussion of self-directed learning in a meeting with colleagues.
- Read books and articles about interdependent learning.
- Explain your own developing views on independent and interdependent learning to others.
- Explore the links between interdependence and emancipatory learning. How might this be fostered in your practice?

Glossary

Asynchronous learning: where learners learn the same material but at different times.

Autonomous: literally means self-rule; independent people who make decisions about their lives and are not subject to the authority of others.

Class: a way of categorising people based on their status measured according to their family's wealth (socio-economic status) and place in society.

Constructivism: a cognitive learning theory. Constructivists argue that learners construct understandings for themselves in an active meaning-making process rather than take in information from others in a relatively unchanged form.

Emancipatory education: education that is committed to removing oppression and injustice in the world.

Pedagogy: is used by Knowles to describe the art and science of teaching children. It is more often used to refer to the whole, complex process of teaching – in pre-school to higher education contexts.

Synchronous learning: takes place at the same time.

Zone of proximal development: the difference between what we can learn unaided and our potential for learning when assisted by someone more knowledgeable than ourselves.

References

Arlidge, J. (2000). Constructivism: Is anyone making meaning in New Zealand adult education? *New Zealand Journal of Adult Learning, 28* (1), 32–49.

Bee, H. L., & Bjorklund, B. J. (2000). *The Journey of Adulthood*. Upper Saddle River, New Jersey: Prentice Hall.

Chickering, A. W., & Reisser, L. (1993). *Education and Society* (2nd ed). San Francisco: Jossey Bass.

Covey, S. (1989). *The Seven Habits of Highly Effective People: Restoring the Character Ethic*. New York: Simon & Schuster.

Daniels, H. (1996). *An Introduction to Vygotsky*. London: Routledge.

Doolittle, P.E. (1997). Vygotsky's Zone of Proximal Development as a Theoretical

Foundation for Cooperative Learning. *Journal on Excellence in College Teaching*, 8(1), 83–103.

Feuer, D., & Geber, B. (1988). Uh-Oh ... Second Thoughts About Adult Learning Theory. *Training* (December), 31–39.

Flannery, D. D. (1994). Changing Dominant Understandings of Adults as Learners. *New Directions for Adult and Continuing Education, 24* (2), 143–161.

Flannery, D., & Hayes, E. (2001). Challenging Adult Learning: A Feminist Perspective. V. Sheared, & P. Sissel (eds), *Making Space: Merging Theory and Practice in Adult Education*. Westport, Connecticut: Bergin and Garvey.

Garrison D. R. (1992). Critical Thinking and Self-Directed Learning in Adult Education: An Analysis of Responsibility and Control Issues. *Adult Education Quarterly, 42* (3), 136–148.

Garrison, D. R. (1997). Self-Directed Learning: Towards a Comprehensive Model. *Adult Education Quarterly, 48* (1), 18–33.

Grace, A. P. (2001). Using Queer Cultural Studies to Transgress Adult Educational Space. V. Sheared, & P. A. Sissel (eds), *Making Space: Merging Theory and Practice in Adult Education*. Westport, Connecticut: Bergin & Garvey.

Hall, C. (1996). Student-Centred Learning as Viewed through a Relational Model of Teaching and Learning. *NZARE Conference Symposium on Student-centred Learning*.

Hayes, E., & Flannery, D. D. (2000). *Women as Learners: The Significance of Gender in Learning*. San Francisco: Jossey Bass.

Joblin, D. (1988). Self-Direction in Adult Education: An Analysis, Defence, Refutation and Assessment of the Notion that Adults are more Self-Directed than Children and Youth. *International Journal of Lifelong Education, 7* (2), 115–125.

Johnson-Bailey, J., & Cervero, R. M. (2000). The Invisible Politics of Race in Adult Education. In A. L. Wilson, & E. R. Hayes (eds) *Handbook of Adult and Continuing Education* (New Edition). San Francisco: Jossey Bass.

Kegan, R. (1982). *The Evolving Self: Problem and Process in Human Development*. Cambridge, Massachusetts: Harvard University Press.

Knowles, M. (1990). *The Adult Learner: A Neglected Species* (4th ed.). Houston: Gulf Publishing.

Leach, L. (2000). Self-Directed Learning: Theory and Practice. Unpublished PhD thesis, University of Technology, Sydney.

Tangaere, A. (1996). Maori Human Development Learning Theory. B. Webber (Compiler), *He Paepae Korero: Research Perspectives in Maori Education*. Wellington: New Zealand Council for Educational Research.

Welton, M. (1987). Vivisecting the Nightingale: Reflections on Adult Education as an Object of Study. *Studies in the Education of Adults, 19* (1), 46–48.

— PART III —

Supporting Learning and Teaching

Overview

In Part III our focus shifts from the learners themselves to some of the things we can do to create an environment that fosters learning. Of course, learners are central to any planning and preparation we do. We explore three clusters of ideas about supporting learning and teaching: plan for all aspects of teaching – from lesson planning to using technology to finding resources; use collaborative learning strategies – a learning–teaching method that builds strong social relationships and results in high quality learning; and design courses and assessment processes that lead to transformative rather than reproductive learning.

An important part of good practice is being well prepared for our teaching. As Robin Graham points out in Chapter 7, learners expect teachers to be well prepared … and it helps our confidence when we have done our preparation! Robin explores a range of preparation strategies: plan content, resources, lectures and individual lessons; practise with equipment; prepare the physical and psychological environment; cater for different learners' needs; organise resources. A feature of Robin's chapter is her discussion of ways we can use technology – not only to access, create and file resources but also for on-line teaching.

There is a growing recognition that learning is a social rather than an individual activity. This makes collaboration central to learning and teaching. In Chapter 8 Linda Leach and Michele Knight explore some ideas about collaborative learning and why it has become popular. They discuss components of collaborative learning and the benefits that result from learning together rather than individually or competitively. They describe two models and six collaborative strategies you might try in your teaching. As with any approach to learning and teaching, there are issues with collaborative learning that need closer examination. The authors explore some of these, using examples from their writing collaboration.

Course design and assessment come under scrutiny in Chapter 9. In the first part of the chapter, Linda Leach, Guyon Neutze and Nick Zepke discuss some principles and offer specific suggestions for practice within the 'outcomes approach'. In the second part, they critique existing ideas and practices and discuss ways to go beyond them – to use curriculum design and assessment for transformative learning. Using examples from their practice, they introduce the idea of a process orientation that challenges the current outcomes-based model, the idea of internal and external fairness that challenges current understandings of reliability, and emerging criteria that challenge predetermined criteria in assessment.

Chapter 7

Preparing for Teaching

Robin Graham

Introduction

In teaching, as in scouting, the motto 'Be Prepared' is apt. "Teaching a course requires careful planning to ensure that what you teach is relevant to the discipline and fits within the development of a body of knowledge" (Robbins, 2001, p. 2). In planning your teaching, you may want to consider the triplet of knowledge, skills and attitudes. Designing a course that reflects the inter-connectedness of these three domains can provide you with a challenge, if your teaching is to recognise and validate the compatibility of all three.

In an era variously known as 'the information age' and 'the knowledge economy', learners and teachers alike can be overwhelmed by the amount of information available. A plethora of options exists for accessing information. As well, recent developments in technology mean a changing environment in relation to on-line learning and the traditional classroom. Yet whatever the mode of delivery, you can use technology to enhance your preparation and planning process.

In this chapter, I discuss some of the factors to consider in preparing for teaching. I do this in seven sections which:

- examine some preparation practicalities
- relate this to creating a positive learning environment
- offer some suggestions for preparing for your students
- examine some strategies for lesson planning, lecturing and on-line teaching
- discuss ways of preparing for information literacy
- suggest how to process information
- suggest ways for organising your resources.

Preparation for practicalities

Those of you who are fitness fans might compare preparing for teaching to preparing for physical exercise. Preparation concentrates the mind and helps to minimise those unexpected (and unhelpful) incidents that can undermine your confidence – and your credibility!

Even as a teacher of many years' experience, I still feel varying degrees of fear before facing a new class. This can range from being ill at ease to full-scale panic! First impressions can be lasting ones, so I like to be prepared to ensure that I get off to a good start. I recently taught a new group for two hours a week over a three-week period. I was really delighted when one student came to me at the end and thanked me for the obvious preparation. That pleased me as I felt her compliment acknowledged my work. However, more importantly, the preparation had facilitated her learning.

Compiling resources

The following tips for preparing to teach could help you and your students.

- Course outlines are useful for yourself and your students. They show dates and times of class, course credits, hours of contact and independent learning, course aims and learning outcomes, assessment tasks, teaching and learning strategies, required and recommended texts and an outline of each session's topics. If you are in a classroom, write the outline on the whiteboard so students may anticipate the lesson format.
- Prepare teaching and learning notes, but remember, "notes are best used as a support and not as the primary medium of communicating ideas" (Robbins, 2001, p. 4). Plan the visuals you will use to illustrate the discussion. "The key to using visuals is to make them part of the learning experience" (Robbins, 2001, p. 4). They can demonstrate relationships more clearly than words.
- Take a register, so you know whom to expect in your class. You can record attendance and observations alongside student names.
- Collect learning resources you will need. These might include overhead transparencies, copies of handouts and pens. I have treated myself to a basket, which contains coloured pens and paper, and I load it up with the pertinent paraphernalia prior to the particular class.
- Check equipment. If you want to use any technological equipment, practise using it beforehand. This includes sophisticated computing gear like 'PowerPoint' or a 'data show' or hooking up your laptop, and the more mundane aids like the video or overhead projector or electronic whiteboard. You may well have a scintillating lesson planned, but if the technology fails, you need to be very enterprising to save face! My workplace has a very high-tech lecture theatre with all mod cons but I have been witness to many embarrassing experiences, where ignorance of the technology resulted in time wasting and much loss of credibility.
- If I am teaching in an unfamiliar classroom, I like to check it out beforehand. This may seem overzealous but since the occasion when I led a new class to our allotted

room only to discover it was the ablution block, I have become more cautious! It is also good to check out the heating, light and noise, not that you can always do anything about these, but 'forewarned is forearmed'.

Preparing the environment

A major responsibility/duty you have as a teacher is to prepare an environment for effective learning. Given "the unflagging movement toward more use of technology and distance education" (Barefoot, 2000, p. 3) the interpretation of what 'environment' really means will vary.

Environment can include the beliefs and values you hold, as these will inevitably pervade your teaching. Knapper and Cropley (in Nichols, 2001) maintain that the attitudes and beliefs of teachers influence the learners' outcomes. It is important to plan how you will create such an environment. I am currently teaching a course on-line and the environment I create is critical to success. I am finding this very challenging as my only means of motivating the students is the communication we have through the medium of e-mail, so the factors that are discussed next, in promoting an environment conducive to learning, become all the more important.

Some factors to consider in planning a positive learning environment can include acknowledging differing learning styles, recognising prior learning, facilitating student interaction and orientation/induction activities, as these may be the factors that help your students to feel comfortable and 'fit' for learning.

Planning for differing learning styles

While we all value our own uniqueness and individuality, we have certain learning preferences and behaviours that can categorise us. This is equally applicable to our preferences for learning. Educators have devised many different tools to assess these learning styles, such as Honey and Mumford and Kolb (see Chapter 5 for more detail on these). A relatively simple yet appealing model is Fleming's VARK model (2001), which enables students to gauge their preferred way of learning – visual, aural, read-write or kinesthetic – and to adopt learning strategies to accommodate these. In preparing for teaching, you can plan how you might best use such a tool. Uses can include providing students with more insight into their own learning and helping you employ relevant and appropriate teaching techniques. For example, for visual learners you can plan using visual aids such as the overhead projector or the whiteboard, for aural learners select a tape or CD, and for kinesthetic learners look for some physical activities.

Recognising prior learning

A tenet of adult learning is recognition of prior learning, the acknowledgement of the merit of learners' past experiences. "Teachers who can identify and use their students' existing knowledge and skills are likely to increase their motivation and application of knowledge and understanding" (Chalmers & Fuller, 1996, p. 50). Your task as the teacher, then, is to interpret and link new knowledge to existing learning. Advocates "of experiential learning argue that linking what goes on in class with students' out-of-class activities creates a synergy that potentially compounds student learning" (Barefoot, 2000, p. 4). Plan strategies you can use to validate students' life experiences as part of orientating them to learning.

Facilitating student interaction

According to McKeachie (in Robbins, 2001), peer learning has both motivational and cognitive benefits in that it provides opportunities for mutual support and stimulation. In planning, think about what activities you can employ to foster student interaction. (See Chapter 8 for a fuller treatment.)

Peer assessment is also a useful technique for encouraging interaction. However, the students need to understand the assessment criteria in order to be able to give valid feedback. As you plan your assessment tasks, keep in mind the value of formative assessment as a tool for teaching understanding of assessment criteria and for teaching students how to give and receive constructive feedback. (Also see Chapter 9.)

The Internet has the potential to enhance the environment in both traditional and non-traditional settings. It gives learners access to current information; it enables them to collaborate readily with others, so is ideal in those disciplines where collaborative group learning is important. Students are increasingly 'techno-savvy', and it makes sense to integrate activities employing the media they use outside the classroom.

Orientation/induction activities

"New student orientation, whatever its precise form and structure, offers ... a unique opportunity to change student attitudes and expectations by including ... activities during the time period when new students form initial impressions" (Barefoot, 2000, p. 4).

As a teacher in a library, I have had ample opportunity to witness the 'checklist' type of orientation, where new groups are subjected to a bewildering array of speakers, each dutifully delivering their particular patter. The teachers appear satisfied that they have fulfilled their duty by covering the fundamental informational needs. Rarely are these instructional sessions integrated with any social peer activities. Time given to activities that encourage peer and teacher relationships and introduce students to basic requirements will foster a good learning environment.

Induction in an on-line environment is equally important. An induction package could include a letter of introduction clearly outlining requirements. For example:

- hardware and software requirements
- details about on-line technical help

- student e-mail addresses
- ways of contacting the teacher
- URL for course
- password for access to restricted parts of course
- training manual or disk or video explaining how to use the system
- warnings about back up of assignments and prevention of viruses
- checklist of minimum technological skills to access course (TAFE Frontiers, 2000).

Inclusive teaching

Find examples and metaphors for different ages, abilities, cultures and genders. (Chapter 5 will give you a number of ideas.)

Preparing for students

Students are the most important thing in your teaching world. The relationship you form with them can be critical to the success of their learning.

Getting to know you

One early important way to establish that relationship is to learn the *names of your students*. Knowing and using their names can help them feel included in the group (Rogers, 2001). Some ways to assist you with names include:

- use name badges big enough to be read easily from a distance
- draw a seating plan and note each student's name as they are introduced
- try games to learn names really quickly. For example, play the picnic game. After the students have introduced themselves, ask them to form a semicircle in alphabetical order of their first names. Then tell them they are going on a picnic and they must bring an item beginning with the first letter of their name e.g. My name is Robin and I'm bringing raspberries. The first person begins and each subsequent student must repeat the name and item of all preceding students. It's fun!

Getting to know *you*. Students will want to know about you too – who you are, your position and/or responsibilities within the institution and your relationship and experience with this programme. "Achieving academic and social integration requires sustained, informal interaction between students and faculty" (Barefoot, 2000, p. 3). Equally the students will want to know about their peers. "The student's peer group is the single most potent source of influence on growth and development during the undergraduate years" (Astin, cited in Barefoot, 2000, p. 3).

Icebreakers enable learners to get to know you and each other in a non-threatening way. The trick is to feel confident and comfortable with the icebreaker you choose. Another important consideration is to be clear about the purpose of the icebreaker. It can be a way of getting to know each other or it can be a teaching method for introducing a topic. The picnic game is an example of an icebreaker.

Acknowledging feelings

It is understandable that students may feel anticipation, apprehension or even complete terror. It may have taken courage for them to enter your foreign environment. The territory is our comfort zone and consequently it is easy for us to forget how formidable it may appear to others. Acknowledging this, either by discussing it or by asking direct questions ("Who is feeling nervous right now?") may allow the student to see that others are feeling the same way. However, I think it is important to 'accentuate the positive'. Some students may feel elated, excited, empowered by the prospect of learning. Don't overlook acknowledging these positive feelings as well. Think about strategies you can use in your initial sessions that facilitate the expression of these feelings. Plan to allow time for the students to talk together in pairs or small groups, for example ask them to introduce themselves and give two adjectives that reflect their feelings. (Chapter 4 has more information on these matters.)

Preparing for teaching lessons

Some useful questions in lesson planning:

1. Who are my students? What do I know about them?
2. How much time do I have available?
3. What do I want the students to be able to do by the end of the session?
4. How much will the students already know?
5. What icebreaker/warm up will I use to introduce the topic?
6. How can I break the task into steps?
7. What different teaching and learning strategies can I use?
8. How will I know they have learned?
9. What resources will be needed?
10. How can I summarise the lesson?
11. What method of evaluation will I use? (Also see Chapter 4.)

Lessons have three main parts:

- introduction (including recapping)
- main part
- summary and future direction.

Introduction

It is important to set the context of the lesson. Global learners will want the big picture, while analytical learners will prefer detail. Therefore you need to recap the main points from the previous session. The function of the introduction is to clarify the purpose of the lesson by linking to the learning outcomes and explaining the structure of the session. Equally important is capturing the students' attention. Sometimes rather than beginning with an outline, you may find it more valuable to point out to the students the benefits they may accrue from this lesson. For example, explain how this lesson can help solve a problem or relate the content to an assignment.

Main part

This is where the saying 'variety is the spice of life' applies. Applying a variety of teaching and learning strategies will help to ensure effective learning occurs. Think about the most appropriate technique for the knowledge and skills you will be teaching. In addition to you lecturing, techniques can include group work such as:

- Brainstorming. This involves an uncensored 'blat' of ideas to solve a problem or remind the learners of what they already know, or generate questions that still remain unanswered (Roberts, 1996).
- Pyramiding or Snowballing. Students work on their own at first, then in pairs and then in fours. One member of the group reports back, according to the teacher's instructions.
- Incomplete handouts. These can be in linear or diagrammatic form. The student fills in the gaps.
- Mind-Maps. These are pictures providing an overview and showing links and relationships between ideas.

Concluding the lesson

Plan to allow time at the end of the session to review the learning outcomes and determine whether they have been achieved. Concisely summarise the main points covered and indicate the content areas to be covered in the next session.

Ongoing evaluation and feedback is critical to reflective practice. Plan to include evaluation in your lessons. Some techniques for gaining immediate feedback include:

- The hand signal. Instruct students to indicate effectiveness or usefulness or enjoyment of the session: 'a little' equals hand close to ground; 'OK' equals hand at desk height and 'great!' equals hand above head.
- Written feedback. Use questions such as "What helped your learning in this lesson?", "What hindered your learning?", "What suggestions do you have for improvement?".

Preparing for lecturing

A well-prepared lecture may both impart knowledge and facilitate understanding. Know why you lecture and prepare learners for lecturing. They can then "recognise that different learning tasks make different demands and start extending their repertoire of learning responses accordingly" (Gibbs, Habeshaw & Habeshaw, 1992, p. 15). Think about the most effective use of handouts to support the lecture. For example, if you plan a PowerPoint presentation, also prepare a copy of the screens with space for the students to embellish your points. Alternatively, you may provide a diagram of the presentation or an incomplete handout.

As the traditional notion of lecturing is very teacher-centred, you can assist the learning process by planning not just the content but also the process of your lecture.

- Think about the language you will use. Is the jargon clearly explained?
- Give clues about the important points. For example, "There are three main points to X. The first is …". Or, "The most important factor is …".
- Plan to include a summary of the main points.
- Plan for 'break outs' where students can discuss something briefly in pairs.
- Plan how you will deal with questions. Will you leave time at the end for this or take them as they arise?

Preparing for on-line teaching

On-line teaching can be seductive and appealing in its novelty and its potential for variety and flexibility. However, a recent study of on-line sites by Mioduser *et al.*, (2002, p. 306) found that the sites mainly promoted "individual rather than collaborative learning, direct instruction rather than inquiry, clicking rather than communicating, automatic feedback rather than guidance, memorisation rather than knowledge construction". Most students value active participation, sharing of ideas, problem-solving and constructive feedback. "Social interactive and affective dimensions of the learning experience remain powerful determinants of successful learning" (McLoughlin & Luca, 2002, p. 442). The role of the teacher is to provide coaching, guidance and scaffolding. McMahon (2002, p. 459) defines this as "forms of learning support provided to bridge the gap between existing skills and potential skills". On-line learning expects learners to be independent. Nevertheless, your role is to reduce their isolation as much as possible.

Think about the following when planning for on-line learning:

- Develop a problem-based approach to the structure of your materials.
- Prepare appropriate learning resources so that students can work through them actively and critically rather than passively. Rather than a back-up reading list, investigate and prepare a list of appropriate and relevant e-learning articles and journals and/or provide links to relevant databases provided by your library.
- Organise the administrative procedures so they are as effective, transparent and student-friendly as possible.
- Incorporate social interactions, for example a goal-setting exercise.
- Schedule time in your day so you can give regular, timely and personalised feedback.
- Plan how you will orientate the learners to this new mode. Is there an instructional programme to introduce them to Blackboard or CT Web, two of the more common e-learning tools?

- Build in exercises where the students can reflect on their learning and give peer feedback.
- Encourage goal-setting and time organisation.
- Think about the relevance and purpose of your course to the overall programme and how you will communicate this.
- Prepare checklists to help learners organise their materials, schedules and resources.
- Prepare assessment that requires group collaboration as well as individual effort.
- Familiarise yourself with the technology so you can use the discussion board and chat rooms to encourage sharing and problem-solving.
- Prepare a study guide outlining an overview of the course.

On-line delivery can take a number of forms.
- web-supplemented delivery where participation is optional
- web-dependent where the web activities are directed but face-to-face learning is also included
- fully on-line with no face-to-face opportunity.

Whatever on-line teaching you are planning, teaching issues should take priority over technological matters and interaction should be built in wherever possible.

Preparing for information literacy

Roe (in Bruce 1997, p. 4) suggests that "the intimidating growth of knowledge and the age of rapid technological change" requires that we "learn to learn". In preparing for teaching, you will use information in new and increasingly complex ways. You will become increasingly information-literate. The student who learns in today's environment must equally be information literate. You may have to plan to teach students information literacy skills.

'Information literacy' may be defined as the ability to access, evaluate and use information. It is a model which serves "the needs of practitioners interested in reflective problem-based and resource-based approaches to teaching and learning" (Bruce, 1997, p. 12). However, there is debate about the ultimate definition of information literacy. I like Bruce's (1997) notion of a relational approach. The 'relational view' disassociates itself from seeing information skills as a discrete set of measurable, transportable skills and instead puts the emphasis on the learner's relationship with the information. Bruce draws attention to the use of information rather than the technology that accesses it. "Adopting this approach ... would be compatible with the emphasis towards reflective and experiential modes of teaching and learning ..." (Bruce, 1997, p. 171).

The saying 'the person who does the work does the learning' is very pertinent to the gathering of resources. By involving your students in this process, you will be helping them, not only to learn how to use the technology to access resources, but also how to evaluate, critique and manage the information for their end purpose. Brandt (2001), however, warns that learners also need to understand the technological environment in which information resources are used, as he maintains that without this conceptual understanding, students may not develop their full information-literacy potential.

Searching for information

It becomes important to plan for students to learn how to find information. Information comes in different print formats (books, journals, newspapers) and electronic formats (videos, CDs and on-line). In selecting information, you need to decide how it will be used. This will help you choose the most useful format. For example, if you need an up-to-date, authoritative range of opinions, you would be more likely to find these in a journal article than in a book.

Libraries provide a range of tools for organising and accessing information. Catalogues generally provide bibliographic information about their physical stock: that is, what books, journals, videos and CDs the library holds. The predominant resource will be books. However, this may be a small proportion of the information available as the library will also offer access 'virtually' (on-line). Journal, magazine and newspaper articles and conference proceedings are available via databases in the form of an index or in full text.

How to search

Regrettably, electronic information sources are not standardised in their commands but generic concepts apply to many. The following section outlines some concepts relating to databases. This term applies to catalogues, indexing and full text databases and Internet search engines. It is advisable to use the *Help* menu to solve particular problems with a database.

- **Keyword Searching:** most databases respond to keyword searches rather than long phrases. For example, using the search term 'information technology and information literacy' will result in a more effective search than typing in 'What is the relationship between information literacy and information technology?'.
- **Truncation:** use of this symbol (often * or ?) enables a search to retrieve singular or plural forms of a word and different endings. For example, teach* will retrieve teach, teaches, teacher, teachers and teaching.
- **Relevancy Ranking:** databases with this feature will rank the order of results by the number of occurrences of your keyword. If you are searching for a phrase, put it in quotation marks ("information technology"). The database will look for those two words next to each other and rank the results based on the number of occurrences of the phrase. An alternative method of sorting results is by date.
- **Boolean Logic:** this gives options in combining key words.
    - If you want to combine two or more words or phrases, use 'AND' to combine them.
    - You can use synonyms in the search term to provide more options: teenagers OR adolescents AND literacy.
    - Putting these terms in brackets (teenagers OR adolescents) AND literacy will help if you are developing a more complex search.
    - *NOT* enables you to exclude results that contain certain words; for example, if

you wanted information about all aspects of education but not primary education your search term would be Education *NOT* primary. Some databases use *AND NOT* instead of *NOT.*
- **Thesaurus and Index:** a thesaurus or list of subject headings is a list of standardised terms which ensure that articles on the same subject will always be described using the same words. An index is an alphabetical list of all the words and phrases in the database. It is useful for checking spelling and formats of names.
- **Add to Search:** talking the same 'language' as the database is a very useful tactic. Scan the results looking especially at the subject headings or descriptors. Many databases have a feature that allows you to highlight terms by double clicking or dragging across with the mouse and then clicking on "Add to Search". Cutting and pasting in Windows will achieve the same result. In web-based databases, simply clicking on the term will usually activate a search.
- **Marking, Printing and Saving Records:** most databases let you mark or select those records that you are interested in and then display, print or save only those. Saving to disk has the advantage of retaining them in electronic format so they can be copied later and pasted into your bibliography or list of references. Another common option is to e-mail the search results (in the case of full text databases, the complete article) to a specified e-mail address.
- **Bibliographic Managers:** software packages such as ProCite, Endnote and Reference Manager assist in the management of a large number of references. These allow you to import correctly formatted references from databases, sort and manipulate the records and then output them in a predefined bibliographic format such as APA, Chicago or MLA. Such software is commonly integrated with word processing packages to enable the management of intext references. These bibliographic managers are available as freeware, shareware and fully commercial products but are probably worth using only if you are dealing with a large number of references (Field, 2000).

Processing Information

Locating information is not enough. An information-literate teacher and student must also be able to process it. In planning for teaching it is useful to think of what an information-literate person can do. In my tertiary institution, such a person may be defined as being able to complete an assignment. To help your students become information-literate graduates, you could plan to teach them information-processing skills via their assignments (see also Chapter 9):

- analyse assignment instructions
- match with the marking guide
- analyse your information need
- decide on your search strategy
- access the information
- evaluate the information

- organise the information
- draft the assignment
- reference
- evaluate feedback.

This framework implies a parallel process for you, the teacher. Table 7.1 includes some suggestions for facilitating this process for your learners.

Table 7.1. Information literacy as learner and teacher activity

Learner	Teacher
Analyse assignment instructions	Write clear and concise instructions which are clearly linked to the learning outcomes.
Match with marking guide	Write a clear and explicit marking guide outlining all aspects of content, structure, research and presentation. If you wish the students to be thinking critically, ensure this skill is reflected appropriately in the weighting within the marking guide.
Analyse information need	Use brainstorming and mind-mapping techniques to assist in developing concepts and terms related to the assignment topic.
Access information	Model use of library tools to discourage dependence on the Internet.
Evaluate information	Teach your students how to be selective with information on the basis of age (of the information!), authority, level of language, relevance, geographical coverage, bias, perspectives, features and accessibility.
Organise the information	Teach the skills of effective reading, i.e. skimming and scanning, as well as summarising and paraphrasing. Show models of information organisation.
Draft the assignment	Teach the structure of an essay/report/literature review.
Reference the work	Explain about the academic sin of plagiarism and teach how to acknowledge sources of information by using acceptable paraphrasing and citation.
Evaluate feedback	Give your learners clear, constructive, explicit feedback on their assignments to enable them to benefit from their mistakes.

Information literacy can provide an intellectual framework for understanding, finding, evaluating and using information. While the integration of information literacy into your curriculum is a desirable outcome, there will be times when this is neither feasible not practicable. This is when you call upon the professional, the librarian, whose expertise is in information retrieval. By using more sophisticated methods of information acquisition, librarians can be your partners in learning and can advise you where and when they can to assist the development of information skills.

Organising resources

When asked to describe, in an informal poll, the best qualities of their best teachers, 50 per cent of those students polled said 'organisation' (Robbins, 2001). "Being well organised in the classroom is a reflection of the real organisation that goes on outside the classroom" (Robinson, 1996, p. 60). Just as technology assists in gathering resources, so it can help in organising our teaching resources by storing and filing them in an orderly and readily accessible manner.

Organising and filing the flow of paper that comes into my office is the bane of my working life, but information that either I create or I am sent electronically is easy to organise. All resides invisibly in my computer.

Think about the different ways you want to organise your teaching material. In my system I have a folder for each of the programmes I teach and within those are subsets for such things as administration, course notes, student information, assessment, moderation and minutes of related meetings. These are saved in alphabetical order and I can transfer to my system any Word documents sent to me by e-mail as attachments.

The ease of accessibility and use of Word allows you to prepare your teaching resources professionally. You can create a template as a master by setting up the fonts, headings and margins and then simply adding text for each new resource. This gives you consistency.

In setting up a logical file structure, you may be helped by thinking of a family tree. Decide on the main topic by clicking on *File* on the tool bar. Then click *New* and, typing in the title you choose for that folder, you can set up a series of folders, a little like a set of Russian dolls. You can then copy or move material into your folders by clicking on the documents and dragging them to the relevant folder. The versatility and flexibility of such a system is very appealing to a tidy and ordered mind. Very regrettably, if you are a messy manual filer, chances are this trait may transfer to the technological territory!

Conclusion and further work

As a teacher you will bring all your prior experience as a learner, and the knowledge of your discipline, to your teaching. This chapter has discussed ways in which you can enhance these skills, knowledge and attitudes by preparing in both practical and psychological ways, by anticipating strategies for fostering a positive learning environment and by preparing interesting and relevant lesson plans. It has shown that technology provides a tool, not only to enhance the learners' competence in technological and information literacies, but also to assist you in the preparation and organisation of resources.

Whether you relate more to the analogy of scouting or to that of exercise regarding preparation for teaching, hopefully you will be motivated to learn more about how you can enhance this and how you can integrate skills, as well as knowledge, into your teaching. This chapter has also pointed out the benefits of using the advances in technology to develop your organisational abilities.

Try some of these activities to develop your planning and preparation skills further:

- Review sample lesson plans and devise a template more suited to your requirements.
- Treat yourself to a practical hard-wearing basket and fill it with goodies such as multi-coloured pens, OHT (overhead transparency) pens, whiteboard pens, newsprint and other related requisites.
- Practise using an OHP (overhead projector), an electronic whiteboard, a data-show, a video monitor, PowerPoint.
- Rewrite a familiar lesson plan incorporating different teaching strategies, e.g. snowballing.
- Identify the implicit generic skills in your assessments and plan a teaching activity to promote the skills.
- Set up an e-mail discussion list with your students and promote discussion and reflection on their learning.
- Plan induction and orientation activities that include social interactions and exclude a litany of lectures!
- Identify a pertinent icebreaker for a topic.
- Check out your institution's library databases and develop at least one resource-based assessment, remembering to include marks for selection, evaluation and management of the information.
- Using the Information Skills Process as a template, rewrite the lesson plans for at least one of your courses.

In order to attempt some of these activities, more reading may be in order. Try these books:

Benn, K., & Benn, C. (1997). *Writing a Thesis using a Word Processor: A Practical Guide.* Palmerston North Dunmore Press.
Booker, D. (1998). *Information Literacy: The Professional Issue.* Adelaide, Australia: University of South Australia Library.
Drew, S., & Bingham, R. (c1997). *The Student Skills Guide.* Aldershot: Gower.
Iannuzzi, P., Mangrum, C. T., & Strichart, S. S. (c1999). *Teaching Information Literacy Skills.* Boston: Prentice-Hall.

Lee, W.W., & Owens, D.L. (c2000). *Multimedia-based Design*. San Francisco: Jossey-Bass.
Meltzer, M., & Palau, S. M. (c1996). *Acquiring Critical Thinking Skills*. Philadelphia: W. B. Saunders.
Muldoon, R. (2000). *Study Skills*. Armidale, NSW: Teaching and Learning Centre, University of New England.
Salmon, G. (2000). *E-moderating: The Key to Teaching and Learning On-line*. London: Kogan Page.
Spitzer, K. L., Lowe, C. A., Doyle, C. S., Eisenberg, M., & ERIC Clearinghouse on Information and Technology (1998). *Information Literacy: Essential Skills for the Information Age*. Syracuse, NY: Syracuse University. ERIC Clearinghouse on Information & Technology.

Glossary

Cognitive: thinking, brainwork.
Data Show: a clever piece of machinery that projects an enlarged computer screen image onto a screen.
Experiential learning: learning that is acquired through experience rather than through theory.
Generic: general and not specific to a particular discipline.
In-text references: acknowledgements to the source of information e.g. author, cited in the body of the text.
PowerPoint: a clever piece of software that provides information in a series of bullet points. Popular with conference presenters!
Template: a pattern to be used as a guide.
Thesaurus: a resource that groups words with similar meanings.

References

Barefoot, B. (2000). Are We Making It Any Better? *About Campus*, 1–5.
Brandt, D. S. (2001). Information Technology Literacy: Task Knowledge and Mental Models. *Library Trends, 50* (1), 73–86.
Bruce, C. (1997). *The Seven Faces of Information Literacy*. Adelaide: Auslib Press.
Chalmers, D., & Fuller, R. (1996). *Teaching for Learning at University*. London: Kogan Page.
Field, G. (2000). Access and Use of Published Literature. Christchurch Polytechnic Education Resource Centre Cyberteam. *Introduction to Research*. Christchurch: Christchurch Polytechnic.
Fleming, N. (2001). *VARK* [Web Page]. URL http://www.vark-learn.com/ [2002, August 12].
Gibbs, G., Habeshaw, S., & Habeshaw, T. (1992). *64 Interesting Things to do in Your Lectures*. London: Technical Educational Services.

McLoughlin, C., & Luca, J. (2002). Enhancing the Quality of the Student Experience Online: Revisiting the Imperative of Learning as Socially Based. *HERDSA*, 442–447.

McMahon, M. (2002). Designing an Online Environment to Scaffold Cognitive Self-regulation. *HERDSA*, 457–463.

Nichols, M. (2001). *Teaching for Learning: Designing Resource Based Learning Courses for the Internet Age*. Palmerston North: Traininc.co.nz.

Robbins, L. (2001). Self-observation in Teaching: What to look for. *Business Communication Quarterly, 64* (1), 19–37.

Roberts, C. (1996). Developing Teaching Skills. N. Zepke, D. Nugent, & C. Roberts (eds), *The New Self Help Book for Teachers*. Wellington: WP Press.

Robinson, C. (1996). Organising Content Material. N. Zepke, D. Nugent, & C. Roberts (eds) *The New Self Help Book for Teachers*. Wellington: WP Press.

Rogers, J. (2001). *Adult Learning (4th ed.)*. Buckingham: Open University Press.

TAFE Frontiers (2000). *Teaching and Learning Online: A Manual for Teachers in Vocational Education*. Melbourne: TAFE Frontiers.

— Chapter 8 —

Collaboration for Learning and Teaching

Linda Leach and Michele Knight

Tau rourou taku raurau kia whài oranga tatou katoa
Your contribution, my contribution for mutual benefits shared

Introduction

It seems that the time is ripe for collaborative learning. Our society is becoming increasingly diverse; the information explosion and knowledge society mean that we must continue learning throughout our lives if we are to understand and take our place in the world around us; teamwork is being emphasised in the workplace. All of these factors support a shift to collaborative learning. In the past, education has been structured according to a view that knowledge can be transmitted, usually from the teacher to individual students. It has tended to focus on the individual and on competition between individuals. In this chapter we promote collaborative learning as an alternative. Collaborative learning engages with diversity, valuing the contributions of all to learning. It values the different types of knowledge brought by learners as well as teachers and helps them to develop the interdependent, teamwork skills and personal attributes desired not only in the workforce but in wider society, nationally and globally.

In this chapter we explore:

- what collaborative learning is and why we use it
- components of successful collaborative learning
- some benefits and issues
- suggestions for practice.

What is collaborative learning?

Collaborative learning occurs when teachers and learners work together to create knowledge. This generates a learning community that embraces and values the voices and contributions of all. "It is a pedagogy that has at its centre the assumption that people make meaning together and that the process enriches and enlarges them" (Menges *et al.*, 1996, p. 103).

Collaborative learning is not new. People have always learned together; educators have known about and used it for centuries. But there are different ways of understanding collaborative learning. Some writers (e.g. Bruffee, 1999; Millis & Cottell, 1998) make distinctions between two major concepts – co-operative and collaborative learning. While these share underpinning ideas, co-operative learning is usually seen as a more structured, organised, focused form of collaborative learning. In this chapter we draw on ideas from both without making a distinction between the two.

Collaborative learning is about people:

- learning together
- having a shared goal
- working interdependently, supporting each other
- jointly constructing knowledge, understanding, insights
- learning *with* each other rather than *from* each other.

Collaborative learning is more than the sum of individual experiences and achievements. The outcome is sometimes seen as 1+1=3. Working together, people interact to go beyond what any one of them could achieve on their own. Together they create something new, something that cannot fully exist for any individual.

Group work is not collaborative learning. Too often it is just "individual learning with talking" (Johnson & Johnson, 1997, p. 2). Here is an example that shows some differences.

> Form yourselves into groups of five or six and discuss the next example in the text. I'll give you 15 or 20 minutes, then we'll hear from all the groups. Any questions? Okay, go ahead" (Ronkowski, 2000, p. 1).

In this situation the teacher is using group work. To make the exercise a collaborative one the teacher would organise learners to work together on specific tasks that enabled them to develop their own and others' understanding of the topic:

> Look at the next example in the book and think about the advantages and disadvantages of the solutions which Clarkson proposes. Think about their economic feasibility. Write down your ideas and then compare them with one of the other students in your usual group of four. Make sure you justify the reasons for your answers, especially if there is any disagreement with your partner. Once you are satisfied that you understand your partner's choices – you don't have to

agree with them – I'll ask you to share your answers with the rest of the group so that we can come up with the main advantages and disadvantages of the proposed solutions (Ronkowski, 2000, p. 1).

This teacher is using a 'think-pair-share' strategy for collaborative learning that we will describe later in the chapter. Notice how the partners are learning together; have a shared goal set by the teacher; are working interdependently, supporting each others' learning; are jointly constructing knowledge about the advantages and disadvantages; are learning *with* each other rather than *from* each other; and may have different views. Individual, small group and whole-class ideas together create a fuller understanding of the situation. This is collaborative learning.

We have adapted ideas from Johnson & Johnson (1997) to expand on the differences between group work and collaborative learning in Table 8.1.

Table 8.1. Some differences between group work and collaborative learning

Collaborative Learning	'Traditional' Group Work
Positive interdependence	Little interdependence
Individual accountability	Less individual accountability
Diverse members	Members usually similar
Shared leadership	One appointed leader
Responsible for each other	Responsible for self
Focus: looking after each other as well as task completion	Focus: only task completion
Social skills directly taught	Social skills assumed or ignored
Teacher: observes and intervenes	Teacher is less actively involved
Group processing occurs as part of the learning	Group process not acknowledged as part of the learning
Mutual assistance	Competitive or individual

For teachers there are other forms of collaborative learning worth considering. In adult learning contexts you can develop learner–teacher collaborations. Because the learner–teacher relationship is a more equal one, collaborative learning partnerships work well. Learners and teachers learn together rather than the teacher being the knowledge holder and transmitter of information. You can be both teacher and learner;

students can be both learners and teachers. You can also learn collaboratively with other teachers. Team teaching, peer mentoring, buddy systems, clinical supervision, peers acting as critical friends, participatory action research and collaborative enquiry are examples of this.

Why collaborative learning?

For a long time learning and teaching were thought to be about transmitting information, unchanged, from one person to another. This idea is challenged now. There is a view that says each person makes their own meaning from their experiences, the information they receive, the world around them. It says that different people can share the same experiences, access the same information and yet understand and communicate it differently. This is why two people might attend a Treaty of Waitangi workshop together and understand quite differently what they have experienced. One may have a new view of the history of relationships between Maori and Pakeha in New Zealand. The other may have confirmed all their existing prejudices.

The theory that explores this idea is called constructivism. Constructivists believe that learners are not passive, empty vessels waiting to be filled by a knowledgeable teacher. Rather they are active, thinking people who make sense of experiences and information for themselves. They need to be actively engaged in the learning process – perhaps questioning, debating, explaining, challenging, but always creating their own understanding.

But there are different views among constructivists as well. Some believe that we develop our knowledge/understanding largely as individuals. Others, social constructivists, argue that we develop our knowledge in association with other people. Vygotsky, for example, argued that we learn in social and cultural contexts and that our learning is of better quality when undertaken with others. (For more ideas about constructivism and how to use it in your teaching, see Chapter 11.)

Ideas about collaborative learning draw on social constructivism. They use the idea that people's learning is better when they learn together. Being 'together' does not mean that they have to be in the same room. With modern technologies people can discuss ideas across time and space. One of us, for example, has students in England and Whakatane who are e-mailing one another about their learning. As well, collaborative learning goes beyond the idea that the teacher is the only person who has knowledge to share with others. Learners too, particularly adult learners, have vast experience and knowledge that is valuable to others in the group.

Components of collaborative learning

Johnson & Johnson (2002) have identified three ways learners can interact with one another: they can compete to see who is best; work individualistically without paying attention to others; or work collaboratively taking an interest in the learning of others as well as their own. They have also identified five components that are essential to successful collaborative learning:

- *Positive interdependence.* Learners believe that they are 'in it together'. They accept that they are responsible not only for learning the material themselves but also for ensuring that everyone in the group understands it. They know that their success depends on the success of the others.
- *Face-to-face promotive interaction.* This means that learners encourage and help one another to finish tasks successfully and achieve the group goals. It is our view that in an increasingly technological age we need to think of ways that learners can encourage and help one another without necessarily being face-to-face. This occurs in collaborative on-line learning, for example.
- *Individual accountability.* Although the focus is on collaboration, individuals are responsible for completing tasks, doing their share within the group, for contributing to others' learning and for ensuring their personal mastery of the learning. 'Social loafing' and 'hitch-hiking' are not acceptable. In collaborative learning, people learn together so that they can perform alone as well as with others.
- *Interpersonal and small group skills.* Collaborative learning relies heavily on interpersonal and small group skills, so these must be taught. Merely telling people to collaborate does not result in collaborative learning.
- *Group processing.* A key aspect of collaborative learning is the way learners work together in groups because the group process will affect the outcome. People need to know about group processes, to be aware of how their group is working together, and how to identify and resolve group issues. Knowledge of and skills in group processing also need to be taught.

If you are going to use collaborative learning you will need to think of ways to incorporate these five components. They also have an explicit link with the framework of this book. Our chapter is a communicative/interpretive one. You can see from these components how closely collaborative learning fits within Habermas's communicative/interpretive level. It embraces communication and dialogue across difference of all kinds. Indeed, learning is better when different views have been heard, interpreted and discussed. Interpersonal skills and group processing are central to students' successful learning – both content and process – and underpin collaborative learning.

Benefits of collaborative learning

From your own experience you will know that much of your education has been done individually and competitively. But there are many benefits from learning collaboratively. In this section we outline seven that have been identified through research (Johnson & Johnson, 2002) and from our own knowledge and experiences. You will find others in your reading as well.

Achievement

One of the main benefits of collaborative learning is illustrated in the old saying 'the whole is greater than the sum of the parts'. What we learn with others is more than what we can learn on our own. Rather than be limited by what we know ourselves, by the sense we can make of something, by our own view of the world, we are exposed to different forms of knowledge, different perspectives and different views of the world. Discussion of these different views results in higher quality learning, higher achievement for individuals and the group, higher level reasoning, more frequent generation of new ideas and solutions and greater transfer of learning to new situations than either competitive or individualistic learning. Understanding developed as a result of collaborative learning is broader and/or deeper and more likely to be retained than information transmitted in a teacher-centred approach.

Understanding interdependence

Humans are social beings. We live, work and play together. We need to learn how to interact with others in social situations, to develop the necessary social skills. For a long time, in Western education, the focus has been on the independent individual. Now it is recognised that in order to live and work well with others we need highly developed teamwork knowledge and skills. An essential feature of collaborative learning is the development of the learning community, group, team, whanau. Support of one another also features. The community does not focus on individuals and competition. Rather, the intention is to ensure the wellbeing and the learning of every group member. Collaborative learning, therefore, fits well with collectivist cultures that value the community and family above the individual. The experience of working collaboratively enables people to understand how interdependent both we and the world are.

Interpersonal relationships and acceptance of difference

Collaborative learning results in acceptance and valuing of difference, more liking amongst learners, more commitment to and caring for others. Membership of the learning group is key in this process. Each group should be diverse, heterogeneous. This enables members to get to know different people, to work alongside them, to develop interpersonal, working relationships with them and to value and care for them. It also ensures that there is a range of knowledge and views available for discussion in the group. As the goal is to ensure the learning of each member of the group, caring for others, regardless of their difference, becomes central to collaborative learning.

Active construction of knowledge

People engaged in collaborative learning are active learners. Rather than sitting passively, listening as a teacher imparts the knowledge, learners process information to construct their understandings. They discuss and debate ideas, forming and re-forming them in the process. They create meanings together. This active engagement in knowledge construction results in higher quality learning and higher achievement.

Self-esteem

Collaborative learning fosters the self-esteem of each learner. Because collaborative learning is an active process of knowledge construction it draws on the knowledge and experience of each person within the group. The individual's knowledge and experience are valued; individual strengths are recognised; and each person makes a contribution to the learning of others. This, along with the feelings of being encouraged and helped, and feeling cared about by others, produces positive effects for individual learners. Peer acceptance fosters feelings of self-esteem.

Perspective-taking

Perspective-taking refers to our ability to understand how a situation appears to someone else and, therefore, why that person reacts to the situation in the way they do. While some collaborative learning strategies deliberately foster this ability (e.g. see our description of academic controversy below), all collaborative learning promotes perspective-taking. Because collaborative learning draws on and values difference, learners are encouraged to listen to and consider perspectives other than their own.

Creativity

Because collaborative learning encourages the generation of many possible responses to problems, it fosters creative and lateral thinking. Working together triggers ideas and responses that might not be generated when working alone.

The benefits of collaborative learning are summarised by Bruffee (1999, p. xii-xiii) in this way:

> ... collaborative learning demonstrably helps students learn better – more thoroughly, more deeply, more efficiently – than learning alone ... teaches students to work together effectively ... so they can work together effectively later on ... to construct knowledge as it is constructed in the knowledge communities they hope to join after attending colleges and universities .... Most important, in collaborative learning students learn the craft of interdependence.

Issues with collaborative learning

There is considerable evidence that a paradigm shift is occurring in teaching (Johnson, Johnson, & Smith 1991; Boehm 1992). This shift is resulting in a changed role for teachers. Collaborative learning is part of this paradigm shift. We can embrace or reject it.

The move towards collaborative learning is not universally welcomed. Embracing it may expose you to challenges from many sources, particularly from students and colleagues. Millis and Cottell (1998) have identified a number of such issues:

- Students may reject classroom activities they regard as frivolous or irrelevant. Students want to learn from an authority figure.
- Students may think teachers are not fulfilling their professional obligations if classrooms seem noisy and out-of-control. They won't understand or appreciate these departures from traditional teaching.
- Teachers don't know how to evaluate students who spend so much time focused on 'group' work.
- Introducing collaborative learning activities will take too much time. There are already too many demands on student and teacher time. Collaborative learning may involve revising the course syllabus and reworking course content.

Writing this chapter has been a collaborative process. Certainly, issues have appeared in our own collaboration, if in a different form. We now reflect on our process. In this very personal examination of collaborative learning we recognise many of the issues noted in the literature but also want to reaffirm that if issues are seen as challenges, they can be overcome. For our reflection we use a framework of questions developed for writing partnerships by Saltiel, Sgroi and Brockett (1998, p. 1):

- How do partners find each other and initiate their work?
- What qualities does each partner look for or find in each other? Why is this important? How does it contribute to the dynamic?
- What factors from the particular setting or context affect success of the partnership?
- How do partnerships change over time?
- What stages do they pass through?
- What role patterns emerge, and what is the relationship of these patterns to the amount of quality learning?
- What problems emerge?
- What strategies are employed to address these problems?
- How do partners either terminate or agree to continue their work (or relationship)?

We are colleagues who had expressed an interest in contributing to this book. We were invited to work together on this chapter. We discussed whether, and how, we could collaborate and decided that we would give it a go. While we talked about the content knowledge we each brought to the task, we didn't discuss the personal qualities we were looking for in each other. In hindsight, we think personal qualities must be discussed. For example, it is important to be clear about what each offers to the partnership and how these qualities are balanced.

There are both issues and benefits from being colleagues and co-authors. Professional workloads meant that there were few blocks of time we could commit to planning and writing. Our collaboration was limited to infrequent, short periods working together. There were even occasions when we cancelled scheduled writing times. On the other hand, working together meant we had easier access to one another than people working in different organisations. Professional and personal circumstances sometimes prevented the preparation and research we had agreed to do. As part of our process we discussed relationship factors identified within our working context. We each had personal, emotional relationship issues that affected the way we worked together.

Our partnership has changed and developed over time. We started out thinking it would be a straightforward mechanical process. We planned the chapter – 2,000 words here 1,000 there – and began work. As we worked with the collaborative model we identified pitfalls in the way we were working. Group processing is certainly central to a successful collaboration. It is essential to identify the issues to bring them into the open to pick them up and address them and to deal honestly and openly with one another to enable progress.

We began by deciding to write together – to brainstorm on the whiteboard, to sit at the computer and write each word together. As time pressed, we tried writing separately. This did not work for us for this chapter. It took more time and created more disagreement between us. So we went back to writing each word together.

Our collaborative relationship was formal, professional and task-focused. This influenced the roles we took: critical thinker; ideas generator; reader; researcher; typist; writer. The key pattern we identified in our relationship was leader–follower. This pattern is not necessarily a negative one. For example mentoring may be seen as a leader–follower relationship but good quality learning will result when it works well. However, in our relationship many of the issues we had to address came from negative aspects of our leader–follower roles. For example, one of us felt that her ideas were not being valued or included; the other felt that she was carrying much of the load for the chapter. While we worked as leader–follower this time, in future we would work towards taking more balanced roles.

There is a new level of understanding, honesty and humour that has developed for both of us from living the collaborative model. There has been pain and anger, frustration and excitement. While we have learned a great deal from reading more widely about collaborative learning, the most important learning has come from living the process – dealing with the issues and developing our interpersonal skills. We celebrate a better working relationship.

In addition to our leader–follower relationship a key problem we had to address was our different writing styles. We decided it was best to write together. Another problem was that we weren't actually talking to one another about issues. Although we are colleagues, our writing collaboration was a new and different relationship that was confined to our writing moments. It took time for us to grow into this relationship and to be able to talk honestly to one another and begin to address the issues. The strategy we stumbled across was to each write our reflections about the process. This enabled us to recognise some of the issues and those that led to our leader–follower relationship for instance, one of us being unfamiliar with the topic and not reading about it. We each had to be open to addressing these issues.

Another problem that emerged was that we worked in different ways. Our process is still developing. One of us prefers to work informally the other has learned to be task focused. Tight time constraints have meant that we have worked in a task and time-focused way. This process has not been ideal for either of us. In future we want to commit larger amounts of time to writing and to working in different settings that allow for informality at times.

To enable our relationship to continue we have identified and discussed issues in our collaboration. Group processing is the key to collaboration. Indeed, we have found that the components Johnson and Johnson (2002) identify are essential in successful collaborative learning (see our discussion of these earlier in this chapter). Bray *et al.* (2000, p. 6) put it this way:

> Collaboration suggests a certain degree of tension found to be part of the 'meaning-making' process. People wrestle with the divergence that emerges from the different lived experiences they bring to the inquiry process – tension that is mediated by varying learning styles and rooted in different situated interests.

Collaborative learning in practice

So far in this chapter we have introduced you to collaborative learning and some of the benefits and issues. Hopefully you are convinced that it is worth trying in your own teaching. We now detail six specific, practical strategies you could try. Each strategy works best when you have already established a collaborative learning environment with learners.

Think–pair–share

Think–pair–share is probably the best-known strategy. If you have not tried collaborative learning before, this would be a good strategy to start with. It is easy to use and even works in large lecture classes.

- Prepare a question that has more than one possible answer and requires some thought.
- *Think:* ask learners individually to think of a possible answer. Allow quite a short time for this: thirty seconds to two minutes. This individual thinking time is really important. You might ask them to write their answers down.
- *Pair:* organise students into pairs to discuss their answers.
- *Share:* ask the pairs to share their answers with the class.

Think–pair–share can be organised very quickly. It means that every learner engages with the question, thinks of an answer and discusses it with at least one other person. More ideas are generated than in a whole-class question and answer session. Everybody talks for a time rather than one or two people answering your questions. A variation of this strategy is 'think–pair–square'. At step four the pairs share their answers with their collaborative teams rather than the whole class.

Send a problem

This strategy gives learners the chance to identify and work on issues or problems that are of interest to them. It is a good idea to prepare some questions yourself too.

- Get the collaborative groups to generate several problems or questions.
- List all of these on large sheets of paper and display them on the wall. If you prefer, these two steps can be done in a previous class.
- Prepare a large envelope for each problem, writing the problem on the outside.
- Each group selects a problem they want to work on and takes the appropriate envelope.
- Each group discusses its problem, generates and records as many solutions as possible on a sheet of paper and places it inside the envelope.
- The envelopes are passed to another group that reads the problem but NOT the first group's solutions.
- The second group brainstorms possible solutions for the problem and places them inside the envelope.
- The envelopes are passed to a third group that reviews the solutions proposed by the first two groups. They may add some of their own but their main task is to select the two most viable solutions to the problem.
- Groups report to the class: the problem, the solutions they have chosen and the reasons for their choices.

One of your tasks is to set times for each of these steps and to act as timekeeper. Alternative ways of using 'send-a-problem' include passing the envelopes around to more groups and having the groups working on the same, rather than different, problems. 'Send-a-problem' generates many possible solutions and encourages learners to use lateral and higher level thinking skills.

Three stay, one stray

This strategy is used after collaborative groups have completed a problem-solving discussion. It requires each group to have its members identified in the same way. For example, each group will have a person labelled 1, 2, 3, 4 or club, diamond, heart, spade.

- The group ensures that each member can report the outcome of their discussions.
- You select reporters using one of the labels for group members. For example, you might say, "The diamonds will be the reporters".
- The reporter moves to another group and reports their group's discussion and findings. It is important that the movement between groups is planned. For example, the reporters may all move clockwise. Reporters can rotate again if the discussion has generated many possible solutions.

'Three stay, one stray' gives learners the opportunity to improve their learning by teaching others. Because reporting is simultaneous it takes less time than sequential group reports to the whole class.

Academic controversy

Collaborative learning includes conflict. One of the social skills we need to develop is ways of dealing with conflict. Academic controversy is one strategy that uses conflict constructively. It has many similarities to debate, but rather than adhering rigidly to their own views, as happens in debates, learners are encouraged to rethink their views, integrating others' ideas with their own. This also develops positive relationships.

- Prepare the task. It needs to be one that has at least two clear positions – e.g. pro and con.
- Prepare the materials. Make sure that each learner knows which position they are to argue for and where they can get information about it. The materials you need to prepare are:

    a) A clear description of the task.
    b) A definition of the position to be argued and a summary of the key arguments for this position.
    c) Resource materials for the position and arguments.

- Conduct the controversy.

    a) Organise the collaborative groups into pairs to prepare their arguments and their presentation.
    b) Have each pair present its position to another pair.
    c) Have each group discuss the issue taking into account both of the positions, exchanging information and ideas.
    d) Have the pairs reverse positions and present the opposing point of view.
    e) Have each group reach consensus and prepare a report.
    f) Arrange for the groups to present their reports to the class.

While academic controversy creates opportunities for learners to defend a position, it also enables them to see the issue from other perspectives, to learn how to deal constructively with having their views challenged, to deal with conflict and uncertainty and to incorporate the information of others into their own position.

Group investigation

This strategy is largely student-directed. After you have introduced a topic and presented the class with a related, complex problem that has no right answer, they work together to determine how they will approach it. There are six steps to a group investigation.

- Each learner identifies sub-topics/questions they would like to investigate. The class is organised into research groups around these topics/questions.

- The groups plan their investigations co-operatively. Each member takes responsibility for researching some aspects/questions.
- Groups carry out their investigations. They may work singly or in pairs. They locate information, organise and record it, report their findings to the group, discuss these, decide if they need more information, decide on their findings. A lot of investigation may take place outside of class time but ideas are shared and interpreted in class.
- Groups plan their presentations, identifying the key ideas they want to convey and how they will do this.
- Groups make their presentations to, and discuss their findings with, the whole class.
- You and other learners evaluate the group investigations and presentations according to agreed criteria. These may include content and presentation.

The benefits of group investigation are that members engage in reciprocal teaching and experience a problem-solving and learning process that they will be able to use for the rest of their lives.

Jigsaw

Jigsaw got its name because it is like putting together pieces of a puzzle to create a whole picture. Each group member becomes knowledgeable about one aspect of the topic and shares that with the others. Jigsaw has four stages.

- *Introduction.* You organise the class into heterogeneous home groups, introduce them to the topic and its importance and identify sub-topics. Each member selects a sub-topic that interests him/her.
- *Focused exploration.* The class reorganises itself into focus groups around the sub-topics. In these focus groups they work together to build ideas and understanding using materials you supply and that they find for themselves.
- *Reporting and reshaping.* Learners go back to their home groups and take turns to tell the others what they learned. Other members ask questions and discuss ideas in depth. As a result, learners begin reshaping their understanding of the whole topic.
- *Integration and evaluation.* You prepare an activity that enables learners to integrate their learning. This may be for individual small groups or the class.

One of the advantages of jigsaw is that learners rely on each other to get the whole picture of the topic. Other versions of jigsaw have been developed (Sharan, 1994).

We hope you enjoy trying some of these strategies in your teaching watching the benefits learners gain from collaboration and finding ways to address any issues.

Conclusion and beginning

Collaborative learning is one more tool to put into your teaching toolbox. It offers a range of strategies that can be adapted to suit your environment. It is not a quick-fix teaching strategy to be used in every situation, but it is an appropriate approach for many. It embraces a wide range of situations, dealing with, for example, cultural diversity, interpersonal relationships, the social creation of knowledge and the development of people who can work well in teams as well as individuals.

There are tensions with collaborative learning. Learners and teachers used to more didactic approaches sometimes struggle to adapt to collaborative learning environments. It can be time consuming, both in preparation and in class time. But the benefits outweigh the costs. Better quality learning, engaged and enthusiastic learners and caring learner relationships are evident. Take up our challenge: try it out yourself and see the benefits – for both learners and teachers.

How to be a collaborative teacher

There are several things you can do to make the transition to collaborative learning a smooth one. We have adapted some ideas from Putnam (1998):

- Start small. Select a collaborative learning strategy that appeals to you, that you think will work with your students and topic, and try it.
- Join or start a collaborative learning study group with your colleagues.
- Seek feedback from a wide range of people about different aspects of your collaborative learning classes.
- Volunteer to observe another teacher's collaborative learning classes. Be honest about what you notice. If you use some of this teacher's ideas in your session, let the other teacher know how he or she influenced you.
- Keep a diary or reflective journal of your collaborative learning sessions, noting what is and what is not working – be honest. Celebrate successes and treat failures as opportunities to invent new lessons.
- Talk to your students about collaborative learning and how it is working for them.
- Read about collaborative learning. Find out more about different strategies and how other people have used them.
- Trace your development as a collaborative teacher, using models such as the one described by Hamilton (1994, pp. 97–100).
- Write an article about how you have used collaborative learning.
- Give yourself lots of gifts, especially the gift of time. It may take two to three years to master collaborative learning strategies, so give yourself time to understand, experiment and succeed with collaborative learning.
- Be prepared to celebrate unexpected, unintended outcomes. Teachers who have used collaborative learning strategies report subtle as well as obvious changes in their students. This is often recorded in the various assessments carried out in the course of the programme by the students. Also be prepared to celebrate the changes in yourself.

Further reading

Bruffee, K. A. (1999). *Collaborative Learning* (2nd ed.). Baltimore: The Johns Hopkins University Press.

Bosworth, K., & Hamilton, S. J. (eds). *Collaborative Learning: Underlying Processes and Effective Techniques*. San Francisco: Jossey Bass Publishers.

Saltiel, I. M., Sgroi, A., & Brockett, R. G (eds). (1998). *The Power and Potential of Collaborative Learning Partnerships*. San Francisco: Jossey Bass.

Slavin, R. E. (1990). *Cooperative Learning: Theory, Research and Practice*. Boston: Allyn & Bacon.

Strategies

Millis, B. J., & Cottell, P. G. Jr (1998). *Cooperative Learning for Higher Education Faculty*. Phoenix, Arizona: American Council on Education and Oryx Press.

Sharan, S. (ed.). (1994). *Handbook of Cooperative Learning Methods*. Westport, Connecticut: Greenwood Press.

Web sites:

The University of California Santa Barbara (UCSB)
http://www.id.ucsb.edu/IC/Resources/Collab-L/CL_Index.html [2002, August 15]
An introduction for adult educators to collaborative learning.

The North Central Regional Educational Laboratory
http://www.ncrel.org/sdrs/areas/rpl_esys/collab.htm [2002, August 15]
An introduction, including theoretical underpinnings and examples from practice.

The Centre for Learning and Teaching, Penn State University
http://www.psu.edu/celt/clbib.html [2002, August 15]
A bibliography for collaborative learning.

The Cooperative Learning Center at the University of Minnesota:
http://www.clcrc.com [2002, August 15]
Provides access to a number of links on co-operative learning.

The Cooperative Learning Network, Sheridan College
http://www.sheridanc.on.ca/coop_learn/cooplrn.htm [2002, August 15]
More links to co-operative learning sites (including the TiCkLe site).

Glossary

Maori: indigenous people of New Zealand.

Pakeha: Maori word used to refer to non-Maori people.

Pedagogy: the science of teaching; used to refer to particular approaches to learning and teaching.

Treaty of Waitangi: a treaty signed in 1840 by Maori and the Crown; the founding document of New Zealand.

References

Boehm, L. (1992). In Wake of Crisis: Reclaiming the Heart of Teaching and Learning. T. J. Frecka (ed.), *Critical Thinking, Interactive Learning and Technology: Reaching for Excellence in Business Education*. New York: Arthur Andersen Foundation.

Bray, J. N., Lee, J., Smith, L. L., & Yorks, L. (2000). *Collaborative Inquiry in Practice: Action, Reflection and Meaning Making*. Thousand Oaks, California: Sage Publications Inc.

Brooks, A., & Watkins, K. E. (1994). A New Era for Action Technologies: A look at issues. *New Directions for Adult and Continuing Education, 43*, 5–16.

Bruffee, K. A. (1999). *Collaborative Learning: Higher Education, Interdependence and the Authority of Knowledge* (2nd ed). Baltimore & London: The Johns Hopkins University Press.

Hamilton, S. J. (1994). Freedom Transformed: Toward a Developmental Model for the Construction of Collaborative Learning Environments. K. Bosworth, & S. J. Hamilton (eds), *Collaborative Learning: Underlying Processes and Effective Techniques*. San Francisco: Jossey Bass.

Johnson, D. W., Johnson, R. T., & Smith, K. A. (1991). *Cooperative Learning: Increasing College Faculty Instructional Productivity*. Washington DC: The George Washington University, School of Educational and Human Development.

Johnson, R. T., & Johnson, D. W. (1997). Cooperative Learning: Two heads learn better than one. *Context, 18*. Available: http://context.org/ICLIB/IC18/Johnson.htm. [2002, February 28].

Johnson, R. T., & Johnson, D. W. (2002). *An Overview of Cooperative Learning* [Web Page]. URL http://www.clcrc.com/pages/overviewpaper.html [2002, March 28].

Menges, R. J., Weimer, M., & Associates. (1996). *Teaching on Solid Ground: Using Scholarship to Improve Practice*. San Francisco: Jossey Bass.

Millis, B. J., & Cottell, P. G. J. (1998). *Cooperative Learning for Higher Education Faculty*. Phoenix, Arizona: American Council on Education and The Oryx Press.

Putnam, J. W. (1998). *Cooperative Learning and Strategies for Inclusion* (2nd ed). Baltimore, Maryland: Paul H. Brookes Publishing Company.

Ronkowski, S. (2000). *TAs as Teachers*. Santa Barbara: University of California. Available: http://www.id.ucsb.edu/IC/TA/hdbk/ta3-5html. [2002, February 28].

Saltiel, I. M., Sgroi, A., & Brockett, R. G. E. (1998). *The Power and Potential of Collaborative Learning Partnerships*. San Francisco: Jossey Bass.

Sharan, S. (1994). *Handbook of Cooperative Learning Methods*. Westport, Connecticut: Greenwood Press.

— Chapter 9 —

Course Design and Assessment for Transformation

Linda Leach, Guyon Neutze, Nick Zepke

Introduction

This chapter explores course design and, a major subset, assessment. On one level these are very practical tasks, so we offer a variety of practical ideas and information. But they also have a deeper level. The question "What are the purposes of course design and assessment?" takes us there. Exploring answers to that question, we are attracted to the notion of transformative learning, and suggest how you may achieve this.

The chapter has two parts.

1. We describe course design and assessment as rational, ordered, technical and outcome focused.
   - We outline a systematic design process, including needs analysis, learning outcomes, content, learning resources, teaching methods, assessment and evaluation.
   - We examine assessment in detail. We discuss normative and criterion-referenced assessment. We discuss key concepts like learning outcomes/elements/objectives, learning domains, validity and reliability, summative and formative assessment. We describe and evaluate a number of assessment tools and methods.
2. We introduce approaches to transformative course design and assessment.
   - We first suggest ways to design courses and assess learning with a process orientation.
   - We discuss internal and external fairness in assessment, emerging criteria and the politics of difference. We also discuss transformative techniques like self and peer assessment, negotiated assessment and assessment of learning rather than product. Finally we raise further questions, including questions about the process we advocate.

Course design

We design to give shape to things: in this case, to learning. Course design gives shape to a cluster of learning events. These can take us in a number of directions. One is to pre-set skills and outcomes, reproductive learning and fitting-the-dominant-culture. We call this an *outcomes approach.*

Outcomes approach

This comes in different models – linear, circular, interactive. All share common features:

- Needs analysis: who is the course for?
- Learning outcomes, elements or objectives: what will the learners learn?
- Content: what topics will be covered?
- Learning materials and teaching methods: how will objectives be achieved, content covered?
- Assessment of learning: how will we decide that the learners have achieved learning outcomes?
- Course evaluation: has the course achieved its purpose?

These features interact and can be covered in any order, or together. Figure 9.1 pictures the process as a continuous cycle.

We now explore these features in greater detail.

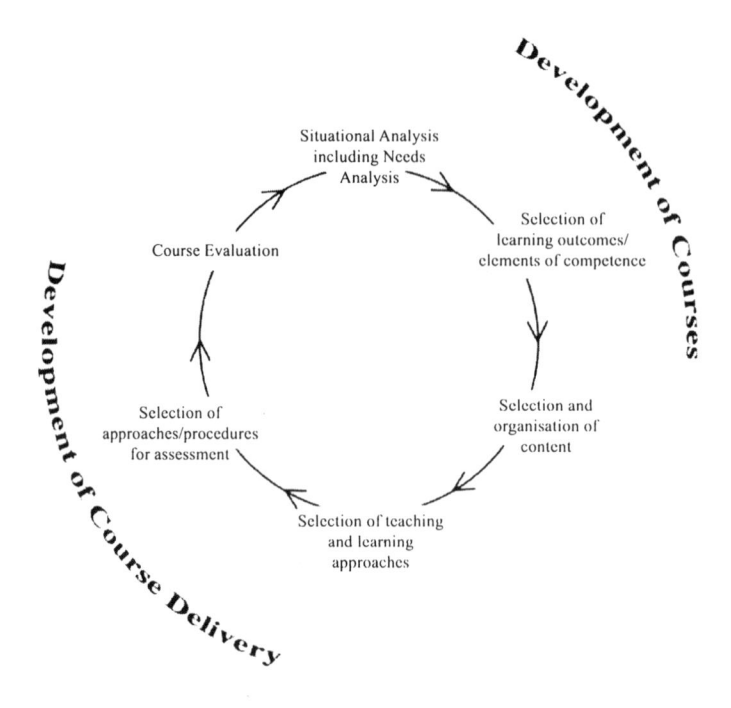

Figure 9.1.   A curriculum design cycle (from Sylvester & Hunter-Reid, 1996)

Needs analysis

First, who is the course for? A number of people may have an interest: students, teachers and employers; the discipline or professional body defining the knowledge and skills required; government funding the course; the institution managing the funding and qualifications; society-at-large which judges the relevance and effectiveness of the course, and the merit and worth of its graduates.

So deciding who the course is for can be complicated. Sometimes different groups' interests conflict. Professional bodies may require content students see as irrelevant; governments have policies teachers disagree with; institutions disagree with teachers about content; or they may all ignore cultural, gender and class differences.

You can untie this knot using needs analysis. Try one or more of the following:

- Look for possible stakeholders and try to identify their interests. Better still, talk with them.
- Look at policy and curriculum documents, contracts and unit standards.
- A variety of methods may establish needs. They include formal processes such as DACUM (**D**esign **a** **C**urricul**um**), Skills Audit and Functional Analysis (who does what). These use the experience of practitioners to identify knowledge, skills and attitudes needed by your students in employment. Research and/or group processes are used. Other more informal methods involve brainstorms and discussions with students, colleagues, industry representatives and graduates. Many educational providers use advisory committees to establish needs.
- After this, write the aims or purposes of the course. These are detailed in the learning outcomes.

Learning outcomes, elements or objectives

A learning outcome describes what a learner will know or be able to do at the end of the course. Three domains are widely recognised – skill (psychomotor), knowledge (cognitive) and attitudes (affective). Outcomes can be written in a simple or a complex way. For example:

Skill domain

Simple: ride a bicycle.
Complex: given a twelve-speed bicycle and a tar-sealed surface, be able to ride one kilometre in three minutes without falling off.

Knowledge domain

Simple: repeat the road-code relating to twelve-speed bicycles.
Complex: under the supervision of a police officer, be able to repeat word-perfectly all the rules of the road relating to the use of a twelve-speed bicycle.

Attitudes domain

Simple: obeys all rules and codes of behaviour relating to bicycles.
Complex: while riding a twelve-speed bicycle, and without being supervised, willingly obey all rules and codes of behaviour relating to bicycles.

Bloom and his colleagues (Bloom 1956; Bloom *et al.*, 1966; Simpson, 1976) developed several levels for each domain. They argued a strict order from simple to complex. We think their approach is useful, but complicated, so here we simplify it.

Knowledge Domain	
Understanding	Knowledge of facts, methods, principles
Application	Knowledge and understanding in practice
Problem solving	Complex thinking skills

Skills Domain	
Imitation	Imitating an instructor or using trial and error
Habit	Performing a skill without needing to think about it
Invention	Discovering new ways of doing things

Attitude Domain	
Openness	Being open to others' ideas, values and beliefs
Appreciation	Valuing others' ideas, values and beliefs
Commitment	Holding to and acting on a set of personal values and beliefs

To use learning domains, decide what your learners need to learn, in which domains, at what levels. Suppose your learning outcome is 'ride a bicycle'. This is in the skills domain at the habit level. Suppose your learning outcome is 'willingly obeys all rules and codes of behaviour relating to bicycles'. This is in the attitude domain, at the commitment level.

The *level* of learning outcomes is shown by a verb. For example, '*Explains* the rules relating to brakes on twelve-speed bicycles' is in the knowledge domain at the level of understanding. '*Creates* an original braking manoeuvre' is in the skills domain at the invention level. '*Initiates* a campaign for maintaining safe brakes on bicycles' is in the attitude domain at the commitment level. We will revisit these when we discuss assessment.

Content: what topics will be covered?

Match your learning outcomes with essential content. The following criteria adapted from Sylvester and Hunter-Reid (1996) could help you.

- *Significance*
  - What minimum content is required to meet the learning outcomes?
  - Is any of this content so important that it must be described as learning outcomes?
- *Validity*
  - Does content match the learning outcomes?
  - Do content and learning outcomes anticipate change?
- *Utility*
  - Are learning outcomes and content relevant and useful?
- *Ease of Learning*
  - Does the course meet the needs of:
    * A large number of students with a wide range of abilities?
    * Students with special needs?
    * Students from different cultures?
- *Interest*
  - Will the content interest students?

Another challenge is to sequence content to the learning outcomes. This is based on sound learning theory. Three key principles apply:

- *Continuity* is provided by vertical or spiral sequencing and is called *stacking*. This stacks courses or lessons in stages, levels or progressions. For example, Stage Two builds on Stage One of a programme, course or topic. It enables the learner to revisit ideas and understand increasingly complex material.
- *Integration* is provided by horizontal sequencing, called *linking*. Subjects, topics or ideas are linked so that their relationship becomes clear to learners.
- *Consolidation* is provided by repetition of learning experiences. Going over content in different ways gives learners several opportunities to grasp new ideas.

Other principles you can use include:

- *Simple to complex*: begin with basic skills and ideas and progress to more involved ones.
- *Known to unknown*: try to relate content to personal experiences before moving to new knowledge, skills and attitudes.
- *Whole to the part*: give learners the whole picture before looking at parts.
- *Concrete to abstract*: relate ideas to tangible things and events before abstracting to general principles.
- *Theory to practical*: work from the principle to its application.

Like all good principles these have exceptions, so be flexible. Learners may prefer to make theory from practical experience; start with a wild concept and link it to something they already know or start with a mystery and solve it (unknown to known).

Learning material and teaching methods

This topic is covered in depth in Chapters 4, 5 and 7. It is important to note that decisions about learning materials and teaching methods are part and parcel of course design.

Course evaluation

Course evaluation is both the last and the first act of course design: last because it looks back at what has happened; first because it gives rise to a new needs analysis, new learning outcomes, and new course design. Indeed, it is ongoing throughout the course. This enables constant adjustments to be made in the interests of the learners. This is known as formative evaluation. However, we need a more formal evaluation at the end of a course to show accountability to stakeholders such as industry. This is known as summative evaluation. A review team with a cross-section of stakeholders – students, teachers, advisory committees – is most suitable for this. One way of doing this is to use a four-step model (Sylvester & Hunter-Reid, 1996).

Step one: Setting criteria

What do you want the course to be judged on? Some possibilities may be:

- learner satisfaction with teacher, communication, assessment
- relevance of aims and learning outcomes
- suitability of resources
- learners' performance in tests
- job placements.

Step two: Investigate how well criteria have been met

Possible approaches include:

- informal discussion with learners
- self and peer evaluation
- observation
- questionnaires
- exit interviews with learners
- small group instructional diagnosis (SGID)
- review team discussions, for example on resources and assessment results.

Step three: Compare data with set criteria
How well did we do? Analyse the information gathered and plan to remedy shortcomings. This is a tricky process. Review-data, and our responses to them, are subjective, based on people's values. We can ignore the results out of shame or arrogance, or be mortified and try to change everything. Both are unhelpful. The whole purpose of evaluation, favourable or unfavourable, is to stimulate a new cycle in the course design process.

Step four: Acting on evaluation results
What do we do with results? This is the sharp end. Some possibilities include:

- look for themes in the data
- prioritise them
- convert them to action statements
- record the action statements for future reference
- act.

Assessment

Assessment is embedded in the design process. In particular it addresses the learning outcomes. Content and teaching methods are also linked to assessment. In Unit Standards, for example, 'range statements' signal content that must be assessed.

Purposes of assessment
Assessment can:

- show whether learners have learned well enough to pass
- give learners feedback on progress and provide opportunities to improve
- provide motivating goals
- tell teachers about learner progress and how to improve it
- maintain standards
- give learners insights into strengths, weaknesses and styles of learning
- measure the success of a course
- give feedback on the success of our teaching.

Assessment requires both technical skills and insights into its underlying assumptions. In this section we deal with the technical skills.

Modes of assessment
Assessment is comparison. Norm-referenced assessment compares the performance of different people. Standards-based, or competency-based assessment compares

performance with set standards. Achievement-based assessment, a sub-set of standards-based, compares performance with *levels of achievement on a set standard*. Figure 9.2 illustrates this relationship.

```
                    Standards-based assessment
                              |
              ----------------------------------
              |                                |
      Competency-based                  Achievement-based
        Assessment                         Assessment
```

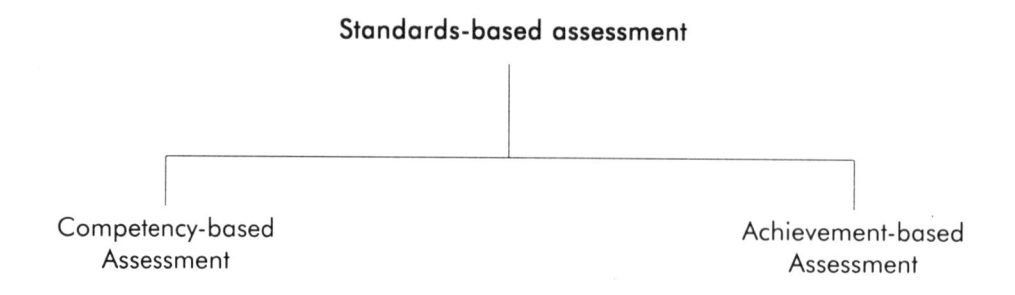

Figure 9.2. **Relationship between standards-based, competency-based and achievement-based assessment**

Norm-referenced assessment

In norm-referenced assessment, every learner is compared with others in a particular group. Teachers working in subjects requiring lots of 'higher level thinking' in the knowledge domain often favour it. It has the following features:

- Comparison takes place within a group. This may be a class or an age group, as with the old School Certificate.
- At its simplest it ranks learners according to their marks, grades or percentages.
- In other situations the actual score a learner achieves is adjusted so the group results fit a normal distribution curve (Bell Curve). This requires that few people achieve the top and bottom grades and most fit around the middle.
- Where assessment is for a selection process, the examiner sets cut-off points and grade boundaries, to achieve the desired result.
- Fans for norm-referenced assessment claim it is good for maintaining even standards.

Standards-based assessment

With standards-based assessment, knowledge, skills and attitudes are described as standards a student must reach. It has the following features:

- The standard is stated as a learning outcome, element or objective, and defined by performance criteria. The learning outcome 'ride a bicycle' is not yet a standard. It requires performance criteria.

- Learner achievement is compared to these criteria. In the case of the bicycle these could refer to distance, time, speed and balance: for example, 'for one kilometre, in three minutes, without falling off'. Performance could now be compared to this standard.
- A learner is judged either competent or not yet competent.
- A 'not-yet-competent' may repeat the assessment until competent. In reality, most institutions limit the number of attempts.
- Assessment is not influenced by artificially set norms. It is possible for all learners in a course to pass.

You judge whether students have achieved the required standard by collecting and analysing evidence from:

- prior achievement outside formal learning
- learning activities set up for students within a learning programme; this is also called 'naturally occurring evidence'
- assessment tasks within formal and non-formal learning programmes; these may be demonstrations, written or oral presentations
- current external performances that you cannot observe first-hand. On-the-job performance is an example.

Achievement-based assessment

Standards-based assessment has often been criticised as denying recognition of excellence. To address this, grade-related standards, usually called achievement-based assessments, have been developed. These describe levels of performance. They include A, B, C and Fail. Features of achievement-based assessments include:

- the allocation of grades rather than pass/fail
- performance criteria for a range of grades
- absence of artificial norms. For example, it is possible for all learners in a course to be awarded an A, or to fail.

Table 9.3 (over page) provides an example of achievement-based performance standards from the field of education.

Quality	C Pass Indicators	B Pass Indicators	A Pass Indicators
Use of Sources	Investigates and locates relevant data. Uses recommended course readings and references. Shows awareness of standard literature.	Uses appropriate search methods. Incorporates references beyond the course recommendations. Shows familiarity with relevant literature.	Researches topic thoroughly. Draws on a wide variety of sources. Makes judicious use of literature in the area of study.
Analysis	Identifies key ideas and information, makes links and comparisons, shows relationships.	Discriminates patterns, trends and relationships; develops conclusions from the analysis.	Examines ideas and information rigorously, and from a range of perspectives.
Reflection	Provides evidence of reflecting on own learning and teaching experiences.	Provides evidence of reflection influencing practice or planning for future practice.	Takes a consistently reflective approach to practice, develops personal insights into praxis.
Awareness of Issues	Identifies and discusses key issues in own context or in wider context (e.g. in literature on the topic)	Acknowledges diversity of views and influences on issues, and is able to articulate own viewpoint.	Discusses and critiques diverse views and influences, develops own clearly articulated perspective on issues.

Table 9.3. An achievement-based marking grid

Two key technical considerations

Validity

Whatever mode you use, it must be valid. Assessment is said to be valid if it properly samples the content and objectives of the course, and can be completed in the time set.

Content and objectives are sampled properly if:

- The form of assessment reflects the domains and levels of the learning outcome. It is invalid to assess the skill of riding a bicycle in a written test.

- Knowledge, skills and attitudes taught in the course are represented, or have had an equal chance of being there.
- The assessment task actually assesses the learning outcomes.
- Different kinds of validity are identified. One is consequential validity. This arises from a belief that social values cannot be ignored. To be valid, assessment must reflect the learner's social context, and consider the consequences of its use (Gipps, 1994).

Reliability

Assessment is reliable if assessment procedures are used 'consistently and accurately'. Reliability is enhanced where:

- marking is consistent; based on sound criteria and not influenced by factors such as tiredness, irritability or presentation;
- learners are treated fairly; study resources are adequate, test conditions are appropriate and undue stress is minimised.

It is widely argued that assessments cannot be valid unless they are also reliable. We don't agree. We take this up later when we discuss internal and external fairness.

Planning assessment

When planning assessments, consider the following questions.

- Why am I assessing?
- When and how often will I assess?
- What will I assess?
- How will I assess?

Why am I assessing?

We referred earlier to some purposes of assessment. It is always important to be clear about these. If you want to be learner-centred, ask 'How will learners benefit?'.

When and how often do I assess?

This will be influenced by the purposes. For example:

- Diagnostic assessment is done early, even before the course starts, so changes to the course plan can be made.
- Formative assessment (usually feedback given without marking or grading) gives learners the chance to practise without penalty, and provides feedback in time to improve performance.
- Summative assessment, which counts towards the final grade, may be end-of-course assessment, or more desirably, continuous assessment as in the world-at-large.

What will I assess?

Some basic guidelines include:

- Assess to the domains and levels of the learning outcomes.
- Observe the requirements of validity
- Ensure your assessments reflect the amount of teaching time, emphasis and level of content. Table 9.4 pictures one possible assessment plan, balancing total teaching time and assessment weighting. You can see how the level is allocated to each topic, and what proportion will be given to each topic.

Table 9.4. Sample assessment plan for an imaginary horticulture unit

Content/ topic	Recall Facts and figures	Comprehension: Knowledge of principles	Application of principles	Problem solving	Per cent of teaching time
Growing media and seeding propagation	5	5	5	10	25
Temperature control	–	5	5	–	10
Moisture control	–	5	5	5	15
Fertiliser and feeding	5	5	5	5	20
Staking and harvesting	–	5	5	–	10
Pest and diseases	5	5	5	5	20
Total assessment emphasis	15	30	30	25	100

(Scott & Scott, 1996).

Course Design and Assessment for Transformation   167

How will I assess?

You look for evidence that the learning outcomes have been achieved. *Evidence* is the magic word. It may take many forms, so you have a wide range of assessment tools to choose from. Some are pictured in Table 9.5 along with their domain use, and this is followed by some more detail about ways to assess in the different domains.

Written tasks and examinations

These ask learners to write on a topic in an organised manner. They include essay and report writing, paragraph-type tasks and formal written examinations. They are useful for assessing creativity, lateral thinking, problem solving, organisational ability and written communication skills.

Setting written tasks

Use these in areas where they will be useful for assessing – like problem-solving. Don't set tasks that measure factual recall. This can best be assessed in other ways. Use key words to emphasise the skill level required. Figure 9.6 lists some key domain verbs you can use for different skill levels.

- Limit the scope of the task by giving students clear instructions for what is expected. Figure 9.7 illustrates this with three examples.

- Give clues as to what is expected. For instance, Example 3 in Figure 9.7 has a number of important clues: It:
  – sets the context for the question;
  – states what is to be done, using clear, bolded directional words (define, state, evaluate).
  – states the weighting of each of the three parts;
  – awards most marks for problem-solving.

- Take care, when setting written tasks:
  – Define the content and objectives you are testing, and make sure students know them.
  – Decide on criteria you will use, or prepare a model answer.

- Consider the student:
  – Make the wording clear and unambiguous.
  – When laying out questions, separate instructions from background information.
  – Provide ample time for students to collect their thoughts, list headings ….
  – When marking, be liberal with comments – but stick to main issues and minimise comments on spelling and grammar (unless this is being assessed).

Figure 9.5. Choice of assessment tools by domain use

Assesment Tool	Knowledge Domain	Skills Domain	Attitude Domain
Assignment	❖		
Case Study	❖		❖
Critique	❖	❖	❖
Demonstration		❖	❖
Essay	❖		
Exams: open book closed book	❖		
Matching exercise	❖		
Multi-choice questions	❖		
Objective Structured Clinical Evaluation (OSCE)	❖	❖	
Observation		❖	❖
Oral assessment	❖		❖
Portfolio	❖	❖	
Practical assessments: Product Process		❖	
Project	❖	❖	
Rating scale			❖
Reflective diary, journal or log	❖		❖
Role play		❖	❖
Seminar presentation	❖		
Short answer	❖		
Simulation exercises	❖		
True/false	❖		
Work-based assessment	❖	❖	❖

Knowledge domain	Key domain words
Understanding	define, list, state, reproduce, explain, summarise, interpret, give examples
Application	apply, solve, modify, predict, demonstrate
Problem solving	analyse, break down, relate, design, plan, create, combine, critique, justify, appraise, contrast.

Figure 9.6. Key words for three knowledge domain levels

Example 1   A poor task question:
'Discuss essay and multi-choice assessment'

Example 2   A better question:
'Contrast essay and multiple-choice test types, paying particular attention to their setting and marking'

Example 3   Better still:
'You have been asked whether essay or multiple-choice questions are better for assessing student problem-solving skills'

(a) *Define* essay and multiple-choice type questions (2 marks)
(b) *State* two examples of problem-solving skills (1 mark)
(c) *Evaluate* the strengths and weaknesses of each type in assessing problem solving (7 marks).

Figure 9.7. Examples of written task questions

Marking written tasks

Marking written assignments and tests is more difficult than setting them. Questions will attract a varied range of answers. To maximise reliability, limit the choice of topics and use a marking schedule. Table 9.3 above, which sets out achievement-based assessment criteria, is also a model for marking written tasks.

To develop your marking schedule:

- identify qualities you want the written work to show;
- write grade indicators for each of these qualities.

Decide how to arrive at a final grade from these qualities. For example, to get an overall A grade, an A may be required in at least four of six qualities. It is important to let learners into your marking secrets, and give them access to marking schedules. Give plenty of feedback.

Assessing practical skills

Valid and reliable assessment of practical skills is challenging. Unless they are properly assessed, overall gradings will be biased towards theory. It is vital that practical expertise is assessed regularly and systematically.

There are two types of practical assessments, product and process.

- *Product* assessment appraises a final product or completed job.
  Assessing the final product is relatively easy. Criteria are usually available for acceptable standards. Construct a minimum list of essential characteristics. Build it while setting course objectives and before you teach. The following are some product-related items:

Task	**Product Assessment**
Hanging a door	Is the door plumb?
Welding two pipes	Is the weld crack-free?
Bandaging wound	Does the bandage cover entire affected area?
Tuning engine	Does it start first time?

- *Process* assessment appraises how well a student has mastered skills for the job. Process assessment is more difficult and takes time and ingenuity. It is often subjective, but can still be reliable. For example, a video may be used to record a learner's work and then be moderated by a group of teachers to achieve consistency. For process, use achievement-based assessment, using pre-set outcomes. Comparison with other students (norm-referencing) has no place in process. Good criterion-referenced assessment measures learning outcomes directly. For example, if the learning outcome is 'The learner will communicate effectively with the patient', the assessment will focus on that.

   When you assess process, construct a list of performances that are absolutely necessary for the task. Do this while setting the learning outcomes and before you teach.

   For example:

Learning outcome: 'The student uses aseptic techniques for hand-washing'.
Necessary performances:

1. Turns on taps without clothes touching sink.
2. Wets hands thoroughly.
3. Applies soap to cover hands completely and washes:
   - palms
   - fingers
   - back of hands
   - forearms.
4. Uses sufficient ... and so on.

Course Design and Assessment for Transformation 171

- Turn performances into a checklist to be marked off 'yes' or 'no'. Process assessment is done by on-the-job observation. This takes time and organisation, so keep to the 'must dos'.
- Tell students what and how you intend marking.
- Ensure you assess what is important – product or process.

Testing for competency

A student has passed a practical test when the specified skill has been achieved on *every* standard set. Remember, grade-related criteria, as shown earlier in the chapter, are also useful in practical assessment.

A word of caution

Remember that your main role is to facilitate learning. Intensive practical assessment may prevent learners from seeking help. Further, when you assess process don't become too task-oriented. Try to assess for strategy and planning. Simple questions such as "What do you intend doing next?" and "How does that meet your objective?" will soon catch the level of thought that has gone into planning. And don't forget that the student may need help with strategy as well as the task.

Assessing attitudes

This involves observing learners and making judgements about their attitudes. Three steps are usual:

1. Prepare the observation.
    - Identify attitudes in the learning outcomes.
    - List these and identify levels of complexity for each. For example, "willingly obeys all rules and codes of behaviour relating to bicycles" is a commitment-level learning outcome.
    - Now list its behaviours. For example, "maintains bicycle well; rides on the left-hand side of the road; is careful of pedestrians; gives way to traffic turning right; is considerate of other traffic; wears helmet".
    - Now, if you use achievement-based assessment, develop suitable criteria. For example, "throughout the observation"; "for most of the observation"; "for some of the observation"; "occasionally during the observation"; and "not at all".
    - Combine into a portable checklist. Figure 9.8 is an example.
    - Decide which standard a student must meet to pass. You may decide that for "bicycle is well maintained" the passing grade is 'mostly'; but for "gives way to traffic turning right" the requirement is 'throughout' the observation. Make sure you tell learners this *before* the assessment.

Observation Assessment Report		
Learner's Name:		
Course Name:		
Date of Observation:		
Instructions		
Circle the statement that you consider best reflects the learner's performance		
Bicycle has been maintained	*Gives way to traffic turning right*	
Throughout	Throughout	
Mostly	Mostly	
Some of the time	Some of the time	
Occasionally	Occasionally	
Not at all	Not at all	
Rides on the left-hand side of the road	*Is considerate to other traffic*	
Throughout	Throughout	
Mostly	Mostly	
Some of the time	Some of the time	
Occasionally	Occasionally	
Not at all	Not at all	
Is careful of pedestrians	*Wears helmet*	
Throughout	Throughout	
Mostly	Mostly	
Some of the time	Some of the time	
Occasionally	Occasionally	
Not at all	Not at all	
Signature of Assessor:		
Date:		

(adapted from Athanasou, 1997)

Figure 9.8. Observation Assessment Report for assessing attitudes

Course Design and Assessment for Transformation   173

2. Conduct the observation. As you can see, most of the work is the preparation; or is it? You may not think so as you run after the bicycle, especially when you drop your pencil!
3. Make a judgement from the recorded evidence.

Getting to transformation

So far we have looked at key technical matters – the 'how' of course design and assessment. But we are not just dealing with toolboxes of techniques. Values, beliefs and educational philosophies underpin everything we do. In this section we surface ideas other than the technical, which may lead to transformations.

It may seem strange to find course design, assessment and transformation in the one chapter. We recognise that people design courses and assessments for a purpose. It is rarely simple or singular. We agree with government and business leaders that courses should prepare people for the workplace and the economy, but believe this focus is too narrowing and reproduces only what already is. This is not a complete preparation for life, which is seeded with change. In this section we explore approaches to course design and assessment that enable transformations to happen.

'Transformation' means many things. In a business environment it often means change so that organisations work more efficiently, more profitably and more adaptively. Translated to course design and assessment, this means we transform students into useful working units. In adult education it can mean change in the way people see themselves and their world (Mezirow, 2000). Translated to course design and assessment, this means both teachers and students change their understanding of these activities. It can also mean people working for social change, and a more just society (Brookfield, 2000). Brookfield holds, for example, that certain belief systems such as capitalism impose one way of thinking on us. This creates inequities in education and society at large. To help counter this, he wants course design and assessment to engage learners in what he calls ideological critique.

We give the term 'transformation' all three meanings. We want courses and assessments to enable people to change the way they think and act in society. Keep this in mind, as you read this section, and critique what we have said in your own way. The reflective, critical reflective and meditative processes described in Chapter 1 may help you. Never underestimate the power of the question, or of silence, in the transformative process.

Process approach

One way to transformation is to use what we call a process approach. This gives us the space, within the official course requirements, to enable learners to transform as individuals, workers and agents in society. In our own work we are experimenting with process approaches. You may use these even when others have written your course. They are not as tidy to describe as outcome approaches, but are more likely to lead to learning transformations. While our approaches vary slightly, we share the following ideas when designing courses.

Our courses are learner centred. Even with very specific learning outcomes, we involve the learner in decisions of interpretation. We ask them to decide: (i) what they make of them; (ii) how they will be useful; (iii) how they can adapt them to their needs or interests; and (iv) what kind of exploration they can invent to meet them. In this, we offer options and cues to enable people to decide their own learning pathways. At the very first session Linda, for example, negotiates content and processes within the framework of the learning outcomes. She offers several assessment options, including "negotiate with me an alternative assessment that shows you have met the learning outcomes".

Learning is negotiated. Some of you work within very specific course prescriptions. Even then, you can negotiate much. For example, content focus and sequencing, learning activities, organisation of assessments, feedback to learners and course evaluations are all negotiable. The looser the course is, the more that can be negotiated. For Linda, negotiation is the key. Adults do *not* all want to learn the same things in the same way or do the same assessments. So learners and Linda negotiate content and processes within the framework set by the learning outcomes.

Focus on learner interest. This follows from the others. We make space for learners to express their unique interests in a subject, then build learning activities and assessments around them. We encourage learners to apply learning to their own contexts, making it authentic. Even with a course set in New Zealand, Nick encouraged a learner from a Pacific nation to design learning that adapted content to his own nation. This focus on learner interest makes learning relevant and potentially transformative.

Structure for breadth and depth. Some learners are interested in most of the features in the course landscape. Others want to examine only one or two, but at great depth. We design courses to enable learners to be explorers or miners. They choose whether to explore widely or dig deeply. Guyon composes his assignments so that learners can make such decisions.

Question. We question to create content, to generate problems, to challenge and deconstruct existing concepts and practices, to encourage learners to question the course, their beliefs, values and understandings, and to keep us in touch with the learning we are all engaged in. Guyon, for example, aims to leave the learner with more questions than answers. That, he believes, is the path to transformation; to realise that, however many answers we construct, the universe remains a question.

Include the big picture. We keep in mind that learners need to understand the wider social, political and economic contexts of the learning outcomes, even when courses are described in detail. Nick, for example, builds in activities that encourage learners to critique commonly held 'truths', including his own, recognise and challenge ideas that ensure dominance for certain social groups and put to the question their own ideas about the world.

Assessment for transformative learning

To create spaces for learner-centred and transformative assessments we need to expose undeclared and hidden assessment agendas. One is that very few people are excellent, many are mediocre and a few are outright failures. This leads to the yoke of the 'bell curve' and the belief that an excellent course must fail some. In our view an excellent course is one where everyone passes, something that is possible in standards or achievement-based assessment.

A second undeclared item is that there is only one true knowledge, one correct way of doing things. To pass, you must have it, or do it. Yet different ways of knowing are part of our daily lives in every sphere. For example, amongst several solutions to a mathematical problem, only one is approved; amongst many ways of slicing vegetables, an international catering authority will only allow one; amongst countless ways of building a staircase, only one is approved by the building inspectors. Knowledge may differ with cultures. In one, the weather changes with currents and wind patterns, in another it changes with the spirit of the people. The view that there is only one form of knowledge constrains teachers and learners and prevents recognition of valid alternatives.

A third assumption is that the power lies with the teacher. Many don't recognise that power is an issue in assessment. They take for granted that teachers will assess 'accurately' and 'fairly' and they have an unchallengeable right in this. So learners who wish to succeed become compliant. They learn to distrust their judgement, as do the teachers. We know of good staircases built in non-approved ways. We know of delicious vegetable dishes sliced in non-approved ways. Given the space to express their own ways of knowing, learners are able to come up with their own solutions.

A fourth is that to be fair, assessment must treat everyone the same. This means learners do the same assessment under the same external conditions and meet the same standards. This is one kind of fairness. We call this *external fairness* (Leach, Neutze, Zepke, 1999). It does not suit all conditions. So we have developed what we call *internal fairness*. This creates space to recognise different cultures, contexts, viewpoints and ways of knowing and doing. It draws on notions of equity. Internal fairness would recognise many ideas, cultures, contexts, ways of doing for making a staircase, not complying with the inspector's manual.

A fifth is the idea that assessment criteria must be set beforehand. The undeclared agenda is that learning is predetermined and must not change. We challenge this with the notion of emerging criteria. Learning is often change: in understanding, behaviour, attitudes. To prevent change is to reduce it to ritual. So we suggest learner and teacher look within the learner's work for emerging criteria by which it may be assessed. This is another challenge to the teacher. Instead of measuring the staircase against existing standards, the teacher discovers new ways to teach about building them.

These undeclared agendas, to a greater or lesser extent, confine learners within a social structure. They will be presumed ignorant; they will need to comply to succeed; different cultures, contexts and ideas will not be recognised; original minds will be penalised; and learning will become a ritual.

So for us the key is to assess what has actually been learned rather than what we would have liked learners to learn. There are a number of ways of doing this.

- Engage with the learner throughout the learning. Be inside the learning process, not outside it, and assess the learning, not merely the product. Then we can better understand actual achievements, validate different forms of knowledge, and be both internally and externally fair.
- Share power. We are experimenting with a number of techniques for this. First, to encourage, but not impose, learner-centred assessment. Techniques include self-assessment, peer-assessment and collaborative or group assessment. Each of these is as possible with large classes as with small.

General principles for self, peer and group assessment

In some cultures, people will not speak about themselves, especially in complimentary terms. "It is not for the kumara to proclaim its own sweetness." Some learners have too little confidence, others too much. Self and peer assessment is not recognised by some professional bodies. So self, peer or group assessments are not always the answer. But they can counter the impact of undeclared agendas. Here are some general guidelines to making the most of them.

- Encourage learners to consider alternative forms, but don't impose them.
- Make a partnership between you and the learners. Create an environment of trust between teacher and students.
- Share the power of assessment, giving equal weight to teacher and learner judgements. Where there is a difference, have moderation available.
- Don't make it merely a self-marking exercise. Include learners in topic development, form of assessment and in identifying criteria.
- Allow criteria to emerge in an ongoing conversation with the learner during the course.
- Give plenty of practice. Introduce assessments early, so that confidence and skills can develop.
- Use self-assessment in formative assessments.
- In group assessments, negotiate whether individual contributions will be assessed, (by the group and/or yourself) or whether the whole group will accept the same grade.
- These forms of assessment don't alter the need to meet the requirements of the course.
- Don't dump learners into them. Develop them together.

What now?

We would like these ideas to lead to some transformations in how you design courses and assess. We recommend that you take transformation seriously to avoid becoming irrelevant in an ever-changing world. Change is not always positive. You might design courses and assessments to enable learners to be critical, to deconstruct, to question, to listen to their silence. You might do the same with the ideas in this chapter.

- Identify ideas in this chapter that attract and repel you. Clarify reasons for this. Brainstorm those that attract you for use in planning and assessment. Develop alternatives to those that repel you.
- Identify ruts you think we are travelling in.
- Decide what 'transformation' means to you and how you would use it in course design and assessment.
- Ask others what they think of it. You may feel like rubbishing it. Do so, but avoid falling back into your own 'rubbish'!
- Read widely about course design, assessment and transformation. The following books are useful:

Suggested readings

Curriculum design

Barnett, R. (1994). *The Limits of Competence: Knowledge, Higher Education and Society*. Buckingham: Society for Research into Higher Education and Open University Press.

Eisner, E. (1994). *The Educational Imagination* (3rd ed.). New York: Macmillan.

Toohey, S. (1999). *Designing Courses for Higher Education*. Buckingham: Society for Research into Higher Education and Open University Press.

Assessment

Broadfoot, P. (1996). *Education, Assessment and Society.* Buckingham: Open University Press.

Cangelosi, J. (2000). *Assessment Strategies for Monitoring Student Learning*. New York: Longman.

Raven, J., & Stephenson, J. (2001). *Competence in the Learning Society.* New York: P. Lang.

Glossary

Assessment: all the activities and processes of measuring and reporting learning.
Course: an organised set of learning content and outcomes.
Course evaluation: the process of making judgements about the course.
Criterion-referenced assessment: methods of assessment involving measuring learners against a pre-set standard.
Formative assessment: assessment to help learners improve by providing feedback. It does not contribute to the final judgement of the learning.
Learning outcomes: statements of what the learner will have learnt, usually expressed in behavioural terms.
Needs analysis: a process that identifies learning needs and prioritises them.

Normative assessment: methods of assessment in which the grades reported describe how well each learner did in comparison with all others.

Process approaches: *how* and *what* learning and assessment is to occur is negotiated between teacher and learner.

Reliability: the extent to which the same assessment tool would give the same results if it could be completed again by the same learner under the same conditions.

Summative assessment: assessment to measure whether the learner has met the learning outcomes and which contributes to the final judgement of performance. Usually a mark or grade is assigned.

Transformative: learning that may confront and examine all points of view and produce significant change of action.

Validity: whether an assessment tool measures what it claims to measure.

References

Athanasou, J. (1997). *Introduction to Educational Testing*. Wentworth Falls, NSW: Social Science Press.

Bloom, B. et al., (1956). *Taxonomy of Educational Objectives*. Vol 1: Cognitive Domain. New York: McKay.

Bloom, B., Krathwohl, D. R., & others. (1966). *A Taxonomy of Educational Objectives*. London: Longman.

Brookfield, S. (2000). The Concept of Critically Reflective Practice. A. Wilson, & E. Hayes (eds), *Handbook of Adult and Continuing Education*. San Francisco: Jossey Bass and the American Association for Adult and Continuing Education.

Gipps, C. (1994). *Beyond Testing: Towards a Theory of Educational Assessment*. London: The Falmer Press.

Leach, L., Neutze, G., & Zepke, N. (1999). Fairness in Assessment: Challenging a Myth. N. Zepke, M. Knight, L. Leach, & A. Viskovic (eds), *Adult Learning Cultures: Challenges, Choices and the Future*. Wellington: WP Press.

Mezirow, J., & A. (2000). *Learning as Transformation: Critical Perspectives on a Theory in Progress*. San Francisco: Jossey Bass.

Scott, C., & Scott, J. (1996). Assessing Student Achievement. N. Zepke, D. Nugent, & C. Roberts (eds), *The New Self Help Book for Teachers* (pp. 94–124). Wellington: WP Press.

Simpson, E. J. (1976). *The Classification of Educational Objectives: Psychomotor Domain*. Urbana: University of Illinois.

Sylvester, G., & Hunter-Reid, P. (1996). Designing Programmes. N. Zepke, D. Nugent, & C. Roberts (eds), *The New Self Help Book for Teachers* (pp. 77–93). Wellington: WP Press.

— PART IV —

Contexts for Learning and Teaching

Overview

Finally, in Part 4 we consider the contexts in which we learn and teach. Our work is always done within contexts. We need to understand these so we can decide how to act to achieve particular purposes in our teaching. We need to be aware of local and global issues; changes occurring nationally and internationally in education; and how these might affect our teaching. We invite you to think about how you might be a more holistic teacher, including emotional and spiritual dimensions in learning, using internationalist pedagogy and constructivist ideas to create transformations both for learners and yourself.

Context has a major, but often unrecognised, influence on our teaching. The social, cultural, political, economic and historical environments in which we live and work have a profound effect on what we do and how we do it. In Chapter 10, Brian Findsen explores contextual issues and discusses some of the international, national, institutional and local 'classroom' factors that influence us and how we work – eg. globalisation, instrumentalism, economic rationalism and the market economy, massification of education and accountability. While he acknowledges that contextual constraints exist, Brian argues that we should critique these and find ways to work transformatively, using more radical pedagogies.

Nick Zepke continues the global theme in Chapter 11. Using the term 'global village', he explores some of the social, economic and political processes at work – economics, technology, diversity and knowledge. He then focuses on knowledge as one key feature of education, one that is at the heart of teaching and learning. Nick discusses three schools of thought about knowledge (realism, relativism and fallibilism), the politics of official knowledge in the New Zealand context and the role of ignorance in learning. Finally he offers us a model of teaching for the global village and some insights into its use in his own practice.

In the final chapter, Dean Nugent introduces us to a spiritual perspective on learning and teaching, linking this to global, environmental issues. For centuries, state-run Western education has separated the spiritual and the secular in education and focused on the development of the rational, cognitive dimension of people. Now there is a growing recognition that we need to find a balance, to work holistically, incorporating physical, social, emotional, intellectual and spiritual dimensions. Dean does this. He describes his own explorations of the spiritual and discusses ways in which we can create a better balance in our teaching, thereby leading to transformative learning.

— Chapter 10 —

Making Sense of Our Contexts

Brian Findsen

Introduction

In my experience as an adult educator in New Zealand and overseas (mainly the United States and the United Kingdom), I have been aware of contextual factors at work, influencing the kinds of learning that are possible. There are a whole host of factors – economic, political, cultural and social – that can have a serious impact on the quality of learning environments. These factors operate at multiple levels – local, organisational, national and global – to produce, for each teacher of adults, unique circumstances that need careful attention and subsequent action. I offer you a framework for analysing your teaching context. My special interest is in *transformative learning*, a deeper form of learning where learners challenge their basic beliefs about themselves and their world and make significant, positive changes in their lives.
In this chapter, I:

- define the domain of *adult and higher education* to make explicit the breadth of this sector of education;
- consider the global or international influences on our work as educators;
- discuss the concept of *globalisation*, including the implications for us;
- develop a set of strategies to create a more *internationalist* attitude to teaching (without giving up some of New Zealand's idiosyncratic features and values);
- examine the national context in which trends in this country's system of adult and higher education are situated;
- argue for a professional and humanistic stance for teaching adults, rather than a technical or instrumental one;
- discuss the institutional context for teachers' work, acknowledging that the history

and the contemporary philosophical positions adopted by the parent institution in a competitive market have a strong influence on what teachers can do;
- focus on the immediate teaching environment and argue for adopting a more liberatory approach to teaching and learning where a critical attitude is continually espoused and practised;
- recommend practices for a transformative learning environment as a basis for future action.

Defining adult and higher education contexts

The phrase *adult and higher education* hides a complex array of agencies and institutions in which teachers of adults operate. The term *adult education* is used as shorthand here for *adult and community education* which itself has been variously described. I have adopted the definition used by Tobias (1996, p. 42), which was ratified by the Adult and Community Education Association (Aotearoa/New Zealand) in 1994. I use it here because it encapsulates the diversity of the field.

Adult and community education covers five main fields:

- adult basic education;
- second-chance education opening the way to further formal education, training and/or employment;
- personal development education which enables an individual to live in a family, group or community;
- cultural education which enables a person to participate in the life of their community;
- education to facilitate group and community development.

The phrase *higher education* (or *tertiary education*) is used in this chapter to incorporate the following institutions:

- eight publicly-funded universities (including the new Auckland University of Technology);
- three whare wananga (Maori tertiary institutions);
- four colleges of education (modified teacher education institutions);
- numerous (several hundred) private training establishments (PTEs) in diverse areas such as language teaching, health promotion, business schools and religious education.

In general, higher education represents the formal end of the adult education spectrum. Typically, these environments are hierarchical and entail formal assessment of students who strive for credentials.

So, the phrase *adult and higher education* encompasses all agencies and institutions identified above in either *adult education* or *higher education*. This represents a huge sector within New Zealand's education system, the majority of teachers within which receive scant training for their educative roles (Findsen, 1996).

Understanding global forces in adult and higher education

In the New Zealand context, we have experienced traumatic changes in our society since the advent of the Fourth Labour Government in 1984 and subsequent 'New Right' ideology and practices. Under 'Rogernomics' (the financial reforms of Roger Douglas, then Minister of Finance, to streamline the political economy) this country underwent the systematic dismantling of the welfare state and the establishment of a market economy based on the *minimal state* (Snook, 1989). At the time, it was not so easy to recognise that these reforms, so dramatically executed in a small democracy, were also part of a world-wide movement towards a free market (or freer market) in which corporatisation, deregulation and privatisation were the hallmarks (Peters, 1997). The term *economic rationalism* has been used by Codd (1997, p. 131) to describe what has been occurring – "the dominance of the economy and economic processes over most areas in society". Its purpose is to "bring the agencies and apparatus of the state into line with the policy prescriptions of neo-liberal (or free market) economics and contractual managerialism". What New Zealand experienced as a result of this change in ideology was echoed in other, primarily Western, countries that also wanted to trim back social spending and promote individual choice and responsibility.

What does this have to do with adult and higher education in New Zealand? Plenty, I think. We do not exist in an economic and political vacuum but as part of a matrix of political and economic alliances with other nations. While we may enjoy some limited autonomy as a country, the harsh reality is that our economic fortunes (and therefore, our political, social and cultural dynamics) are inextricably linked to those of major trade partners such as the USA, Asia, Australia and the UK. Our education system, including higher education, is similarly bound by economic, political and cultural movements.

Globalisation and internationalism

I use the term *globalisation* to depict those international forces that impact on the New Zealand economy and our system of adult and higher education. With respect to this trend, Stalker (1996, p. 366) points out that at its most basic level, globalisation can be said to "foster homogeneity rather than diversity, sameness rather than difference and unity rather than variance. Its impact is independent of national boundaries." Obviously, globalisation affects what we think of as knowledge in our society. (See Chapter 11 for a discussion of this.)

Drawing upon the work of Barnett, Codd (1997) explains that the "ideology of instrumentalism" favours some forms of knowing over others, which then become marginalised. The emphasis in the workplace, and in adult and higher education, too often becomes concentrated upon skills to be performed, new technologies to be mastered and knowledge to be absorbed. According to this view, knowledge becomes defined as a product, a commodity or a performance. In a stinging attack on higher education in this country, Codd argues that viewing knowledge as a commodity amounts to a denial of the distinction between academic and vocational learning. He favours knowledge that is intrinsically worthwhile, that does not have to *produce* something and that can be pursued for its own sake. He argues for universities to continue to operate as the "critic and conscience of society", one of the fundamental roles of a university as recorded in their charters. Otherwise, universities could be reduced to an overly-instrumental function of producing non-critical thinkers for the marketplace.

At a global level, Collins (1998) discusses the idea of an *internationalist pedagogy* from within a liberatory framework. He argues that while there has been a growing sense of humanity's shared destiny, as part of the global village and the end of Cold War politics, there are still entrenched inequalities throughout the world – between countries, between groups within and outside nations – and unmitigated violence is still pervasive. Improvements in communications technology, a major factor in the spread of globalisation, have not brought benefits to all because some peoples still have disrupted daily lives and undergo widespread alienation. There is an absence of "popular democratic input" (Collins, 1998, p. 172) into the way new technology is deployed. He also challenges the global interests of big business wherein the multi-national corporations can virtually ignore nation states' policies and wishes. This means that these huge companies can exert considerable financial and political clout to reduce the impact of country-level social policies. He urges educators to resist this anti-democratic trend and to adopt in their classrooms an internationalist perspective that is moral and political. He advocates "an undertaking on the part of educators to embrace their roles as members of a world community and to incorporate this understanding into their teaching practices" (Collins, 1998, p. 175). More specifically, this role could entail:

- being kept informed of world events whatever our teaching discipline might be;
- resisting seeing ourselves as isolated from world events;
- maintaining an informed, critical attitude towards mass media productions of what is happening in the world;
- engaging in critical dialogue with our students about the significance of international events;
- being prepared to forego preconceived curriculum in favour of teaching practices which seriously investigate international events;
- taking opportunities to travel in foreign countries, especially developing countries, and adopting a risk-taking attitude, with lower expectations towards personal comforts.

Collins challenges all of us to broaden our frames of reference to include an internationalist pedagogy and to embrace a critical stance on any form of oppression and injustice.

Understanding adult and higher education from a national perspective

Global dynamics directly affect events at national, organisational and local levels. They intertwine with New Zealand perspectives and events. So we should ask, "What has been the impact of globalisation on New Zealand's higher education system?"

Globalisation and regionalism

Before I trace the effects of globalisation, I remind you that globalisation may have different consequences in different geographical areas; that is, it does not have a consistent effect across time and place. According to Dale and Robertson (1997), neo-liberalism has been a dominant, organising ideology that encourages competitiveness, deregulation, privatisation and restructuring. They also identify a countervailing phenomenon of *regionalisation* – "the emergence of geographically and economically distinct trading blocs in the pursuit of stable trading markets and mutual security" (1997, p. 210). So, they argue, globalisation is not an homogeneous trend that neatly maps onto the New Zealand landscape. We need to be aware of, and value more, indigenous or local ideas and social movements, which typify this region of the South Pacific and help to make it distinctive.

Snook (1989, cited in Findsen & Harre-Hindmarsh, 1996, pp. 196–7) points to political and economic imperatives that contribute to our uniqueness as New Zealanders.

- A long-standing commitment to equality; even though New Zealand is not a classless society, many hold firm to the ideal of egalitarianism.
- A tradition of a strong central state that has been manifest in social welfare and education. It may be difficult to overthrow the centralism of the past.
- The co-existence of Maori (as tangata whenua) and Pakeha, and a deep-seated belief that 'we are one people' living harmoniously. Importantly, the Treaty of Waitangi acts as a founding document as one basis to promote Maori sovereignty and to redress inequities (e.g. land confiscations).

It appears that Dale and Robertson and Snook are saying something quite similar. The effects of globalisation are not uniform (this point is also discussed in Chapter 11). It would be unwise to argue that the effects of a global free market are felt in the same way by each of us as individuals or as members of groups, whether dominant or subordinate. In this country we have our own ways of doing things that uphold our distinctive identities, as Kiwis, as tangata whenua, as Pacific Nations peoples, as new immigrants, as whoever. This 'regionalism' or distinctive New Zealand identity has embedded within it a set of values and beliefs that reflect our perspective on the world. We need to be simultaneously 'international pedagogues', so that we understand what is happening in the world and this country in a broader, critical paradigm, and 'regionalists', who uphold a unique set of values and perspectives that reflect our idiosyncratic location. The dictum 'think globally, act locally' captures this concept. We need to adopt a balanced perspective – maintaining a sound knowledge of international events and trends while being aware of our New Zealand and regional cultures and idiosyncrasies.

Recent changes in higher education and their implications

With the technological advances associated with a market economy, there have been distinct changes in the higher education system over the last two decades. These are similar to changes in other Western democracies. Evans and Abbott (1998) characterise the significant changes in the UK system as increasing student numbers or "the massification of higher education" and the greater centralised control of the state, accompanied by intense concern over quality assurance. As they point out, "at the core of these changes has been the government's wish to increase the take-up of university education by people representing a broad spectrum of the population" (Evans & Abbott, 1998, p. 8). This type of change is also evident in New Zealand. University education, and to a lesser extent polytechnic education, has moved away from its élite base to encourage the participation of a wider range of adults. The polytechnics have always had a diverse range of students (Zepke, 1996), so charges of élitism have not usually been thrown at them.

Pluralism in higher education has put pressure on our systems to change. For instance, there is greater awareness of the need to bridge marginalised students (e.g. Maori and Pacifika students) into the system and to retain them once they are there. Even in traditional universities such as Auckland there have been bridging or staircasing programmes, for example New Start and Wellesley, to increase the probability of success. Age-mature students, an increasing proportion of students in higher education, can participate in these programmes and maximise their chances of academic success. Most higher education institutions recognise the 'typical' tertiary education student is stereotyped as a high-achieving, white, middle-class adolescent fresh from seventh form. This stereotype now has dubious validity. Fortunately, in line with current expressions of the importance of lifelong learning, adults of any age and background may find themselves engaged in general or vocational education provided by either the state or private education agencies.

Another consequence of greater diversity of students has been the struggle to retain what most tertiary teachers would see as decent working conditions. A major problem for all educators is having to deal with "the intensification of work" (Apple, 1981) associated with higher education institutions chasing EFTS (the colloquial term for equivalent full-time students) while trying to retain quality of provision. It is no accident that quality assurance mechanisms have coincided with increased numbers and types of students. In much of higher education, behaviourism is to the fore in the use of learning outcomes, performance indicators and staff appraisal. These are not necessarily negative strategies (they can be introduced in a humanistic fashion) but they are suggestive of an overall structure of surveillance and diminished teacher autonomy. As noted by Evans and Abbott (1998, p. 14), "the reforms designed to increase quality and accountability and the creation of a mass system of higher education have imposed heavier workloads on individual members of staff". This is evident in New Zealand today, for example in the plight of secondary teachers whose work conditions are deplored by citizens wanting a decent school system for their adolescents.

As part of the dismantling of an élite higher education system, there has been a diversification in the types of institutions and what they offer. While there is still a hierarchy of types of educational providers (a large traditional university holds greater status than a small regional polytechnic) and the types of knowledge taught (a medical degree has more status than a hairdressing course), the distinctions seem less stark than in the past. In addition, better articulation between institutions (for example cross credits and recognition of prior learning), now enables students to move more freely within the overall system. So, Lockwood Smith's (former Minister of Education) notion of 'seamless education' has become something of a reality. In particular, the New Zealand Qualifications Framework has established greater transparency of learning outcomes and enabled clearer staircasing to occur, principally through a unit standards approach.

Technocratic or professional teaching?

Depending on our values and beliefs, our views on what is occurring in higher education may be positive or negative. Codd (1997) argues that a new language of learning has been introduced which reflects the economic origins of recent educational reforms. Terms such as 'consumer', 'efficiency', 'audit' and 'competence' have entered our day-to-day vocabulary in a hegemonic way (i.e. we accept the language uncritically). He argues that there is a political struggle between two opposing views of teaching. Those who accept the reforms he labels as 'technocratic-reductionist' with respect to their view of teaching. From this perspective, teaching is treated as producing specific learning outcomes in an administrative context of 'efficient management' where the teacher is viewed as a 'skilled technician'. On the other hand, from a 'professional-contextualist' perspective, the goal of teaching is to produce a person with diverse human capabilities in an administrative context of 'professional leadership' where the teacher is seen as a 'reflective practitioner'. Codd further emphasises the differences between these two paths by alluding to the underlying motivation of these two types of educators. In the technical domain, teachers are assumed to be motivated by extrinsic rewards such as merit pay; in the professional track, teachers are intrinsically motivated, deriving their satisfaction from involvement in a social enterprise, creating a learning community. In most settings, there are elements of both positions that are not necessarily in opposition. For example, a teacher may be a skilled technician but operate from a professional attitude of enhancing the capabilities of students. I think Codd's distinction between two types of teachers help us to appreciate the effects of national educational changes and their impact on educators' work contexts.

Understanding adult and higher education from an institutional context

While higher education institutions share some common characteristics, each organisation has its individual character. This specific character is framed by history and philosophy. For the moment, consider the very different histories of some agencies in this diverse field. The Workers' Educational Association (WEA), transplanted here in 1915 from its British origins (Dakin, 1992), began as a mechanism to ensure that workers could access education relevant to their lives. Auckland University of Technology (AUT) is a new university that unapologetically has its roots in technical and vocational education. Both these adult education institutions come from a largely vocational tradition. In contrast, the Whitecliffe College of Arts and Design in Ponsonby and the University of Auckland have very different antecedents in a more liberal and progressive tradition. Each institution has its own unique history (occasionally herstory) in which teachers locate themselves and work.

We need to understand the philosophies of institutions (and prominent individuals within them) to get to grips with their character. The purpose of each of the above institutions is quite distinctive, and often publicised in a mission statement or a charter. These statements are likely to reflect the type of institution (for example, a university or a polytechnic) and the actual geographical location (an urban or rural constituency). The institution's surrounding region will also play a significant role in helping it to establish its particular identity. Yet for larger institutions, and with the growth of distance learning, the notion of geographical boundaries is almost meaningless. For instance, in Auckland City there are numerous higher education providers – Auckland, AUT and Massey being the prominent universities at this stage. These universities try to capture market niches by referring to their particular histories, major philosophical positions and distinctive contemporary character.

In the past, one of the defining features of an institution was whether it was established for service (funded by the government) or for profit (in the case of private providers). This demarcation appears less significant these days amid the proliferation of providers because, as critics point out (e.g. Peters, 1997), they behave much more like corporations and need to hunt for extra finance to boost their research capabilities. Conversely, private providers want to provide a quality learning experience for their students in addition to making a profit to survive. In other words, economic and educational goals of tertiary education institutions often intersect and collide in the bid to achieve both short term and longer-term strategic goals. Much of the internal turmoil within specific departments or schools in tertiary institutions amounts to having to do as much as possible with very limited funds – maintaining the quality of education for students in an environment of depleting resources. This seems to be a challenge all educators face in New Zealand.

Teachers of adults do not always find themselves in an *educational* organisation. Learning can occur anywhere in life, in both informal and non-formal contexts, as well as informal learning establishments. Some educators work for agencies in which education is a peripheral activity or one subsumed in the major focus of the organisation. For example, a museum may identify itself primarily as a place to display artifacts and collections rather than as a learning organisation. (This would be a pity because the orientation of the institution would be quite different if it were to promote itself as a learning organisation.) Many people employed by museums are adult educators even if they and their employer do not recognise this. In the best-case scenario, such workers would be educated for both their museum profession and their education profession.

The culture of an organisation, or of a sub-unit within it, can make or break our commitment as educators. By 'culture', I mean the norms, expectations and ways of doing things in a place. In this instance, the culture of a department in an institution is probably the most vital ingredient in a teacher's ongoing motivation and commitment to the profession. This is where the rubber hits the road. In my experience, effective leadership is a key factor in promoting dialogue among staff and in helping to create a shared vision to which people are committed. But it is not the only component for success. Good communication channels, clear job descriptions, effective feedback to teachers on performance, collegiality, fun in the workplace and sufficient resources to do the job are important too. While the parent institution sets the general parameters for how a department may manoeuvre, there is still relative autonomy for the sub-unit. In my own case at the Auckland University of Technology, the School of Education is one of several in a Faculty of Arts; the faculty being one of four in the institution. Part of the skill for middle managers such as myself is to create sufficient space for teachers to enjoy the job, to gain professional development opportunities and to engage in creative and rewarding teaching. Too often, as a result of insufficient funding, complaints about poor working conditions outnumber positive comments about what staff valued from their day's work.

Hence, the institutional context can have a pervasive influence over all staff. The bottom line of providing excellent service to students often results from the sterling effort of committed teachers who frequently have fewer resources than they need. I believe that a positive outcome really depends on the creation of a collegial culture of co-operation that builds on the special characteristics of the parent institution.

Understanding adult and higher education at the 'local' level

At the *local* level – the actual classroom or location in which teaching takes place – the constraints and opportunities of the situation show in the work of the teacher. It would be easy to let the constraints of globalisation, government policy, national interests, institutional frameworks and departmental culture overcome our commitment to do better for our students. While I acknowledge the constraints of the environment, and am openly critical of some of them with peers and students, it is my role as an educator to evoke excitement for learning and to foster students' inquiring minds. In adult education, there are many inspirational voices of emancipation to draw upon. Myles Horton, bell hooks, Jane Thompson, Paulo Freire, Ira Shor and Jack Mezirow come to mind as people with a liberatory and self-reflective approach to teaching. We need to be comfortable with who we are as individuals and professionals before we can encourage students to fulfill their potential. A good starting point is to establish a working philosophy (see Apps (1973) and Pratt (1998) for some guidelines). In this we make explicit our own values and beliefs about effective teaching. If we do not have a firm statement of our intent for teaching, how do we know whether we have progressed or regressed or whether there is a positive relationship between our teaching and students' learning?

My own position as a teacher is based on Paulo Freire's and Ira Shor's work (e.g. Freire, 1984, 1985; Shor, 1980, 1992). Of course, this approach is modified to the specific context in which I find myself. Teaching from a set of adult learning principles, especially those based on a more radical pedagogy, is not always compatible with a higher education context. This is because principles are often expressed as 'ideals' to be followed and because higher education is frequently reduced to how to impart a curriculum to the largest number of students in the most economical way – usually by lecture. I have written about how effective principles can be adapted from Freire's work to apply to a higher education context (Findsen, 1999, p. 76). I restate them here as a set of guidelines for adult educators working from a transformative learning framework:

- An adult educator does not impose knowledge on others but works with them to jointly construct knowledge.
- Adults should be encouraged to take increasing responsibility for their own learning and not be dependent on the teacher (outside expert) to interpret their world for them.
- Teachers and learners are co-learners in a situation where mutual respect must operate.
- Learning is not something done *to* learners but is a process, and the result of what learners do *for* themselves.
- The teacher does not enforce choice but rather encourages learners to make decisions and choices for themselves.
- Responsibility and freedom are primarily in the hands of learners, but the teacher is not exempt from exercising responsibility and on occasions intervening in the situation.

This framework for transformative learning assumes certain teacher capabilities: prepared to be self-analytical; to consider curriculum as a negotiated process rather than a given; to be participatory in the use of teaching–learning methods; to be democratic in decision-making; to situate knowledge in the reality of students' lives; and to be a risk-taker. In my own classroom pedagogy, I try to take no knowledge as a *given*, as something that is unchallengeable, but rather as something that is socially constructed and is subject to criticism. I advise students that we are examining what, for the moment, passes for conventional knowledge. As a technique, I quite often ask students to brainstorm their ideas on a topic as a whole group (recorded on the whiteboard) or as small groups (recorded on large posters and reported back to the entire class). For example, in looking at what constitutes 'effective teachers', I drew upon their collective ideas (some of which we argued about) before declaring what some experts had written. Very often the 'two knowledges' coincide. Their collective viewpoints, based first on individual then shared experiences of effective teachers, and those of the expert recorded in a book, are similar. This validates students' knowledge and demystifies the authority's position. Again, we need to be selective about when to use particular approaches, depending on the ultimate purpose of the teaching.

In summary, here are some considerations for a classroom teacher wanting to promote transformative learning.

- Be yourself and make explicit your values and beliefs about why and how you are approaching a topic.
- As a group, establish ground-rules that allow ideas to be challenged and individuals to be supported.
- Where feasible, use participatory learning approaches and techniques that validate the students' own knowledge of a topic but which also challenge them to inquire further.
- Do not consider knowledge as inert but as something to be created both individually and collectively.
- Reflect upon the setting in which you find yourself, especially the backgrounds of the students, and develop a collegial atmosphere that enables you to incorporate experiences from the group.
- Think carefully about how to best manage group dynamics, being conscious of cultural variations among students.
- Connect local issues with global trends so that issues are exposed in their fuller economic and political implications.

Conclusion

I have explored contextual aspects of adult educators' environments using a multi-layered approach. I outlined the effects of globalisation and their implications for us in New Zealand, to make them more transparent. I considered the advent of economic rationalism in our political economy and how instrumental approaches to education often appear as common sense and natural. One way to avoid an introverted, narrow approach to teaching is to adopt an 'internationalist' strategy, wherein we continually connect local issues to the wider scene of global justice. While overseas trends, such as the language of reductionism, inevitably find their way into our systems, there are other important features of this country and its people that help to establish and maintain our distinctive identity. As a teacher in the New Zealand context I advocate social equity and justice as valuable attributes to be retained.

At an institutional level it is necessary to establish a collegial and supportive context in which to work, even if working conditions are not ideal. We need to advocate strongly for a professional approach to our work rather than have it reduced to a set of technical skills. While our work is always coloured by the particular historical and philosophical stance of the parent institution, there is still considerable autonomy at the departmental level to collectively organise for more humanistic approaches to our colleagues and students. Within the immediate teaching environment, we can employ more liberatory approaches to teaching that encourage our students to think critically. We can develop a 'learning community' in which we challenge traditional knowledge and develop new knowledge based on a negotiated curriculum. While there are undoubtedly constraints in our system of adult and higher education that need to be continually fought against, we also need to spend time on building alternative structures and strategies to maximise the quality of students' learning.

Some suggested activities

These activities correspond to the sequence of discussion in this chapter.

- Using the five fields within adult and community education, find examples from your own localities. What are the proportions practising in each field? What dominates provision? What is less visible?
- Consider how economic rationalism has changed the face of adult and higher education in New Zealand. Should privatisation of this field be encouraged further? What evidence is there to support deregulation or more advanced regulation in higher education?
- What features of globalisation are evident in your adult and higher education context? What effects (positive or negative) are evident in your locality?
- What evidence do you see of regionalism in your local context? Has this been in opposition to or in support of globalisation?
- Collins (1998) suggests some strategies for being an internationalist in our teaching of adults. Which are appropriate to your teaching? What other strategies might you try?
- How has the massification of higher education affected your local adult and tertiary institutions? How effective have institutions' responses been to this new pluralism?
- Debate whether teaching has become more or less technocratic. What are the qualities of a professional adult teacher? What are the limits on you being an effective professional?
- Find out about the history of the agency you work for or have regular contact with. How has this history affected what happens in the institution today?
- How would you describe the culture of your organisation? What features of this culture need improvement to encourage better teaching?
- Write a brief statement on your personal philosophy of teaching adults. In what ways does your practice match your espoused beliefs?
- What is meant by a 'critical pedagogy'? If you teach from such a perspective, what strategies would you adopt with adult students? What opportunities and constraints are there in your context to teaching in such a way?
- Consider the extent to which principles of transformative learning can be accommodated in a tertiary education context.

Further reading

- Michael Collins' (1998) book *Critical Crosscurrents in Education* provides an excellent source for contemporary issues in education, with special relevance to adult learning contexts.
- For a very good practical view of British teaching and learning in higher education, look at Linda Evans and Ian Abbott's book *Teaching and Learning in Higher Education*. In particular, it provides a sound analysis of how the massification of higher education has impacted on teachers.

Making Sense of Our Contexts

- As a starting point for encouraging transformative learning through a critical pedagogical approach, Ira Shor's books provide plenty of ideas for imaginative teaching. His book *Critical Teaching and Everyday Life* is a great base from which to explore this kind of teaching further. Do not be put off by the date (1980) – it is as relevant now as it ever was.

Glossary

Behaviourism: a philosophical position that suggests that we can shape people's behaviour by changing elements in their environment.

Critical analysis: an ongoing review of a phenomenon that examines fundamental assumptions and the 'taken for granted'.

Economic rationalism: a system that privileges economic arguments over others and redefines issues in mainly economic terms.

Hegemony: a term coined by Italian Antonio Gramsci to explain the ways control is maintained in societies. Generally, the state maintains control through consent from citizens. When this breaks down the state may bring in force (e.g. military) to quell dissent.

Ideology: a set of prevailing beliefs in a society or culture. For example, the 'ideology of individualism' relates to how North American society reveres the rights and choices of the individual as distinct from the collective.

Learning organisation: an organisation that places learning at the forefront of all that it does. Every part of the organisation (individuals, work-teams, departments) has a responsibility to promote learning opportunities from which the organisation will benefit, for example, by better service or increased profits.

Liberatory education: an educational practice through which people are empowered to take action to improve society, usually as part of a collective.

Negotiated curriculum: a teacher works collaboratively with students to develop a programme of study rather than deciding what students need to learn.

Neoliberalism: a system of beliefs and practices that promotes individual decision-making and choice.

Pedagogy: the approach to teaching and learning used in a particular context.

Pluralism: refers to the diversity of students in educational institutions with respect to their age, ethnicity and socio-economic background.

Privatisation: describes how education and other social services have become controlled increasingly by private individuals rather than the state.

Reflective practitioners: educators who engage in critical reflection on their practice through a continual action–reflection cycle.

Seamless education: a notion promoted by former Minister of Education Lockwood Smith who wanted to diminish the divide between different forms of education, for example between the upper end of secondary education and entrance levels for tertiary education.

Transformative learning: focuses on significant, positive changes in meanings held by individuals or groups. It is distinct from instrumental learning, which concentrates on learning for jobs or technocratic purposes.

Working philosophy: a set of personal beliefs about teaching and learning which are embedded in and tested out in practice.

References

Apple, M. W. (1981). Reproduction, Contestation and Curriculum: An essay in self-criticism. *Interchange, 12* (2–3), 27–47.

Apps, J. W. (1973). *Toward a Working Philosophy of Adult Education*. Syracuse, New York: Syracuse University Publications in Continuing Education.

Codd, J. A. (1997). Knowledge, Qualifications and Higher Education: A critical view. M. Olssen, & K. Morris-Matthews (eds), *Education Policy in New Zealand: The 1990s and Beyond* (pp. 130–144). Palmerston North: Dunmore Press.

Collins, M. (1998). *Critical Crosscurrents in Education*. Malabar, Florida: Krieger Publishing Co.

Dakin, J. (1992). Derivative and Innovative Modes in New Zealand Adult Education. *New Zealand Journal of Adult Learning, 20* (2), 29–49.

Dale, R., & Robertson, S. (1997). 'Resiting' the Nation, 'Resiting' the State: Globalisation effects on education policy in New Zealand. M. Olssen, & K. Morris-Matthews (eds), *Education Policy in New Zealand: The 1990s and Beyond* (pp. 209–227). Palmerston North: Dunmore Press.

Evans, L., & Abbott, I. (1998). *Teaching and Learning in Higher Education*. London: Cassell.

Findsen, B. (1996). The Education of Adult and Community Educators. J. Benseman, B. Findsen, & M. Scott (eds), *The Fourth Sector* (pp. 297–312). Palmerston North: Dunmore Press.

Findsen, B. (1999). Freire and Adult Education: Principles and practice. P. Roberts (ed.), *Paulo Freire, Politics and Pedagogy: Reflections from Aotearoa New Zealand*. Palmerston North, NZ: Dunmore Press.

Findsen, B., & Harre-Hindmarsh, J. (1996). Adult and Community Education in the Universities. J. Benseman, B. Findsen, & M. Scott (eds), *The Fourth Sector* (pp. 193–209). Palmerston North: Dunmore Press.

Freire, P. (1984). *Pedagogy of the Oppressed*. New York: Continuum.

Freire, P. (1985). *The Politics of Education: Culture, power and liberation*. South Hadley, Massachusetts: Bergin & Garvey.

Peters, M. (1997). Neo-liberalism, Privatisation and the University in New Zealand. M. Olssen, & K. Morris-Matthews (eds), *Education Policy in New Zealand: The 1990s and Beyond* (pp. 228–250). Palmerston North: Dunmore Press.

Pratt, D. &. A. (1998). *Five Perspectives on Teaching in Adult and Higher Education*. Malabar, Florida: Krieger Publishing Co.

Shor, I. (1980). *Critical Teaching and Everyday Life*. Montreal: Black Rose Books.

Shor, I. (1992). *Empowering Education: Critical Teaching for Social Change*. Chicago: The University of Chicago Press.

Snook, I. (1989). *Educational Reform in New Zealand: What is Going On?* Trentham, NZ: New Zealand Association for Research in Education.

Stalker, J. (1996). New Zealand Adult and Community Education: An international perspective. J. Benseman, B. Findsen, & M. Scott (eds), *The Fourth Sector*. Palmerston North: Dunmore Press.

Tobias, R. (1996). What Do Adult and Community Educators Share in Common? J. Benseman, B. Findsen, & M. Scott (eds), *The Fourth Sector* (pp. 38–64). Palmerston North: Dunmore Press.

Zepke, N. (1996). The Role of Polytechnics in Community Education. J. Benseman, B. Findsen, & M. Scott (eds), *The Fourth Sector*. Palmerston North: Dunmore Press.

— Chapter 11 —

Teaching and Learning in the Global Village

Nick Zepke

Introduction

We are observing a Tourism class. Students have taken the roles of tourist operators. Their task is to come up with a recipe for keeping 'Western' tourists happy. They brainstorm a list of ideas that includes:

- instant communication with loved ones back home
- contact with different and unique cultures
- access to people who speak English
- access to familiar foods and drinks
- local people who understand the needs of tourists
- availability of money machines and other banking facilities
- easy and unusual shopping opportunities.

The teacher observes that the list contains some services that are purely local and others that are global in scope and asks, "How can tourist operators provide such services?" A moment's silence follows. Then one of the students replies that anywhere in the world we can enjoy both the local and the global at the same time. Another says that communications, particularly computer technologies, are so advanced that instant connection between continents is possible. A third observes that things are particularly good for Americans, as corporate giants like Coca-Cola, Microsoft and Bank of America can be found all over the world. A fourth student concludes that we seem to be living in a kind of global village: a place where local customs still apply but where global influences, too, are very important.

The term 'global village' stands in the place of 'globalisation'. Both terms describe a world:

Teaching and Learning in the Global Village

- networked by electronic communication technologies such as computers and television;
- dominated by a marketplace outlook valuing individual enterprise, free trade and huge transnational businesses;
- immersed in a global popular culture ranging from music to film.

It seems, no matter where we live, we are connected to other members of the global village by the fruits of Western, particularly American, enterprise. This picture of an orderly, connected world is, of course, illusion. Seething beneath the seemingly calm surface are many points of difference and contradiction.

- Benefits are shared unequally; some regions and people get poorer as others enrich themselves. Various members of the village community break its conventions to advantage themselves.
- Local cultures resist the global blanket by asserting their own traditional religious, legal, political, economic and technological ways. Life in the global village is a living process with uncertainty the only constant. In trying to describe the process of globalisation, Perry (1998, p. 167) decided that it is only ever "glimpsed, but not grasped".

Why is knowing about the global village important for you? The scale of the global village is one answer. Whether you live in its poor, outer reaches or rich west, whether you accept it or fight it, you cannot escape it. The complexity and contradictions of the process provide another answer. Its effects on our lives are never simple. Free trade brings us magical goods to enrich our lives while at the same time our long-term existence is threatened by a dangerous breakdown in environmental health. Science and technology prolong our lives while millions don't have the means to live. While we anticipate the changes wrought by new wonders of science, we regret the loss of traditions they replace. In short, as teachers we work in a maelstrom of change, a maelstrom we must understand in order to help our students navigate its turbulence. In my view, attempting to make sense of globalisation is an ethical responsibility for teachers. In this chapter:

- I offer some bird's-eye views of the social, economic and political processes that make the global village work.
- I then examine education in the global village with a particular focus on knowledge, education's keystone.
- Finally, I discuss teaching practice in the global village environment.

Bird's-eye views of the global village

This section looks at the global village as a bird looks at a landscape, picking out notable features. Four features of the global village are glimpsed: economics, technology, diversity and knowledge.

Economics

Economics drives the global village. Western products and services, like telecommunications, finance and electronics, penetrate and overwhelm national and cultural borders. Huge multinational concerns, often bigger than nation states, shift capital and the sources of labour around the world to suit their bottom line. Ever more sophisticated goods and services result. These require applied research and a highly skilled labour force to develop and maintain them. Consequently knowledge and skills become key sources of competitive advantage in a global marketplace.

Underpinning this is the view that economics holds sway over all aspects of life; that purely economic and technical methods can solve all social problems. This thinking reduces all human actions to economic explanations. Human behaviour only serves self-interest. In pursuit of self-interest, we produce goods and services for the marketplace. In this process we always compete for dominance. No one, including the state, should interfere with the free operation of the marketplace.

We feel this economic imperative personally when we hear the language of economic growth and survival from our leaders. "Compete in the global village or die" is the message. Even closer to home we hear, "Develop courses that put bums on seats and prepare students for the market". Educational providers have become businesses selling a staple commodity – education.

Technology

Technology supports capitalism. Telecommunication and computer technologies shrink boundaries and facilitate market penetration. Deals are negotiated and completed with the push of a button. Daily television images demonstrate the wonders of capitalism and suggest goods we should buy, goals we should aspire to. The confusing cultural messages of Western popular music infiltrate every nook of the village. Engineering marvels, like the modern aeroplane, speed goods to market and bombs to those parts of the village that don't comply with the world order. Such technologies have an ever-increasing impact on education.

The Internet, arguably, has the greatest impact. Prestigious universities offer programmes worldwide. They employ leading experts and teachers in state-of-the-art productions in partnership with computer houses like Microsoft and media giants like Turner Broadcasting. The sheer technical excellence of their programming represents the visible hand of capitalism in education. The Internet also encourages diversity. Learners can escape the confines of any virtual course and explore a vast variety of learning resources, including those putting alternative views. Using e-mails, they can consult peers and contact experts excluded by their teachers. A student enrolled in an adult education course in New Zealand contacted one of the world figures in the field, asked a question and received an answer almost instantly. Searching 'adult education', the same student could also have gained access to unlimited pornographic sites.

Diversity

The global village is not entirely in the thrall of Western values and practices. While Western ways have spread over the globe, this very happening creates pressures for recognising difference. The seeming conformity of the global village has changed but not removed diversity (Jameson, 1998). Yes, globalisation represents a triumph of capitalism and the marketplace; but market capitalism itself also encourages local challenges to a white, male-dominated, 'Eurocentric' culture.

Modern communications enable the emergence of different ways of seeing the world. For example, First People in Africa, the Americas, Australia and New Zealand assert their own traditional cultures via television, music recordings, the Internet and education. In New Zealand, tino rangatiratanga (self-determination) for the indigenous Maori people was built into the Treaty of Waitangi in 1840. This defined the relationship between Maori and colonial Britain. Maori have long proposed a bilingual approach in education to safeguard Maori language and lobbied for the creation of higher education institutions controlled by Maori. While bilingualism in higher education has not been achieved, Maori universities, called Wananga, have. Funded by the state, they offer degrees in Maori language and teach a range of subjects based on Maori knowledge such as Maori law, medicine and philosophy.

Knowledge

Globalisation has changed the kinds of knowledge valued in the village. Knowledge underpins capitalism, produces technology and safeguards diversity. As teachers we are deeply involved in its construction. But the whole meaning of the word 'knowledge' is not as straightforward as it appears. It can mean truth, information, fact, understanding acquired through experience, rational conviction, intuition, justified true belief, absence of ignorance. At least some of these meanings assume that knowledge is provisional, relevant to its own context but not beyond this. It therefore undergoes constant re-interpretation in a continuous debate between competing claims.

Because commerce is central to the global economy, much of what is taught in formal education espouses technical knowledge to satisfy economic needs. Knowing how to do and make things useful to the market becomes a priority. Formal adult education's mission is to create efficient 'autonomous choosers' – people who are able both to sell their knowledge and buy its products in the marketplace. But other knowledge claims flourish also. Inner knowledge gained through intuition, spirituality and belonging, for example, is essential in validating the inherited understandings and genealogies of first-people cultures. It also brings into the spotlight the special nature of women's knowledge that has not been valued in the commercial marketplace.

Knowing the global village

To make sense of all the complexities of teaching in the global village is beyond the scope of one chapter in a book. So we will focus on one key feature of education –

knowledge. Knowledge enables the global village to be, to maintain itself and to grow. It is also at the heart of teaching and learning: of everything we do, feel and believe.

The competing claims for true knowledge

Just think about some of the most ordinary things you do consciously – getting dressed, going to work, cooking; relating to colleagues, friends, partners; working, studying, teaching; listening to God, nature, your inner self. You cannot do these things without knowledge. Yet we rarely give the nature of knowledge a second thought. We assume that it is just there – safe, certain, true and without question.

Yet questions about knowledge are like fleas on a pet: abundant, alive, active, irritating, challenging, while largely unseen. Every philosopher worthy of the name seems to have said something about knowledge. Opinions, though, have varied greatly and many schools of thought can be identified. Realists, relativists and fallibilists are just three of the many fleas on the beast.

- If you teach in the traditional 'hard' sciences you may be expected to take a realist or objective view of knowledge.
- If you teach in the community or in a social field you could well lean, when pressed, towards a relativist view.
- If you teach in areas at the leading edge of globalisation – business, technology, education, 'soft' science – you may well confess to being fallibilist.

Realism ...

... was the dominant tradition in Western thought well into the twentieth century. Essentially it holds that true knowledge corresponds to a real world independent of social perception and construction. Scientific methods became the preferred way of testing and inferring knowledge from sense experience. Science allows us to explain the reliability of observations and inferences and so reveal truths. The scientific view of knowledge was fine-tuned by a group of thinkers who rose to prominence in the 1920s and were dominant until the 1960s, at least in English-speaking countries. This group recognised scientific observation as the only form of knowledge. Nothing in the universe can be known if it cannot be known scientifically. They even argued that everything beyond the reach of science is meaningless.

Relativism ...

... originated in fifth-century Greece. Sophists argued that nothing exists outside of the perceptions of individuals. So no person's opinion is more correct than another's. The truth-value of knowledge is relative to whatever is accepted as true by people and cultures. This line of 'relativist' thinking, long rubbished by realists, revived in the late nineteenth and early twentieth centuries. Some thinkers, Nietzsche for example, denied that knowledge exists as the representation of a real world. It is never more than interpretation. To many scholars working in the 'new' sociology of knowledge, knowledge is socially constructed to suit the interests of dominant groups. A number of thinkers have tried to bring order to the confusing. Habermas, for example, visualised three kinds of human interests that give rise to different kinds of knowledge. There is technical knowledge that informs the world of work; practical knowledge that informs communications; emancipating knowledge that leads to empowerment.

Fallibilism ...

... moderates both 'relativist' and 'realist' positions. Kuhn (1994) gives a very persuasive account of how beliefs in science change over time, sometimes fundamentally. He argues that normally science is organised under a governing set of rules and practices – a paradigm. There are times when the scientific community abandons one paradigm for another. Paradigm-change can only occur when anomalies are so numerous and fundamental that there is a general sense of crisis. But a new paradigm will only be acceptable if it deals satisfactorily with most of the anomalies. Kuhn's work challenged the very idea that scientific findings correspond to truth and put realists on the defensive. Popper (1992) helped to restore the realist position somewhat. He argued that there is a reality, even if we cannot know it definitively and can only guess at its truth. Truth operates as a standard at which to aim. We cannot ever know with certainty whether we have reached it. This line of argument mirrors that of Kuhn while maintaining the idea of an external reality. Our perceptions and theories are merely attempts to describe reality.

Two questions could now be asked:

- What is your own position on the nature of knowledge and how might this affect how you teach?
- How do these competing claims about the nature of knowledge affect education in the global village?

The first question is for your reflection. We will explore the second together.

The politics of official knowledge

A small case study allows us to address the second question. The New Zealand Qualifications Authority (NZQA) is a statutory body set up to regulate a National Qualifications Framework (NQF). Unit Standards are the building blocks of the NQF. They are written as competencies and describe actions, processes and operations derived from knowledge, skills and attitudes. In the Framework sub-field of *Adult Education and Training*, for example, unit titles describe operations like "write job procedures for training adults" and "provide guidance for individual adult trainees".

Such renditions of learning are firmly planted in the plot of instrumental/operational knowledge. They enable people to carry out practical and useful work in the global village.

Unit Standards have attracted both champions and detractors. Positions seem to be taken, at least partially, on the basis of self-interest. Traditional occupations (medical doctors) and educational élites (universities) are generally opposed. In part at least, this could be in response to the threat the NQF poses to their traditional dominance. Opponents malign competency standards as denoting merely good or satisfactory work. They seek excellence – performance well beyond competency standards.

Those with little traditional power tend to support the educational changes promised by the Framework. Emerging occupations, such as alternative health professionals and private training providers, especially among Maori, champion the Framework. They see in competency standards transparent, practical, useful and democratic measures of performance.

This analysis, however, is too simple. Deep ideological divisions over the nature of knowledge also contribute to the debate. In New Zealand a long established consensus about education – that the state evens out inequalities in a market economy – broke down in the late 1960s. This resulted in fierce debate about the nature and purpose of education among competing ideologies. A 'new right', based on doctrines of economic rationalism, wanted to privatise education. A 'new left' wished to correct education's tendency to reproduce social and economic inequalities. A third group held to the ideas of the previous consensus. It still pursues the ideal of equity achieved through the state (McCulloch, 1990). It supports the work of NZQA, as agent of the state, in its drive to use operational knowledge to achieve greater equity. Both the 'new right' and the 'new left', however, reject aspects of the NQF. The 'new left' regrets the Framework's blindness to critical knowledge leading to social change and a just society. The 'new right' wants the Framework to embrace excellence by ranking learners' efficiency to further economic usefulness and conformity to what is.

While the case study comes from Aotearoa/New Zealand, this struggle between competing interests over what should count as true knowledge is played out throughout the global village. Wherever and whatever you teach, you are involved in this struggle. Apple (1995) refers to this struggle as the *politics of official knowledge*. He believes that technical knowledge supporting wealth creation and economic development is winning out. Certainly the latest buzzword, the 'knowledge economy', suggests he is right. The 'knowledge economy' stands for education's role in developing people who can contribute immediately and actively to economic and technical development.

But even within the privileged technical domain, different knowledge types battle. There is Mode 1 knowledge, for example (Giddens, 1990). This includes knowledge from traditional disciplines like conventional science. Mode 1 knowledge is said to be losing its pre-eminence to Mode 2 knowledge. Note that science numbers in universities are shrinking. Mode 2 knowledge is contextual, applied, trans-disciplinary and diverse. It is accountable to the market; what the global market wants and values defines its nature and quality. Note the oversupply of students in business, law and technology-related courses.

Ignorance: Knowledge's useful shadow

Many of us teach in this technical, 'how to' domain. We usually teach to learning outcomes that specify precisely what is to be learnt. Outcomes focus on what is known and ignore what is not known. Indeed, ignorance is portrayed as some kind of unmentionable disease. Blake *et al.* (2000) warn that to ignore or decry ignorance is a grave mistake. They argue that recognition of its existence enables knowledge to be broadened and, indeed, to be raised to a higher order. To them, knowledge and ignorance go together. We do not make the most of our knowledge unless we are also aware of our ignorance. They assert that "someone who knows how much she doesn't know lives in a 'bigger, wider world' than someone who has no such awareness of ignorance" (Blake *et al.*, 2000, p. 210).

I can relate to this as I reflect about teaching adults in the global village. I realise I know a lot about different forms of knowledge – technical, practical and emancipatory – but am largely ignorant of spiritual knowledge. I know that by filling that gap I will access even more knowledge – about being in the world and in nature; about being a citizen teacher in the global village.

By seeing ignorance in this way we can begin to think about it as a higher form of knowledge. Blake and colleagues (2000, p. 213) even suggest, "ignorance is not extraneous to knowledge. It is its undetachable shadow ... A true appreciation of ignorance is the deeper part of wisdom". I go along with the notion that valuing ignorance is wise. Realising I was ignorant of spiritual knowledge encouraged me to find out about it. I even found a non-religious definition that appealed to me: "an awareness of something greater than ourselves, a sense that we are connected to all human beings and to all of creation" (English & Gillen, 2000, p. 1).

This has opened for me the possibility of exploring the spirituality of others in the global village. This has both identified further yawning gaps and opened up new areas of exploration. I realise the limits of my knowledge about reflection, for example, as I start to explore meditation as a reflective technique. I have also learned much about the 'unknown' pane in my Johari Window while beginning to recognise how much I have yet to learn (see Chapter 1 for more about Reflection and the Johari Window). Recognition of my own ignorance has enabled me to learn about life in the global village. I will be a better teacher for it.

Kerwin (1994) teases ignorance into six different types.

- Known unknowns – include all the things we know we don't know. We know that we don't know how to cure AIDS. I know that I don't know everything about the global village, or teaching or reflection.
- Unknown unknowns – include all the things we don't even know we don't know. There are no handy examples because I don't know any!
- Unknown knowns – includes all the things we know but don't realise we know. Until I started to write Chapter 1, I did not know that I had been doing crude meditation for years.
- Error – includes all the things we think we know but don't. I thought I was up to

date with reflection in learning; after all, I had written two book chapters about it. It took my discovery of meditation and spirituality to recognise my error.
- Taboo – includes all the things in society that we don't want to admit exist. This type of ignorance is particularly painful for me as I have always pursued rational knowledge. The existence of spiritual knowledge distressed me and I did not admit to it for a long time. It was only the discovery of a secular version that persuaded me to drop the taboo.
- Denial – includes all the things in our lives that are too painful to admit exist.

Ignorance, then, is not just a gap, a constraint on knowledge. It is knowledge's companion: a rich source of learning about the nature of knowledge in the global village.

Practice in the global village

You have probably noticed that my glimpses of the global village show a kaleidoscope of ever-changing forms rather than a still photograph of village life. This variable glimpsing leads me to make some very strong assumptions about teaching:

- Teaching does not take place in an isolation tent. It is out in the world, affected by every change and uncertainty out there.
- Teaching takes place in a very unstable world where nothing is what it seems.
- Teaching is effective where it enables students to thrive in the world, to be at ease with all its complications no matter what learning outcomes grace our course prescriptions.
- Teaching cares for the whole person, not just for our rational side, for life in the global village is not always rational.
- Teaching enables learners to make use of what is constant and secure and to work out for themselves how to deal with what is not.
- Teaching is about the absorption and construction of knowledge. Because we will never know all we need to, recognising our ignorance is a priceless asset when taking and making knowledge.

In short, teaching in the global village gives learners access to information that is constant and stable while enabling them to make sense of what is not. The former is achieved by what I call teacher narrative, the latter by learners constructing meaning. In this third section we will explore a model of teaching based on these assumptions.

Towards a model of teaching

In this model, teachers and learners interact in a specific learning context such as a classroom. Their life experiences shape these interactions. Through critical reflection on experiences, teachers and learners alike construct and adapt their views of the world. In the classroom, two processes link teachers and learners. One is *discursive* action, such as teacher explanation, instruction and examples: teacher *narrative,* in short. The other is *interaction*, such as discussion and research. In both processes teacher and learners combine to construct knowledge. On the discursive side it is constructed mainly from narrative provided by the teacher. On the interactive side, the main actor is the learner, with the teacher bridging "the difference between what a person can do by themselves and what they could do with help from people more experienced than themselves" (Vygotsky, cited in Tiffin & Rajasingham, 1995, p. 22).

The model, adapted from Laurillard (1996) visualises what I think happens in my classrooms.

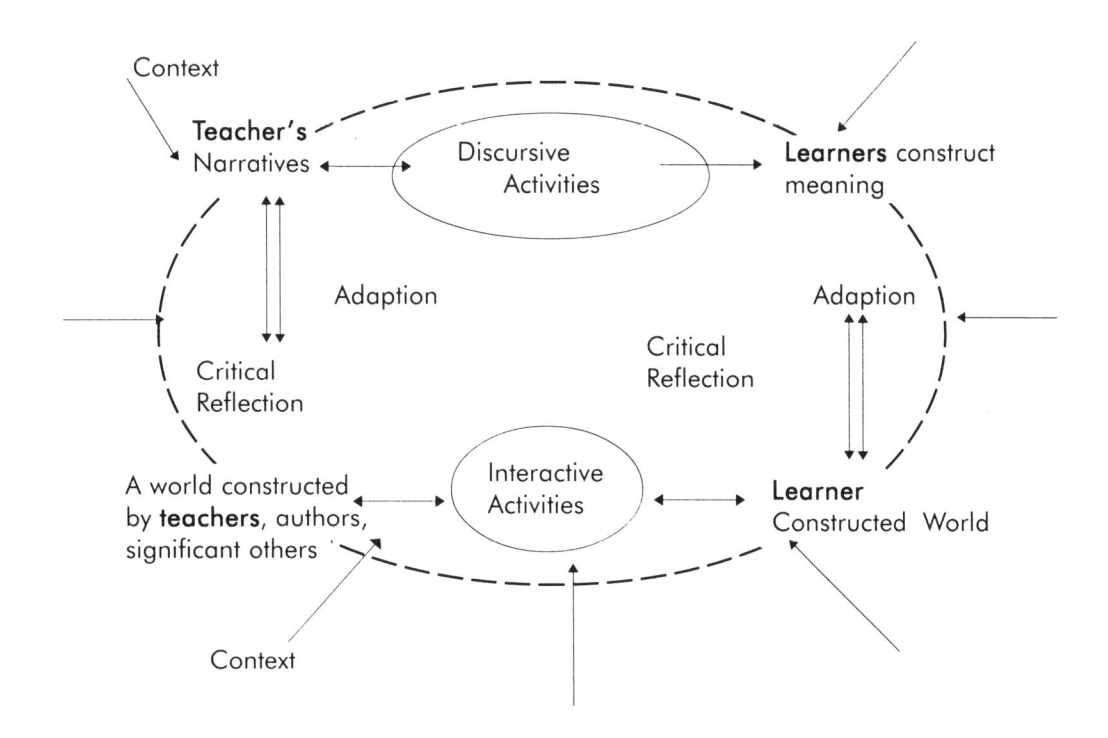

Figure 11.1. A model showing relationships between narrative and meaning construction

Narrative

In Western education, teacher narratives follow set rules. They are expected to flow logically from beginning through the middle to the end. This ideal of teacher narrative comes from Aristotle who insisted that a narrative had to be rational, with logical structure, facts and argument being more important than the personal or language, and with a conclusion flowing from reason. But such rules may be unduly limiting. They privilege rationality over the emotional and spiritual: what is known over what is not. They disadvantage groups of people, such as Maori, who don't place rationality at the pinnacle of learning. They certainly don't recognise the value of ignorance as in the Aristotelian scheme of things there is no pride of place for the unexplainable, unknown and intuitive.

Yet, in my view, narratives could be really effective where they don't deal with certainties where intuition is valuable where ignorance is king. In short, narratives do not have to be 'told' in their entirety by teachers; they can be based on open-ended questions and take the shape of problems to be solved. Problems have a venerable role in teaching. According to Popper, a fallibilist, the very act of learning is initiated by a problem – when a mismatch between expectations and experience occurs (Bailey, 2000). So narratives can be linear and rational, factual and without a sliver of ignorance. They can also be in the form of problems with the teacher asking some key questions.

- Linear and rational narratives include:
  - lectures, demonstrations, textbooks, study guides, documentaries, films;
  - learning outcomes and course scaffolding that enable the outcomes to be achieved, skill-building exercises, assessment tasks;
  - teacher-directed learning on field trips, site visits, going to theatres, films and Internet chat rooms.
- Problem-based teacher narratives are based on open-ended questions using teacher supplied/recommended resources. I use them in three ways:
  - To work through case studies and role-plays. Questions probing these can focus on intuitive solutions as well as rational ones. For example, questions can ask "What do you feel?" as well as "What do you think?".
  - To challenge learners to try out new ways of thinking. My questions put up 'straw(wo)men' which students are invited to attack, defend or critically examine. Such straw(wo)men give structure to discussion as they guide thinking and lay out alternative pathways. For example, "Why will globalisation ruin life as we know it?".
  - To highlight the unknown and enable learners to explore it. Such problems may be couched in open-ended questions to highlight areas of ignorance or uncertainty. For example, "What is a good teacher?"

Constructing meaning

Just as the notion of narrative in teaching is complex, the second pillar of my teaching model, construction of meaning, also requires some unpacking. In practical teaching terms it means simply that students construct meaning from their experiences. But *constructivism* is not as simple as that. You can have at least six different versions. I use both individual and social variations. Individual versions focus on the brain and thinking. The thinking person actively builds up knowledge by adapting experiences and perceptions to new situations. Some constructivists see knowledge from a relativist perspective where a single external reality is but a figment of imagination. Others take a fallibilist view: objective reality exists but we never access that reality.

In the social version, learning takes place in a specific cultural environment. Beliefs, customs and language are determined within a culture that may be defined by ethnicity, class, gender and even academic disciplines. Two cultures may have quite different beliefs, customs and languages, although they may also share some. Japanese and European cultures, for example, have both similarities and differences. In Japan, capitalist 'Coca-cola' culture lives cheek-by-jowl with traditional Japanese culture. Gay and straight cultures interact in any city in the world. Maori culture intertwines with European, even in Maori education institutions for example, when Western technology is used to teach traditional knowledge. Members of cultural communities decide what is true knowledge in their context. The world, like a literary text, is open to many interpretations.

In constructivist classrooms a teacher's role will focus on guiding, encouraging and supporting the learning process "to create information rich environments where students think, explore and construct meaning" (Nicaise & Barnes, cited in Arlidge, 2000, p. 30). Learning will be active, focused on solving authentic problems. Learners are expected to take ownership of their learning and make content relevant to their cultural community's expectations. They will engage with other students and the teacher, working collaboratively to test the viability of their newly constructed knowledge. Knowledge is problematic, subjective and fallible. It is constantly negotiated in the classroom. Teachers and learners play multiple roles. They are at the same time teachers and learners, questioners and reflectors, problem posers and solvers. Knowledge, skills and attitudes required by both teachers and learners include collaboration, goal-setting, questioning, challenging, valuing prior experience, discussing, negotiating, critical thinking and reflecting.

I use four approaches to enable meaning-making through constructivism. They are useful in helping students come to grips with life in the global village.

- I try to create a learning place where students feel empowered to critique and change my narratives and their own views of the world. Critical questioning is the tool I use. (You will find a rationale for this, and possible critical questions, in Chapter 1.)
- In all my courses I teach for difference – different knowledges, different ways to make meaning, different explanations and interpretations in a world where little is certain (see Chapter 5).
- I try to find a way to celebrate ignorance. Reflection on what we don't know is a necessary foundation for building knowledge. In some courses, mapping our ignorance is the starting point.
- A practical project is central to my teaching. This enables groups of learners to construct knowledge from reading, listening, talking, viewing, reflecting or surfing the Internet. These projects:

- are authentic and useful to students
- are based on negotiated topics within set course learning outcomes
- recognise the context within which students work and live
- involve group effort
- involve variable data-gathering: reading, listening, talking, viewing, reflecting on personal or group experiences, surfing the Internet
- are question driven: Why is this happening? What is wrong with it? How can this be improved/fixed? What changes do we want to see? How can changes be achieved?
- Have 'published' results in print form, on video or on the Internet.

The model in practice

Teacher narrative and constructivism are not mutually exclusive. They reinforce one another. I conclude this chapter with an example of how they work together in practice. I have chosen to describe a course I am planning called *Computer-mediated learning in post-school education and training*. This will be a second-year course in a Bachelor of Education taught at a New Zealand university. (If you don't work in a university, don't be put off. I am sure you will find ideas that fit your own situation.) It will be 13 weeks long and have a printed book of readings, but will otherwise be delivered on-line. I have chosen this example because it encapsulates the roles of technology and teaching in the global village.

Narrative

The course will use four quite different narrative techniques.

- *Learning outcomes* define the minimum standards to be achieved. Learning outcomes for this course focus on knowledge construction, skill development and attitude formation about on-line learning in the post-school sector. While I must state learning outcomes, I try to make learners aware that meeting them will only start their learning journeys. They are markers on a learning map; they do not define the learning.
- *Scaffolding for learning* is provided in a number of ways. There is a course timetable that suggests possible topics to study on a week-by-week basis. A written introduction attempts to clarify my various positions in the learning process – as teacher, learner, male, researcher, examiner, technophobe. It also attempts to outline the rationale for course processes and content and I try to explain key concepts and jargon. Reflective exercises focus the learner's attention on key content areas.
- *Readings* provide the narrative content for the course. Each is introduced and questions are provided to enable learners to access the material. The questions are important. They encourage critical reflection and thinking beyond the readings. I find resources on the Internet.

- *Assessment topics* guide student learning perhaps more than we would like. While assessments must show that learners meet the requirements of learning outcomes, I try to have them challenge students to think beyond them. One assessment asks learners to evaluate a number of web-based courses and develop their own principles from this evaluation. The other asks them to develop an on-line module for their own students.

Construction of meaning

Learners will, of course, construct meanings without my plotting. But this course will include three elements designed to expand knowledge beyond the stated learning outcomes.

- *A celebration of ignorance* is a first step. In the first session learners will be introduced to the notion of ignorance and its key part in the construction of knowledge. They will be introduced to the Kerwin model outlined above. They will be asked to reflect on the rational 'known-unknowns', and the more emotional taboo and denial aspects of ignorance. This process will begin a learning plan for the course.
- *Research on the Internet* will first of all facilitate use of the web for educational purposes. Second, it will encourage learners to ask questions like: What is being done here? Why is this course constructed the way it is? What learning theories are used here? What is the teaching approach? What are the strengths of this approach? What could I have done better? What kind of people would enrol in this course? Will this course take learners beyond the limits of what is? How sensitive is this course to issues of gender, social class and ethnicity? Questions like this will enable students to develop criteria for their own project.
- *The project* is seen as the jewel in the crown. It will take about one-third of course time, apply narrative knowledge in a useful way and enable learners to construct new knowledge from their areas of ignorance. They will design an on-line module or course in their own teaching area using the criteria they developed.

Summary for more beginnings

In this chapter I argued that your teaching does not take place in a vacuum. It is situated in a context. Right now your context is global. Economic and technological developments have unified the world. The process by which this occurs is often called globalisation. It results in what I call the global village. But life in this village is never simple. Globalisation creates both sameness and difference. I illustrated this by showing how knowledge is perceived differently and the effects this has on education. Finally, I constructed a model of teaching that I claimed is serviceable in the global village. I finished this chapter by showing how the model works in a course on computer-mediated learning.

Hopefully this chapter will lead to further learning. Some books to light your way include:

Books

Globalisation

Edwards, R., & Usher, R. (2000). *Globalisation and Pedagogy: Space, Place and Identity.* London: Routledge.

Finger, M., & Asun, J. (2001). *Adult Education at the Crossroads: Learning Our Way Out.* London: Zed Books.

Kelsey, J. (1999). *Reclaiming the Future. New Zealand and the Global Economy.* Wellington: Bridget Williams Books.

Knowledge

Apple, M. (1995). *Cultural Politics and Education.* Teachers College Press: New York.

Fricker, M., & Hornsby, J. (eds) (2000). *Feminism in Philosophy.* Cambridge: Cambridge University Press.

Power, R. (2000). *A Question of Knowledge.* Harlow: Prentice Hall.

Adult Education

Mayo, M. (2000). *Cultures, Communities, Identities: Cultural Strategies for Participation and Empowerment.* Basingstoke: Palgrave.

Sheared, V., & Sissel, P. (2001). *Making Space: Merging Theory and Practice in Adult Education.* Westport, Connecticut: Bergin & Garvey.

Wilson, A., & Hayes, E. (eds) (2000). *Handbook of Adult and Continuing Education.* San Francisco: Jossey Bass.

Activities

Reading is not the only vehicle to carry you beyond this chapter. Try some of these activities.

- Note down everything you know you don't know about globalisation and its effects on *your* teaching. Include things you have never dared to think about before and things you have always denied. Plan ways to use your ignorance to develop insights into your teaching in the global village.
- Work out how you think about the knowledge you teach. Does your subject take a realist, relativist or fallibilist view of knowledge? Do you agree? If not, why not? How would your teaching change if your view of knowledge changed?
- Develop your own teaching model to fit your place in the global village.
- Use the following and other questions to critique the ideas in this chapter.

- How well supported are the generalisations?
- How does the argument match your own experience/knowledge?
- What are the assumptions underpinning this chapter? Are there any hidden ones?
- What world view/ideological standpoint do they have?
- How well do the assumptions match your experience?
- Do you want to challenge any assumptions? In what way?
- What is your interpretation of the meanings in this chapter?
- How does this differ from mine?
- Who will be oppressed if the ideas in this chapter are accepted?
- What needs to be changed in this chapter to avoid oppressing anyone?
- Who might help you challenge the ideas in this chapter?
- How can you achieve personal truth?

Glossary

Constructivism: describes a view of learning in which the learner takes an active part in making meaning of experiences.

Discourse: in a general sense this can apply to any conversation, but it is more frequently used to describe communications, discussions or arguments based on rules agreed to or imposed on parties to the communication.

Eurocentric: beliefs and practices that are modelled on the European way of thinking and doing.

Ideology: a set of ideas about social life based on very tightly defined beliefs, values, sense of history and place in society.

Objectivity: letting the facts speak. Making decisions only based on facts. Not taking account of personal values or preferences.

Popular culture: culture of ordinary people such as working-class people.

Scaffolding: the practices used by a teacher to support learning.

Transnational: large corporations that cross national boundaries that are well known in countries other than their country of origin.

References

Apple, M. (1995). *Cultural Politics and Education*. New York: Teachers College Press.

Arlidge, J. (2000). Constructivism: Is anyone making meaning in New Zealand adult education? *New Zealand Journal of Adult Learning, 28* (1), 32–49.

Bailey, R. (2000). *Education in the Open Society: Karl Popper and Schooling*. Aldershot: Ashgate.

Blake, N., Smeyers, P., Smith, R., & Standish, P. (2000). *Education in an Age of Nihilism*. London: Routledge.

English, L., & Gillen, M. (2000). Addressing the Spiritual Dimensions of Adult Learning: What educators can do. *New Directions for Adult and Continuing Education, 85*.

Giddens, A. (1990). *The Consequences of Modernity*. Cambridge: Polity Press.

Jameson, F. (1998). Notes on Globalization as a Philosophical Issue. F. Jameson, & M. Myoshi (eds), *The Cultures of Globalization*. Durham: Duke University Press.

Kerwin, A. (1994). Lingua Franca: Ignorance is Strength. *The Review of Academic Life (April)*. Mimeo copy, page nos deleted.

Kuhn, T. (1994). *The Structure of Scientific Revolutions* (2nd ed.). Chicago: University of Chicago.

Laurillard, D. (1996). Multimedia and the Learner's Experience of Narrative. *World Conference on Educational Multimedia and Hypermedia:* Boston.

McCulloch, G. (1990). The Ideology of Educational Reform: An Historical Perspective. S. Middleton, J. Codd, & A. Jones (eds), *New Zealand Education Policy Today*. Auckland: Allen and Unwin.

Perry, N. (1998). *Hyperreality and Global Culture*. London: Routledge.

Popper, K. (1992). *Unended Quest: An Intellectual Autobiography*. London: Routledge.

Tiffin, J., & Rajasingham, B. (1995). *In Search of the Virtual Class: Education in an Information Society*. London: Routledge.

— Chapter 12 —

Transformative Learning: A Spiritual Perspective

Dean Nugent

I remember at a very early age asking my mother about where we came from. She replied that we came from 'God'. I don't recall pursuing this matter of 'God' any further with her at the time. The next memory I associate with that moment is standing outside our house and looking across the paddocks to the nearby hills and blue Hawke's Bay sky above and wondering about 'God'. I guess most people can remember similar ponderings in their childhood. Such moments, very early on in our lives, are an invitation for us to contemplate the mystery of life, or being.

The terms 'religion' and 'spirituality' mean different things to different people. Some recent researchers are adamant about distinctions between them. English and Gillen (2000, p. 1), for instance, point out that "religion is based on an organized set of principles shared by a group, whereas spirituality is the expression of an individual's quest for meaning". They define spirituality as "awareness of something greater than ourselves, a sense that we are connected to all human beings and to all of creation". In this chapter I make no such distinction between 'religion' and 'spirituality' and use the term 'spiritual' to include notions of religion, wisdom and the sacred.

In this chapter I suggest that spiritual practice offers us a radical form of transformative learning. Obviously, I cannot hope to do justice to the thousands of years of human spiritual endeavour. I speak, therefore, from the point of view of my own spiritual practice and invite you to consider your own experience.

I have constructed the chapter in four sections:

- I comment on the need for transformative learning in this difficult time in human history.
- I call for an understanding of the human spiritual project as a learning process.

- I describe how spiritual understanding informs my teaching and offer some practical tools for spiritual development.
- I outline the role of intimate and co-operative communities of practitioners for effective learning and the relationship with the secular state.

The need for a transformation point of view

In Chapter 4 I described how I consider teaching to be helping others to:

- recognise new possibilities for growth
- develop critical insight
- participate creatively in the times and circumstances into which they are born.

I explained that I consider my teaching–learning encounters to be within an experiential learning framework. Thus everything that occurs is an experience that can be perceived, felt emotionally and considered conceptually. I described how I try to create an environment that encourages learners to reflect on *their* experience, *their* understanding of whatever is happening. From this experiential learning framework I find I can embrace a number of other adult learning perspectives.

For instance, probably the most widespread point of view throughout our institutions and society is that education is *skill training*. From this point of view a course of study should be well designed and managed. This maximises opportunities for the largest number of participants to learn skills relevant to their effective and efficient functioning as workers and citizens. I have noticed, however, that if I focus exclusively on *effective management of course content* I do not ask questions about the *nature* of the course content (*who* decided *what* content and for *whom?* for instance). I may neglect the *learning purposes* and *needs of the learners* and I may forget to facilitate an environment that encourages *interactive understanding* and *sharing of meaning*.

A second viewpoint I incorporate, therefore, is that of adult learners as *self-directed*. By this I mean that they have unique learning needs and goals and the capacity to judge whether they have met those goals. I can help learners clarify their goals and act as a resource and support person. Our relationship is based on the sharing of meanings and specific agreements between us. This point of view honours the integrity of the learner and encourages the teacher to stay attentive to the learners' perceptions of what they need to learn. This viewpoint can be a limitation, however, if we assume a self-sufficient independence of the learner and fail to recognise that learning is a complex, interdependent relationship with others and things (see also Chapters 5 and 6).

Another perspective identifies the *external constraints* on learning. This notes the limitations placed by our historical and social circumstances. For instance, we may see the present predominant 'instrumental' and 'skills' approach to education as a constraint on learning (see also Chapter 10). As educators, we can help learners, through dialogue, to explore how these constrain their goals and the ways they learn. But this point of view is limited if it merely 'raises consciousness' and does not encourage action in the form of social and political change.

Transformative Learning: A Spiritual Perspective

A fourth perspective is the *internal barriers to learning* – the attitudes, beliefs, values and emotions that inhibit learning. This point of view emphasises a highly supportive and respectful environment to help learners explore their attitudes and values as well as their learning needs. The teacher gives full attention to the learner with empathy and respect.

All four points of view can be embraced by a transformative learning perspective. Self-directed learners, aware of the external constraints on learning as well as their own subjective limitations, can discuss all aspects of their learning experiences. They can identify and undertake training in specific skills and take social action.

With these viewpoints in mind I consider *transformative learning* as learning that:

- uses the experience of the learner to confront, evaluate and consider all information, facts, propositions, arguments, ideas, theories, ideologies, beliefs and practices;
- recognises that our learning and understanding is dependent upon our point of view – our motivations, attitudes, emotions and values;
- involves the whole being (physical, emotional, spiritual and mental) in relationship with all others and things;
- is able to be reflected upon with others.

> **Activity**: Describe your point of view on adult learning. Compare and contrast it with what I have been describing.

These difficult times

I argue that a transformative point of view applies to these very difficult times for humanity. We see massive social upheaval throughout the world and such grotesque human behaviours as genocide, slavery and systematic rape of women. We know that billions live at bare subsistence level. Changed climate patterns throughout the world are wreaking havoc. The AIDS pandemic shows no sign of having peaked in its destructiveness. Our forms of government, of authority, of societal infrastructure seem barely adequate. Large numbers of species (plants, insects, fish and animals) are disappearing. The abundance of life on earth and in the seas is dying before our eyes. Humanity's very life support system is in doubt.

There are signs throughout the world that more people are alarmed at the decisions being made about their lives, their communities, their fellow earth-kind and their planet by the rulers of the global-imperial, military-industrial complex. Our participation in these times requires great responsibility and our profound understanding of the purpose of our existence. I believe that more people are sensing in their hearts that we are being obliged to participate in dramatic change that is about much more than the global marketplace. People are noticing their dis-ease and are looking for forums to discuss their concerns with others, to connect with others and to learn new ways. We have to acknowledge our interdependence and to find ways of acting from that understanding.

Adult education, informed by transformative learning, has a significant role to play in nurturing such forums (see also Chapter 10). There are urgent considerations, such as:

- How are we to co-operate?
- What do we need to learn?
- Who are the leaders in this time?
- What needs to be done?
- How are we to transform our institutions?
- Who is making decisions for whom, about what?
- How do we think and act globally and locally?
- What is right life?
- How do we protect nature?
- How do we work within limits?
- How do we transform 'business-as-usual'?
- How do we practise 'fairness for all'?
- How are we to create sustainable community and sanctuary that nurtures the highest of human aspirations for all?

> **Activity**: What questions about social and political change would you want to add to the above list? How would you answer them?

These are social and political questions that require examination of our values and our taken-for-granted patterns of living. We are required to feel and act from a deep sense of our interdependence with everyone and everything.

I also feel that there is a need for forums that can reconsider the world's spiritual traditions. This is necessary, not only to understand the variations on the spiritual project as it has been manifested throughout history, but also because it is here – in the wisdom traditions – that we find the heart's question most fully addressed. The deep roots of human behaviour and suffering are described and 'ways out' indicated.

The spiritual project is a learning process

For thousands of years, human civilisations and cultures have been informed by spiritual understandings brought to them by teachers of unique experience and realisation. Humanity has been slowly accumulating an understanding of existence. Every so often brilliant flashes of insight are brought to us by rare beings, who are great signs of how to grow in our understanding and experience.

We can make distinctions between the various spiritual learning goals and processes.

Transformative Learning: A Spiritual Perspective 217

I will make two general distinctions. Many have taught about spiritual activity in the context of the earth and the cosmic domains of Nature whereby all beings are considered to be 'spirits', or to be made of energy. A schema of learning was provided in which beings sought to achieve improved destinies in the world of their present embodiment and a transition, at death, to a higher destiny, made possible by an ascent to higher planes. Others have taught a radical Transcendentalism whereby, through understanding, self and cosmic Nature are completely transcended (Adi Da Samraj, 1982, p. 19–61).

My own learning has led me to investigate life and learning in spiritual terms – more specifically, in terms of the Transcendental religion of Adidam (www.adidam.org). I have written elsewhere of this practice (Nugent, 1996; 1999) which is given by the living Western-born Spiritual Master and Realiser, Adi Da Samraj. I have concluded that the spiritual point of view offers the most complete explanation of reality and the analysis of what has to be ultimately transformed (that is, the life of the *self* or *ego*), and it provides the *instruction book*. First and foremost then, spirituality is to be understood as a learning process.

Tolerance

The assumption that spirituality is a means to continue growing, a learning process, has very important implications for religious tolerance. When we assume it, we will be less inclined to think of religion as 'beliefs' and 'behaviours', but rather as learning 'practices': indeed, as forms of 'reflective practice'. We will also see that different traditions and cultures have used different 'performance assistance' to facilitate this learning process (Adi Da Samraj, 2001, p. 492).

Besides traditional wisdom, these days there are many investigations being undertaken relative to more recent social and spiritual movements. The enormous variety and complexity of such movements can be seen in work like *Spirituality and the Secular Quest* (Van Ness, 1996). This refers to recent examples of the search for spirituality amongst movements as diverse as deconstructive aestheticism, New Age thinking, holistic health practices, psychotherapies, twelve-step programmes, feminism, gay movements, scientific enquiry, recreation, ecological activism, arts, sports and games. Participatory and experiential forms of inquiry and learning, such as those discussed in this book, are ways of exploring the spiritual. John Heron (1998, p. 2) describes "an increasing number of spiritually-minded people" involving a "growing and significant minority of people across the planet" who are "seeking open and constructive dialogue".

There are three broad types of political arrangements regarding spirituality today. You can live in a culture that has intact agreements and understandings relative to its traditional spiritual practices, in a politically absolutist society that either denies any spiritual expression or prescribes what spiritual beliefs and practices can be, or in a postmodern context as described by Van Ness and Heron. This latter context may seem to offer tolerance and freedom, but the true, pluralistic post-modern is relatively rare. Spiritual tolerance and freedom of expression cannot be taken for granted even in the so-called Western democracies (see http://www.cesnur.org). Of course, when religions become associated with political power and are used as instruments for consoling and controlling people they are no longer spiritual in the sense I am using here.

How spiritual understanding informs my teaching

> There is only relatedness, no separateness, only mutuality, interdependence. If anything has arisen, there is only relatedness. Yet most of the time you do not observe that fact, you do not *observe* relatedness. Most of your time is spent being obsessed with your separateness. This separateness is not True. But all the time you are thinking this separateness. All the time you are acting as if it were so. All the time you are meditating on it. All the time you are seeking to become free of it. And yet, among all things that arise, this thought is not True, and it is truly the least valuable of all that arises. Understanding is the re-cognition, or knowing again, of that presumption of your separateness (Adi Da Samraj, 1995, p. 204)

I have been involved with Adidam spiritual practice for many years, a practice that we can term 'transcendental'. One aspect of its process is the understanding and transcendence of self, and of changing realities and points of view. We practise critical investigation and understanding of our egoic selves. This resembles the experiential learning cycle and reflective practice. It is fruitful to observe what the self is up to in our relations with others. Teaching, because it involves relationships with many people, gives me lots of opportunities to observe the patterns of emotional states, thoughts and behaviours that comprise my 'self'.

Activity: Recall a 'peak' moment in your teaching when everything seemed to go really well. Your relationships with all your learners seemed very satisfactory, wonderful! Describe the circumstance. What happened? What colours do you associate with it? What smells? How did you feel? What words would you use to describe this moment?

When I have done this exercise with teachers, they have given me words like: *happy, open, loving, giving, shining, radiant, stimulated, flowing, at ease, connected, excited, synergistic.*

Now take a few moments to recall a really bad moment in your teaching. Describe the circumstance. What happened? What colours do you associate with it? What smells? How did you feel? What words would you use to describe this moment?

Teachers have given me these words: *angry, fearful, despair, self-doubtful, hopeless, hurt, dark, get-me-out-of-here, judgemental, frustrated, closed off.*

In many of my teaching moments I have observed in myself patterns of fear, anxiety, self-protectiveness, self-doubt, urges to control circumstances and others, and defensiveness. I have observed other moments when I have felt relaxed and connected to others and able to enjoy the moment. I have also observed these patterns in other teachers.

Self-contraction

We can generalise about these two moments. In one, we felt open, receptive, flowing, giving, connected, and outward-directed: Non-contracted. In the other, we felt closed off, blocked, dissociated and inward-turned. Adi Da Samraj describes this as 'self-contraction'.

In my spiritual practice I observe closely what happens when I turn inwards and close off. If I observe and feel profoundly enough I will notice that I *do* the action. I *could* choose to remain open and radiant no matter what the circumstance that seems to be happening and apparently 'causing' me to close down. This is the process of self-observation and self-understanding – when I see that *I am doing the action* of closing down, I can take responsibility and practise openness and radiance instead. I can, therefore, transcend my usual reaction. I can make a counter-egoic gesture. This is spiritual practice.

Spiritual principle: We are all transmitters

Why should we be interested in observing, understanding, and going beyond our usual 'self'? We can appreciate the purpose in terms of the principle: *we are all transmitters*. Have you noticed how the moods and states of others affect us when we are around them? If someone is very happy we tend to become happy ourselves, and someone who is sullen or contracted will affect us negatively. Everybody is transmitting their state, their mood or their energy to others. If a teacher is open, connected and radiant, this will be transmitted to the learners and they will tend to feel similarly. Their communication about, and openness to, their learning will be enhanced. Our own freedom to attend to others and to encourage deeper understanding is also enhanced. Because a teacher is in a position of leadership, his or her transmission wields a significant influence on the learning situation.

We are always animating contraction

Self-contraction has many dimensions. Our fear and defensiveness is likely to be related to deep presumptions and past experiences about our 'OK-ness' or self-esteem, for instance. (Consider for a moment what you most seem to fear in your teaching. To be exposed as not knowing what you're talking about? To lose control and authority? To be vulnerable?) What we observe over time is that even in our very best moments there is still a *limitation* on our freedom and openness. You may even have found that it was difficult to locate a peak moment in your teaching. You had an intuition in your being of what such a moment of flow and openness and happiness *could* feel like, but it was difficult to actually locate such an experience in reality. This is because, even in our great moments, there is still a limit on our capacity to *be* completely open, completely free, completely happy, completely loving, completely giving and receiving, completely in relationship.

> **Activity**: Describe the notion of self-contraction and how it might relate to your teaching practice.

Spiritual principle: Change of action is the secret of how to change

But, while observing all sorts of limitations in ourselves, we *can* begin to make a different presumption, and change our action in any moment:

> You want to manipulate your subjectivity – your feelings, your thinking, your conceptions, and your feeling-conceptions. You want to change them before you will change your way of life. You want to be free inside before you will love, before you will act differently. You must act differently first, and not be concerned that the feeling and thinking aspect of the being remains full of tendencies. You must not be concerned about them. They are just the signs of the old way of living. You must act in love, in radiance, with energy, with life, in all your relations, in your disposition moment to moment, under all conditions. You will observe in the midst of such action that the subjective dimension is also gradually penetrated and transformed. Its negativity, its reactivity, becomes unnecessary and ultimately obsolete by virtue of your different action (Adi Da Samraj, 1977, p. 268).

The test of practice

I must point out, however, that this practice requires discipline and a growth in our moment-to-moment awareness. The patterns of reactivity and contraction are powerfully programmed into our body-minds, as people and as teachers. This is not a mere self-watching exercise. If our self-understanding is to deepen to any significant extent, we have to practise in the context of other processes of study, self-discipline and meditation. And, most importantly, we have to come into relationship with the transmission of complete happiness and freedom from the Realiser who takes responsibility for the self-contraction. And it is this transmission that progressively reflects back to us all the details of our own egoic patterning. Ultimately, we will see that we are doing only one fundamental act – the *avoidance of relationship* or the act of *separation* and *separativeness* – and we will realise what we *are*, always already, prior to this action. Our ability to locate our fundamental act of self-contraction and to take responsibility for it is a significant understanding. I have yet to demonstrate this as a fully established practice.

Practical wisdom tools for spiritual growth

There are some basic wisdom tools that we can use daily. I offer these, along with the communication strategies I proposed in Chapter 4, for use in your teaching. The basic mechanism of our body–minds consists of four faculties, each of which can register self-contraction:

- body (experiencing comfort or discomfort)
- breathing (shallow, deep or hardly at all)
- mind (or the faculty of *attention*)
- emotion (or the faculty of *feeling*)

Spiritual principle: We become what we meditate on

These faculties are all dependent upon one another, playing together like an orchestra. This is important when we consider another spiritual principle: *we tend to become whatever we meditate upon or give consistent attention to*. You might notice that, if your body is in pain or discomfort of some kind, your attention very quickly fixes on it; similarly if you are experiencing emotional upset. So we must give our consistent attention to our highest aspiration.

> **Activity:** As a person and as a teacher, to what or whom do you give most of your attention? What are the consequences of this? To what or whom might you aspire to give your attention?

Spiritual practice as energy and attention

Breathing is principally a spiritual process and is associated with all other faculties. It is particularly useful to notice breath's relationship to our emotional states. If we are angry, for instance, the exhaled breath is strong and aggressive, but the receptive phase, or inhalation, is inhibited. When we are sad the tendency is to inhale and exhalation is suppressed. If we observe ourselves in moments of fear, we notice that the whole cycle of the breath, both inhalation and exhalation, is inhibited (Adi Da Samraj, 1974, p. 196–197).

For teachers, fear and anxiety at various levels are common experiences, so our awareness of the full cycle of our breath is especially important. We can bring our attention to our breath throughout the day. The breath should be full, easy, naturally open, pleasurable. Inhalation and exhalation should be equal. Here is an activity to help you develop an awareness of your breathing. You may wish to tape the instructions or have someone read them to you while you practise.

- Breathe through your nose, with your mouth closed.
- Initiate your breath from your heart (the conscious, feeling, psychic core of the body-being) – with the power of emotion, whole-body feeling, through and with your throat, to your navel.
- When you inhale, draw in, relax into and conduct the life-energy of the universe with your whole being – through the entire skin surface of the whole physical body head to toe, down into the vital centre, the great life region, whose felt centre is behind and below the umbilical scar. Feel the life-energy at and from this life-centre, radiating through your whole being as fullness.
- Inhale fully, with deep feeling of heart and body, completely filling the lungs with air and the whole body with life-force.
- When you exhale, do not discard the energy itself or allow it to dissipate, but release and relax all hold on it, allowing it to radiate, from the vital centre and the whole body. Exhale fully and with deep feeling of heart and body. Let the energy pervade the whole body and the universe to infinity, and release, via that radiating and expansive energy, all accumulated conditions, positive or negative, so that inhalation may bring what is new and thus become an instrument of change and refreshment.

Clearly, it is not air that is being drawn into the navel and lower regions of the body. It is life-force, energy, 'prana' or 'spirit'. Physical air, and the process of biochemical respiration in the lungs, constitutes only secondary, grosser aspects of the dynamics of the breath. This is why breathing is principally a spiritual process. It directly involves the higher physics of the etheric or pranic body and only secondarily involves the elemental or physical being. So it is also natural, especially as practice matures, to feel the 'in-spiration' or reception of life-energy, not only through the valve of the throat, but through the entire skin surface of the physical body. When the breath is felt in this way, the conscious being is beginning to include direct perception and enjoyment of the subtlest of the gross elements, which is ether or life-energy, along with its perception and utilisation of the denser elements, which are earth, water, fire and air (Adi Da Samraj, 1974, p. 55).

In summary, we can understand our body-minds as involving *attention* (mind) and *energy* (breath, body and emotions). We *direct* our attention and we *conduct* and *re-cycle* the life energy. One way of describing non-contraction, then, is that it consists of free feeling-attention and unobstructed flow of energy. Growth in spiritual practice, as I am speaking of it, is growth in the capability to be responsible for our energy and attention – capabilities that are relevant for us as teachers.

> Over time, without urgency or anxiety, you relax more and more in a graceful, feeling economy of motion, rest, and equalizing rhythms or cycles of breath under all conditions. The breath deepens, becoming full of feeling, subtle, and exquisitely

Transformative Learning: A Spiritual Perspective

pleasurable to the whole body. You are not busy exalting in any personal transformation or change of state. You realize an altogether different relationship to bodily life and the world, in which you no longer spend time in thinking about and demanding attention to yourself, but live unselfconsciously and wisely as a genuine servant of others (Adi Da Samraj, 1974, p. 9).

Spiritual principle: Reality always already Is

It is important that I don't leave you with the impression that this Transcendental practice is simply about adopting a number of techniques to manipulate the body–mind. The fullest practice of self-observation and understanding of the self-contraction takes place in the context of a life of study, self-discipline, meditation and, most importantly, direct relationship to the Spiritual Teacher, Adi Da Samraj, whose constant communication and transmission is the 'Point of View' of the completely transcended condition. Whenever you give attention to this 'Point of View', for instance through study, you will be drawn into contemplation. (See also Chapter 1.)

Try the following study. Sit comfortably and relax the body. Breathe fully, allowing the energy to fill the body. Recite slowly but with appropriate emphasis for meaning. Do not be concerned that you may not follow all of this argument. Allow it. Contemplate.

> Consider this: If a group of people are sitting in a room, each one is looking at the room from a particular position within the room – and, if a photograph were taken from the position of each person's eyes, then there would be a different image to represent each one's separate point of view. Each person would be seeing the room from a particular point in space, and even from a particular point in time, and (therefore) the perceptual view of any particular person would be different from that of any other.
>
> And, yet, even though the room would be seen (and pictured) from many different positions (or angles, or points of view), the room *as a whole* (not limited to the view from any particular point of view) *exists* all the while.
>
> Therefore, the room *itself* exists *only* as it can be viewed from *every* possible point of view (in space and in time) – *simultaneously*.
>
> But if you (or any one) were to see the room from every possible point of view in space and time simultaneously, what would the room look like? What would be its perceived characteristics? What would be the 'image' photographed, simultaneously, from every possible point of view in both space and time?
>
> It cannot be imagined. And, yet, *that* infinite space-time 'room' (or even the *Totality* of space-time, It self) *is* the *only* room being seen (and, necessarily, limited) by the perceptions registered by each person (or present-time point of view) within it!
>
> *Totality* – In and *As* Unqualified (or Non-qualified) Reality – *Is* the *Only* (and, necessarily, Indivisible) 'Room' In Which (or, Really, *As* Which) any and every conditionally manifested being is (in any moment) living, breathing, experiencing, and knowing.
>
> And, if 'That One and Only 'Room' is, because of the limitations (and the limiting effects) of point of view, *never* known, then *all* presumed knowing (and even all conditioned experience) is better described as 'ignorance'!

As a result (or sign) of that characteristic ignorance, *no one* (in any moment) knows *What* any 'thing' (or everything, or Totality) *Is*.

Even though you are suffering the complications of presuming to be a particular 'point' in space-time, it is (or must become) completely and tacitly obvious that (in any and every moment) the Totality *Exists*, and that the Knowing of Reality from the Position of Totality is (necessarily) infinitely unlike any kind of knowing from a particular 'point' in space-time.

In this very moment, you tacitly (Inherently, Prior to body-mind, self-contraction, point of view, or ego – 'I') *know* that the Totality *Exists*. Therefore, if you grow to understand how to Know from the Position of Totality, rather than merely (and by means of, or as a result of) knowing from your apparently separate point of view in space-time, that 'radical' understanding will constantly provide immediate tacit proof of the Real Existence of Real God (or of Truth Itself, or of Reality Itself).

Real God (or Truth Itself, or Reality Itself) *Is* Totality, and Totality *Is* That Which Inherently *Transcends* both particularity and the total sum of parts. Whatever That Totality *Is*, it is (or should be) obvious That *It* (or Reality Itself) *Always Already Exists* – and, therefore, logically (and at heart), *It cannot be denied!*" (Adi Da Samraj, 2000, p. 200). (See Chapter 11 for more on ignorance.)

Attention, breathing, energy and contemplation are some of the practical wisdom tools that inform my spirituality and my teaching. I hope that you will find some of them useful to you in your development and practice.

Communities of practitioners

Our capability to co-operate and work with others in order to bring about changes in our patterns of living is critical. However, our competitive and individualistic patterning is a deep vein in our civilisation. So an important aspect of spirituality as a learning process is the company of, and interaction with, other practitioners. The community of spiritual practitioners has traditionally been highly valued. This is not because of some urge to exclusiveness or to flee from the ordinary demands of life. Rather, it is very useful to spend significant time with others undertaking the same process. When I go to work as a teacher I am coming out of a home environment which is dedicated to growing beyond. The community of practitioners has its collective attention on self-surrendering, self-forgetting and self-transcending life. Besides friendship and human intimacy, we bring each other inspiration and expectation. We presume the practitioner in each of us. It is my experience that spiritual life is a collective venture. Only very rare individuals can 'do it' 'on their own'.

I live in a community where the transcendental 'Point of View' pervades all aspects of our life, including sexuality, conception, birthing, child-rearing, food preparation, food-taking, schooling, higher and vocational learning, social relationships, celebrations and parties, relationships between the sexes, intimate relationships, relationships to all others, co-operative living, bodily exercise, work, health care, healing, radiant life, regular retreat, architecture of living, our relationship to non-humans, care of the environment, art, music and theatre, the right use of science and technology, communications, economic management, illness, dying and death.

To me, the intimate, co-operative and spiritual community is fundamentally liberating. The intimate, co-operative and democratically responsible community creates a free and sacred refuge, a servant of developmental adaptation to spiritual life, while also taking responsibility for managing the availability of the necessary goods and services for its members. In contrast, I see the secular, or corporate, state as a rather abstract, fixed and potentially binding, even enslaving, condition. Obviously, a spiritual co-operative community, without a benign, and self-limiting secular (or non-sectarian) state to protect its rights, is (inherently) in fear. There can be no true sanctuary. Therefore, its members cannot fully release their energy and attention toward the out-growing of their egoic and developmental limitations. Ideally then, the function of a representative, secular state would be to serve the common requirements of all the intimate, co-operative human communities within its sphere.

Conclusion

I wrote this chapter in the context of a planet in crisis. Transformation, however, is also about our capability to participate with conscious awareness and a full and open heart no matter what the moment. Although I have only been able to write from my own experience and understanding, I hope that I have been able to offer tools and principles that resonate with your experience, as teachers and as people. I have tried to write in the spirit of open and constructive dialogue.

I praise The Ruchira Avatar Adi Da Samraj whose wisdom and teaching is a gift available to all in this time and who offers a Way for those who may recognise and respond to this Revelation of Liberation.

The Universal World-Prayer

(A Prayer To The Heart Of Reality,
Proposed By The Divine World-Teacher,
Ruchira Avatar Adi Da Love-Ananda Samraj,
For Non-Sectarian Use By All Of Humanity)

Beloved, *Inmost* Heart of *every* heart,
do not Let our human hearts be broken
by our merely mortal *suffering* here —
but *Make* our mortal human hearts break-*Free*
to an *unconditional* love of *You*,
that we may, *Thus*, love *all* living beings
with Love's *own* True, and *Truly* broken, Heart.
(Adi Da Samraj, 2001, p. 477)

Further reading

Transformative learning and the urgency of these times

Britton, D. (1996). *The Modern Practice of Adult Education: A Post-Modern Critique.* New York: State University of New York Press.

Finger, M., & Asun, J. M. (2001). *Adult Education at the Crossroads: Learning Our Way Out.* London: Zed Books.

O'Connor, M.A. (ed.) (2002). Expanding the Boundaries of Transformative Learning. Great Britain: Palgrave MacMillan.

O'Sullivan, E. (1999). *Transformative Learning: Educational Vision for the 21st Century.* London: Zed Books.

Scholarship on new religions

CESNUR: Centre for the Study of New Religions
http://www.cesnur.org

The complete transcendental teaching and revelation in this time

Adi Da Samraj, Ruchira Avatar (2000 & Forthcoming). *The Five Books of the Heart of the Adidam Revelation & the Seventeen Companions of the True Dawn Horse.* California: The Dawn Horse Press.

Transcendental teachings from two other traditions

From the Canon of Mahayana Buddhism
Price, A. F. & Mou-Lam, W. (trans.) (1985). *The Diamond Sutra.* Boston: Shambhala.

From Hindu Advaitism
Swami, Sri Ramanananda Saraswathi (trans.). (1980). *The Tripura Rahasya.* Madras, India: The Jupiter Press.

Glossary

Ego: not a state or entity but rather an *activity* – the activity of self-contraction, or separation. As the ego we think and feel ourselves to be separate entities. We contract to a 'point' of view. It is as if we see from the point of view of a separate wave rather than as the ocean. We speak of the 'egoic' self to distinguish from the Divine or Transcendental Self.

Religion: the root meaning of the word means 'to bind' or 're-connect' to the 'Divine'. Or we can use other terms, such as 'Consciousness', 'Reality', 'Being', 'Self' or 'God'. It resembles the Eastern term *yoga* – to 'yoke'.

Spirituality: living in contact with the moving force, or presence, of the Divine. I understand that this spirit energy that is living in all beings can be felt and realised to be all-surrounding and all-pervading. To be spiritual, then, is to locate, and to allow, and, eventually, to be consciously lived by that presence. Traditionally, it has been understood that unique individuals, or Realisers, are powerful transmitters of such a presence, and holy and sacred places are established and maintained where the spirit force is especially invoked. One goes there to contemplate, to rest, to be refreshed, to be restored.

Transcendental: describes the condition of having gone beyond the point of view of the ego and therefore of all realities perceived and conceived from that point of view.

Wisdom: understanding and knowing attained via spiritual practice.

References

Adi Da Samraj, Ruchira Avatar (1974). *Conscious Exercise and the Transcendental Sun*. California: The Dawn Horse Press.

Adi Da Samraj, Ruchira Avatar (1977). *The Paradox of Instruction*. California: The Dawn Horse Press.

Adi Da Samraj, Ruchira Avatar (1982). *The Fire Gospel*. California: The Dawn Horse Press.

Adi Da Samraj, Ruchira Avatar (1995). *The Method of the Siddhas*. California: The Dawn Horse Press.

Adi Da Samraj, Ruchira Avatar (2000). *The Seven Stages of Life*. California: The Dawn Horse Press.

Adi Da Samraj, Ruchira Avatar (2001). *Eleutherios*. California: The Dawn Horse Press.

Center for Studies on New Religions (2002). URL http://www.cesnur.org (2002, March).

English, L., & Gillen, M. (2000). Addressing the Spiritual Dimensions of Adult Learning: What educators can do. *New Directions for Adult and Continuing Education, 85*.

Heron, J. (1998). *Sacred Science*. United Kingdom: PCCS Books.

Nugent, D. (1996). Teaching and Learning for a Changing World. N. Zepke, D. Nugent, & C. Roberts (eds), *The New Self Help Book for Teachers* (pp. 264–282). Wellington: WP Press.

Nugent, D. (1999). The Words of Adi Da as Transformative Learning Tool. N. Zepke, M. Knight, L. Leach, & A. Viskovic (eds), *Adult Learning Cultures: Challenges, Choices and the Future*. Wellington: WP Press.

Van Ness, P. H. E. (1996). *Spirituality and the Secular Quest*. New York: The Crossroad Publishing Company.

Author Note

I wish to thank Christine Phippen for her critical help in the shaping of this chapter. Her devotional life and her teaching practice are always an inspiration to me.

Index

Action research 52–65
— Cycle 56–60
— Cefinition of 55
— History of 53–55
— Solitary 63–64
— Spirals 56–60
— Technical, practical, emancipatory 52, 62, 63, 64
Adult education 181–182
Assessment 46, 161–173
— Achievement-based 163
— of Attitudes 171–173
— Fairness in 175
— in Knowledge domain 168–169
— Norm-referenced 161–162
— Peer assessment 116
— of Practical skills 170–171
— Purposes of 161
— Reliability 165
— Standards-based 161–162
— Tools for 167
— and Transformative learning 174–176
— Validity 163–
Autonomy 106, 110, 186
— Andragogy 106, 111
— Independence 105–111, 190
— Self-directed learning 27–29, 91, 105–111, 112–113, 214

Carr, W. 55, 56, 61, 62, 63
Collaboration/collaborative learning 52, 63–64, 112, 115, 126, 139–152
— Benefits of 143–145
— Definition of 140–141
— Components of 142–143
— Co-learners 190
— Interdependence 108, 116, 139, 144, 145, 218
— Issues with 145–146
— Strategies for 148–151
Competence 171, 187
Contexts 181–182, 183, 184–191
Communication 83, 112, 143, 189
— Feedback 83, 165, 189
Constructivism 18, 96, 103, 118, 107, 142
— Social constructivism 26, 112,
— Constructing meaning 107, 117, 205, 206, 207, 209.
— Construction of knowledge 96–97, 140, 141, 144, 145, 190
— Meaning making 100–101, 111, 113, 114, 117, 140, 142, 148
Contemplation *see* meditation
Cooperative/collaborative learning 34, 81, 140, 214, 224–225,
Course design 156–161
— Course evaluation 160–161
— Outcome approach 156–161
— Needs analysis 157
— Process approach 173–174
Critical theory 52, 61
Culture 90, 109, 188–189

Diversity/difference 13, 89, 90, 139, 144, 186, 199
— Individual differences 90, 92
— The politics of difference 97–98

Domains of learning
— Knowledge, skills, attitudes 157–158, 167, 168

Emancipation / emancipatory learning 111, 112, 191
Emotional climate/environment 79–80, 96, 128

Gender 13, 90, 101, 110
Globalisation 55, 181, 183–185, 197, 210

Habermas, J. 7, 34, 52, 61, 63
— and human interests 7–8
— and communicative action 34–35
Hegemony 62, 187, 193

Ideology 26, 33, 183, 193, 211
Ignorance 203–204, 223
— Johari Window 20–21

Johnson, D. & Johnson, R. 140, 141, 142–145

Kemmis, S. 54, 55, 56, 62, 63
Knowledge 199–200
— Politics of official knowledge 201–203
Knowles, M. 106
Kolb, D. 18, 56, 94

Learning 8, 21, 22, 10, 34, 91, 92
— Experiential learning 18, 72, 214, 218
— Holistic learning 8, 29, 96, 101, 115
— Learning in groups 81, 115, 140, 143, 150–151, 176
— Learning outcomes 40, 78, 157–159
— Learning resources 124, 135
— Learning styles 92, 94, 95, 125
— Multiple intelligences 92–93
Learning environment 79, 114–115
Learning organisation / learning community 75, 188, 191
Liberatory education See Emancipation and transformation

McNiff, J. 54, 55, 60
Meditation 30–32, 223–224

Negotiation 99–100, 113–111

Pedagogy 184, 193
Philosophy of teaching 189–190,
Pluralism 186, 193, 217,

Reflection 17, 18, 21, 23, 25, 37, 96
— Being critical 26–29
— Critical reflection 25–29, 37–39
— Critical reflective dialogue 45, 48
— Reflective practitioner 187, 193
— Reflective practice 21, 32, 217, 218
— Reflective learning 19, 34

Spirituality 29, 90, 94, 101, 115, 213, 217
— Definitions 29, 213
— Spiritual project as learning 216–217
— Practical wisdom tools for 221–223
— and Teaching 218–219
Storytelling 37, 39, 40, 46, 49
— Ethical issues 46
— Levels of engagement 42–44
— Multiple perspectives 38
Stringer, E. 54, 60–61

Teaching 71, 72, 76, 83, 90, 98
— Facilitator of learning 72, 107, 171, 214
— Inclusive teaching 89–90, 99, 100–101, 127
— Lecturing 84–85, 129
— Managing learning 72
— Narrative in teaching 205, 208
— Peer teaching 116
— Preparation for teaching 124, 125, 128
— Resources 124, 135
— Self-development 17, 18
Technology 198
— Online learning/teaching 85, 116, 130–131
— Information literacy 131–135
Transcendentalism 217, 218, 224
Transformation / transformative learning 155, 173–176, 181, 190–191, 193, 213–216, 225,

Vygotsky, L. 112, 205

Contributors

Maxine Alterio currently works as a staff development coordinator at Otago Polytechnic, Dunedin, New Zealand. In her teaching role she encourages academic staff and postgraduate students to use formalised storytelling processes to enhance reflective learning and bring about thoughtful change to practice. She is also a prizewinning short story writer with work published in literary magazines, journals and edited collections.
   Email: maxaa@tekotago.ac.nz

Pip Bruce-Ferguson is a Senior Lecturer at Auckland University of Technology. She learned to use action research while doing tutor training in the late 1980s. In her position as a staff developer at the Waikato Polytechnic she helped to develop the institution's research culture by including an action research course in the tutor training programme. Pip is passionate about improving teaching, her own and her colleagues', using action research. Her PhD thesis reported on this work.
   Email: ferguson@xtra.co.nz

Brian Findsen is Associate Professor of Education at the Auckland University of Technology. He has an extensive background in adult and community education and has spent 20 years as an adult educator in higher education settings. His research interests include adult education in universities, the training of adult educators, the sociology of adult education, international adult education and educational gerontology. He has published widely on these topics.
   Email: brian.findsen@aut.ac.nz

Robin Graham is the Information Literacy Programme Leader at Christchurch Polytechnic Institute of Technology in Library and Learning Services. Her career in tertiary education has spanned working in faculty, Staff Development and in Learning Services, where she developed a particular interest in the integration of generic/ transferable skills into the curriculum and in supporting student learning. Latterly she

has focused predominantly on promoting Information Literacy and developing this in e-learning.
   Email: GrahamR@hermes.cpit.ac.nz

Michele Knight is a Senior Lecturer at Massey University, Wellington. She worked as a secondary teacher for nine years, then in New Zealand polytechnic and Australian TAFE contexts for more than 10 years. Michele is also a professional chef and has owned her own business. She is particularly interested in New Zealand's cultural and equity issues; action research and collaborative enquiry. She lives on a lifestyle block where she grows flowers for export and produces honey.
   Email: M.Knight@massey.ac.nz

Linda Leach is a Senior Lecturer in the College of Education, Massey University and is based at the Wellington Campus. Initially a primary school teacher, she has worked as an adult educator in community, polytechnic and university contexts for over 20 years. She teaches in Bachelor and Master of Education (Adult Education) degrees, both face-to-face and extramurally. She has a particular interest in adult learning theories and grapples constantly with assessment issues.
   Email: L.J.Leach@massey.ac.nz

Janice McDrury currently works as an educator and health researcher at Otago Polytechnic, Dunedin, New Zealand. She has 18 years' experience as a nurse educator and is presently a senior lecturer. Her use of storytelling developed when she recognised its ability to surface multiple perspectives of practice events. Her PhD studies were in the area of self-assessment and reflective practice.
Email: janicem@tekotago.ac.nz

Guyon Neutze is a Senior Lecturer at Massey University, and has for some time been concerned with the uses and abuses of the ritual of assessment, which seem to him to reflect and promote old and widespread habits in the wider culture. He has worked in mental health, community education, the motor industry, and a standards institution, all of them areas where these habits are particularly evident. He also teaches and writes about meditation.
   Email: G.G.Neutze@massey.ac.nz

Dean Nugent likes to work in a variety of adult education fields. He has enjoyed many years "educating adult educators" from many different walks of life and also mentors individual trainers and teachers. He facilitates classes on religion as well as relationship counselling from a spiritual perspective. Dean leads a life very focused on the contemplative spiritual practice given by his Teacher. He is also interested in forms of co-operative community living, Green politics and Mac computers.
   Email: dean@adidam.org

Anne O'Brien Kennington is Programme Manager in the Community and Continuing Education Department of the Waikato Institute of Technology. She started work at the Institute (then the Waikato Polytechnic) in the late 1980s. She did an action research course during 1994, when she was a literacy tutor with particular strengths in computer-assisted learning. She remains a strong, committed educator who strives for continued improvement in her own and others' practice.
   Email: ceatk@wintec.ac.nz

Nick Zepke is an Associate Professor in the College of Education, Massey University and is based on the Wellington Campus. For 30 years now he has had great fun teaching and learning in adult and community education settings, earning his keep in colleges of education, polytechnics and universities, but he has also loved teaching in primary and intermediate schools. He has particular research interests in the sociology of knowledge, futures studies and assessment issues.
   Email: n.zepke@massey.ac.nz